Palestinian Colloquial Arabic Vocabulary

Matthew Aldrich
with
Ahmed Younis

lingualism

Table of Contents

Introduction

Vocabulary, much more than grammar, is the key to effective communication in Arabic. You need words to speak; you need words to listen and understand.

Knowing grammar inside and out won't save you if you don't have the right word to plug into the structure. You can walk into a shop armed with grammatical structures such as "I would like some __." or "Do you have any __?", but if you don't know the word for the thing you want, you may very well leave the shop empty handed. On the other hand, if you walk into that same shop and simply say "sugar", you're almost certain to get what went there for.

And without an extensive repertoire of vocabulary, you will understand very little of what others are talking about. Spoken Arabic, to your foreign ears, will remain little more than gibberish. But once you can understand the majority of what you hear, something magical happens. The input becomes manageable–you will be able to use contextual clues from what you do understand to guess the meaning of new words and start to make rapid progress in Arabic.

It is therefore very important to build up a large store of words as soon as possible. **Palestinian Colloquial Arabic Vocabulary** is an enormously effective means to this end. By presenting practical words and phrases categorized by topic and arranged with a logical flow, mental connections that assist in vocabulary retention are fostered. The page layout in parallel columns of English translation, phonemic transcription, and Arabic script provides a variety of ways to study the vocabulary by allowing you to cover columns and test yourself.

The accompanying MP3s, free to download and stream from our website at **www.lingualism.com/pcav**, make up an invaluable part of the learning process, allowing you to hear and mimic native speakers' pronunciation, pitch, intonation, and rhythm. Additional study materials (Anki digital flashcards, premium audio, e-book) are available separately from our website and provide even more powerful tools for rapid vocabulary acquisition.

Although extremely important, vocabulary still only makes up one aspect of learning a language. **Palestinian Colloquial Arabic Vocabulary** is the ideal supplementary tool to reinforce vocabulary acquisition. However, it is not meant to be a stand-alone course. It is expected that you have followed, are following, or plan to follow, a course in Palestinian Colloquial Arabic (PCA). Alternatively, you may have studied another dialect of Arabic, or Modern Standard Arabic

(MSA), and are curious to learn more about PCA and tune your ears to the idiosyncrasies of this beautiful dialect.

I would like to extend a special thanks to Ahmed Younis for collaborating with me to make this book possible, providing authentic Palestinian Arabic translations of the items in this book, proof-reading the text, giving me valuable feedback and cultural insights to ensure the accuracy of the information, and recording the audio tracks.

Audio

Visit **www.lingualism.com/pcav**, where you can find free accompanying audio to download or stream (at variable playback rates).

How to Use This Book

Palestinian Colloquial Arabic Vocabulary is made up of 57 thematic sections, each dedicated to a different topic.

You may study the sections and individual vocabulary items in any order or work through the book systematically. It is encouraged that you mark up and highlight the book as you use it. Make it your own. There is also a Notebook after the last section where you can add in more words you have learned from other sources.

Many words could logically belong to more than one topic. While some words do appear in more than one section, to avoid superfluous repetition of words, most appear only once. To your surprise, you might not be able to find common animals such as *cow* and *horse* in the section "Animals", for instance. This is because farm animals appear in the section "Agriculture" instead. This might not be entirely intuitive, so to solve this, an Alphabetical English index can be found at the back of the book.

- For nouns and adjectives having an irregular plural form, the plural appears in parentheses.
- If a noun is listed in its dual or plural ([pl.]) form, this is indicated.

- A noun ending in ﺔ is feminine, and a noun *not* ending in ﺔ is masculine. The gender is marked [m.] and [f.] for nouns which do not follow this rule.
- All countries (except those marked [m.]) and all cities are feminine. Keep this in mind as countries and cities are not marked [f.].
- Normally, only the masculine version of nouns denoting humans is listed when the feminine equivalent can be formed by adding ﺔ. For example, أُسْتاذ is a male teacher. A female teacher would be أُسْتاذة.
- For the sake of consistency and simplicity, the masculine singular form is used in expressions. You will need to use your knowledge of Arabic grammar to produce the feminine or plural equivalents.
- Each verb appears in its base form (its most basic form without any prefixes or suffixes), which is the masculine singular past tense, literally "he did"; however, the English translation appears in its standard citation form: "to do". In order to use a verb in a sentence, it must be conjugated. See our book 'Levantine Arabic Verbs' for details on conjugating verbs.
- The Arabic script reflects common spelling conventions used by Palestinians. Of course, as there is no official spelling in a dialect, variations occur among native speakers. In this book, we strived for some consistency in spelling and style.
- A few words, which are vulgar or taboo, do not appear on the audio tracks because of their sensitive nature. These are marked with an asterisk.

Pronunciation

Palestinian Colloquial Arabic (PCA) is a spoken dialect with no official status or rules of orthography. Native speakers tend to borrow spelling conventions from Modern Standard Arabic with some accommodations to account for PCA pronunciation. Arabic script, however, is ill-suited to show the actual pronunciation of PCA, including word stress and sound changes that occur when verbs are conjugated. Even if you are comfortable with Arabic script, it is advised that you pay close attention to the phonemic transcription (and audio tracks) to determine a more precise pronunciation of verbs. IPA (International Phonetic Alphabet) symbols are found in [square brackets] in the descriptions below.

Consonants

The following sounds are also found in English and should pose no difficulties:

			examples
b	ب	[b] as in **bed**	*bána* بنى *(build)*
d	د	[d̪] as in **dog**, but with the tongue touching the back of the upper teeth	*dáfa3* دفع *(study)*
đ	ذ	[ð] as in **this** (used in some words borrowed from MSA)	
f	ف	[f] as in **four**	*fātūra* فاتورة *(bill)*
g	ق	[g] as in **gas** by the majority of Palestinians, especially in Gaza. Some speakers in urban areas (and especially among women) may pronounce ق as a hamza sound ء [ʔ].	*gára* قرا *(read)*
j	ج	[ʒ] as in **pleasure** and **beige**	*jísim* جسم *(body)*
h	ه	[h] as in **house**	*hájam* هجم *(attack)*
k	ك	[k] as in **kid**	*ákal* أكل *(eat)*
l	ل	[l] a light *l* as in **love**	*líbis* لِبِس *(get dressed)*
m	م	[m] as in **moon**	*māt* مات *(die)*
n	ن	[n] as in **nice**	*nísi* نِسي *(forget)*
s	س ث	[s] as in **sun**	*sána* سنة *(year)*
š	ش	[ʃ] as in **show**	*šū* شو *(what)*
t	ت	[t̪] as in **tie**, but with the tongue touching the back of the upper teeth	*ta3āl* تعال *(come)*
ŧ	ث	[θ] as in **thin** (used in some words borrowed from MSA)	

w	و	[w] as in **w**ord	*wēn* وين *(where)*
y	ي	[j] as in **y**es	*yíktib* يِكْتِب *(he writes)*
z	ز ذ	[z] as in **z**oo	*zār* زار *(visit)*

The following sounds have no equivalent in English and require special attention. However, some exist in other languages you may be familiar with.

r	ر	[ɾ] tapped (flapped) as in the Spanish **cara** or the Scottish pronunciation of t**r**ee	*ráma* رمى *(throw)*
ɣ	غ	[ɣ] very similar to a guttural **r** as in the French Pa**r**is or the German **r**ot	*yēr* غيْر *(different)*
x	خ	[x] as in the German do**ch**, Spanish ro**j**o, or Scottish lo**ch**	*áxad* أخد *(take)*
ħ	ح	[ħ] like a strong, breathy **h**, as if you were trying to fog up a window	*ħubb* حُبّ *(love)*
3	ع	[ʕ] a voiced glottal stop, as if you had opened your mouth under water and constricted your throat to prevent choking and then released the constriction with a sigh	*3írif* عِرِف *(know)*
ʔ	ء	[ʔ] an unvoiced glottal stop, as [ʕ] above, but with a wispy, unvoiced sigh; or more simply put, like the constriction separating the vowels in uh-oh	*ʔíbil* قِبِل *(accept)*

The following sounds also have no equivalent in English but are emphatic versions of otherwise familiar sounds. An emphatic consonant is produced by pulling the tongue back toward the pharynx (throat), spreading the sides of the tongue wide as if you wanted to bite down on both sides of your tongue, and producing a good puff of air from the lungs.

ḍ	ض	[dˤ] emphatic **d**	*ḍárab* ضرب *(hit)*
ṣ	ص	[sˤ] emphatic **s**	*ṣúbiħ* صُبِح *(morning)*
ṭ	ط	[tˤ] emphatic **t**	*ṭálab* طلب *(ask)*
ẓ	ظ	[zˤ] emphatic **z**	*ẓábaṭ* ظبط *(fit)*

Vowels

In PCA, vowels have some fluidity to their quality—their pronunciation is affected by neighboring consonants. The phonemic transcription offers an approximation based on the Arabic script. However, you should rely on the audio tracks to mimic a more precise pronunciation. Foreign words, in particular, may deviate from the rules below. Final vowels may be marked as long, but in reality, are often pronounced somewhat shorter.

examples

a	ـَ	The most versatile of the vowels, **a** may be pronounced a number of ways, most commonly [æ] as in c**a**t (but with the jaw not quite as lowered as in English); sometimes [ɛ] as in b**e**d, but sometimes more open, as the French é [e]; [a] as in st**o**ck when in the same syllable with *ḥ* or *3*; usually [ɑ] as in f**a**ther (but shorter) when in the same word as *q, ḍ, ṣ, ṭ, ẓ* or, in most cases, *r*	*kátab* كَتَب (write) *ḥaṭṭ* حَطّ (put) *ma3* مَع (with) *ḍárab* ضَرَب (hit) *áṣyar* أَصْغَر (younger)
ā	ـا	[æ:] / [a:] / [ɑ:] as with *a* above but longer	*nām* نام (sleep) *jā3* جاع (get hungry) *maqāl* مقال (article)
ē	ـيْ	[e:] as in pl**ay** (but without the glide to [j])	*wēn* وِيْن (where)
i	ـِ	[ɪ] as in k**i**d; [ɛ] as in b**e**d when in the same syllable with *ḥ* or *3*; when in the same word as *q, ḍ, ṣ, ṭ,* or *ẓ* [ɨ] with the tongue pulled back a bit	*3ílim* عِلِم (science) *líbis* لِبِس (undress) *ḍidd* ضِدّ (against)
ī	ـي	[i:] as in sk**i**; [ɛ:] and [ɨ:] as with *i* above (but longer)	*fī* في (there is) *ybī3* يْبِيع (he sells) *iṣṣīn* الصّين (China
ō	ـوْ	[o:] as with **o** above but longer	*nōm* نوْم (sleep)
u	ـُ	[ʊ] as in b**oo**k	*yúṭlub* يُطْلُب (he orders)
ū	ـو	[u:] as in m**oo**n	*šū* شو (what)

Also to Note:

- The pronunciation rules laid out above are guidelines, rules of thumb. There are many exceptions to these simplified pronunciation rules. Sound changes occur in many instances, according to grammatical inflections such as verb conjugation. A treatment of these, pertaining to grammar, lies outside the scope of this book.
- Attempts have been made to maintain a consistent orthography (spelling) in the Arabic script throughout this book. You will, of course, see various spellings of words by native speakers, as there are no official spelling rules for dialects. *Tashkeel* (diacritic marks) are not normally used by Arabs in their writing but are used in this book for the benefit of learners. To avoid clutter and make the text more readable, fatha (ً) is assumed to be the default vowel and is not normally written. Also, some very common words and affixes are written without tashkeel:

ـية	*-íyya*
الـ	*il- / li-* (followed by shadda when assimilated before certain consonants ("sun letters").
اللي	*ílli*
و	*w*

1 Life and Death

life	ḥayā	حَياة
to live	3āš, y3īš	عاش، يْعيش
I live in Gaza.	ána 3āyiš fi ɣázza.	أنا عايِش في غزّة.
alive	3āyiš	عايِش
to be born	inwálad, yinwílid	اِنْوَلَد، يِنْوِلِد
birth	wilāda	وِلادة
baby, infant	raḍī3	رضيع
to be breastfed, suckle	ríḍi3, yírḍa3	رِضِع، يِرْضَع
to breastfeed	ráḍḍa3at, tráḍḍi3 [f.]	رضَّعت، تْرضِّع
diaper	ḥaffāḍa	حفَّاضة
child; boy	wálad (wlād)	وَلد (وْلاد)
girl	bínit (banāt)	بِنِت (بنات)
well-behaved	muʔáddab	مُؤدّب
naughty, mischievous	šági	شقي
mature(-acting)	wā3i	واعي
adolescent, teenager	murāhiq	مُراهِق
to grow up	kíbir, yíkbar	كِبِر، يِكْبر
person	šáxṣ (ašxāṣ)	شخْص (أشْخاص)
people	nās [pl.]	ناس
young man	šabb (šabāb)	شابّ (شباب)
young woman	bínit (banāt)	بِنِت (بنات)
man	zálama (zlām)	زلمة (زْلامِ)
woman	mára (niswān)	مرا (نِسْوان)

adult	kbīr (kbār) wā3i (wā3yīn)	كْبير (كْبار) واعي (واعْيين)
young people, youth	šabāb [pl.]	شباب
young	ṣɣīr (ṣɣār)	صْغير (صْغار)
in one's fifties	fi -lxamsīnāt	في الخمْسينات
middle-aged	b-nuṣṣ 3úmru	بْنْصّ عُمْرو
old; old man	xityār 3ajūz [invar.]	خِتْيار عجوز
old woman	xityāra 3ajūz	خِتْيارة عجوز
to age, grow old	xátyar, yxátyir 3ájjaz, y3ájjiz	خْتْيَر، يْخْتْيِر عجّز، يْعجّز
Everyone gets old.	ilkúll bi3ájjiz.	الكُلّ بيعجّز.
childhood	ṭufūla	طُفولة
in one's childhood	b-ṭufūltu	بْطُفولْتو
adolescence	murāhaqa	مُراهقة
in one's youth	b-šabābu	بْشبابو
old age	3umr kbīr	عُمْر كْبير
birthday	3īd mīlād	عيد ميلاد
Happy Birthday! – Thank you!	kull 3ām w ínta b-xēr! – w ínta b-xēr! 3īd mīlād sa3īd! – šúkran!	كُلّ عام وإنْتَ بْخيْر! – وإنْتَ بْخيْر. عيد ميلاد سعيد! – شُكْراً
Happy birthday and may you have many more!	kull 3ām w ínta b-xēr w 3ugbāl ilmīt sána!	كُلّ عام وإنْتَ بْخير وعُقْبال المية سنةْ!
When is your birthday?	wagtēš 3īd mīlādak?	وَقْتيْش عيد ميلادك؟

My birthday is in May.	*3īd mīlādi b-šáhir xámsa.*	عيد ميلادي بْشهِر خمْسة.
age	*3úmur*	عُمُر
life span	*ṭūl il3úmur*	طول العُمُر
all one's life	*kull ḥayātu*	كُلّ حَياتو
How old are you?	*gaddēš 3umrak?*	قدّيْش عُمْرك؟
I'm 20 years old.	*3úmri 3išrīn.*	عُمْري عِشْرين.
to turn __ years old	*ṣār [55] (3úmru) __ sána*	صار (عُمْرو) __ سنة
He's turning twenty next week.	*ḥáyṣīr 3úmru 3išrīn sána lisbū3 ijjāy.*	حَيْصير عُمْرو عِشْرين سنة الإسْبوع الجّاي.
a fifty-year-old woman	*mára 3úmurha xamsīn*	مرا عُمْرُها خمْسين
When were you born?	*wagtēš inwáladit?*	وَقْتيْش اِنْوَلدت؟
I was born in 1980.	*inwáladit sant alf w tisa3míyya w tamānīn.*	اِنْوَلدِت سنْةْ ألْف وتِسعْمية وتمانين.
death, passing	*mōt*	موْت
to die	*māt, ymūt*	مات، يْموت
dead, deceased	*míyyit (mītīn, amwāt)*	مِيَّت (ميتين، أمْوات)
to pass away	*twáffa, yítwaffa* *xállaṣ [55] 3úmru*	اِتْوَفَّى، يِتْوَفَّى خلَّص عُمْرو
corpse, body	*jússa (júsas)*	جُثّة (جُثث)
funeral	*janāza*	جنازة
to bury	*dáfan, yídfin*	دفن، يِدْفِن
coffin	*ná3iš (n3ūš)*	نعِش (نْعوش)
cemetery	*mágbara (magābir)*	مقْبرة (مقابِر)
grave; burial	*gábur (gbūr)*	قبِر (قْبور)
gravestone, headstone	*šāhid (šawāhid)*	شاهِد (شَواهِد)

to mourn	ḥízin, yíḥzan	حِزِن، يِحْزن
mourning	ḥidād	حِداد
period of mourning	ayyām il3áza	أيّام العزا

2 Family

(extended) family	*3ēla*	عيْلة
immediate family; household	*dār*	دار

> دار *dār* also means 'house,' but Palestinians use it as the family that lives under one roof—sometimes siblings or cousins share the same building, one apartment each.

relatives	*garāyib* [pl.]	قرايِب
I have some relatives that live in New York.	*3índi garāyib 3āyšīn bi-nyūyōrk.*	عِنْدي قرايِب عايْشين بِنْيويوْرْك.
is related to	*byígrab (la-)*	بْيِقْرب (لـ)
Are you two related?	*íntu -litnēn btígrabu la-bá3ḍ?*	إنْتو الاِتْنيْن بْتِقْربوا لبعض؟
I'm not related to him.	*ána ma bágrablu.*	أنا ما بقْربْلو.

father	*ábu (abbahāt)*	أبو (أبّهات)
mother	*amm (ammahāt)* [or *imm (immahāt)*]	أمّ (أمّهات)
my mother and father	*ámmi w abūwi*	أمّي وأبوي
dad	*yāba*	يابا
mom	*yámma*	يمّا

> Some people say بابا *bāba* 'dad' and ماما *māma* 'mother.'

Hi, Dad!	*márḥaba, yāba!*	مرْحبا يابا!
Where are you, Mom?	*wēnik yámma?*	ويْنِك يمّا؟
parents	*áhil*	أهِل

son, (male) child	*íbin (wlād)*	إبِن (وْلاد)
daughter, (female) child	*bínit (banāt)*	بِنِت (بنات)
Do you have any children?	*3índak wlād?*	عِنْدك وْلاد؟

How many children do you have?	kam wálad 3índak?	كَم وَلَد عِنْدك؟
They have triplets.	3índhum tálat táwāʔim.	عِنْدْهُم تلات تَوائِمِ.
siblings	ixwāt [pl.]	إخْوات
brother	áxu (ixwāt)	أخُو (إخْوات)
My brother and my friend's brother came with me.	axūwi w axū ṣāħbi áju má3i.	أخُوي وأخُو صاحْبي أجو معي.
sister	úxut (xawāt)	أُخُت (خَوات)
older brother	ákbar áxu	أكْبر أخُو
younger sister	áṣyar úxut	أصْغر أُخْت
Do you have any brothers or sisters?	3índak ixwāt aw xawāt?	عِنْدك إخْوات أوْ خَوات؟
I have two older sisters and one younger brother.	3índi uxtēn ákbar mínni w wáħda áṣyar.	عِنْدي أُخْتيْن أكْبر مِنّي ووَاحْدة أصْغر.
I'm the youngest in my family.	ána áṣyar wāħad fi -l3ēla.	أنا أصْغر واحد في العيْلة.
I'm the middle child/son.	ána -lwálad ílli bi-nnúṣṣ.	أنا الوَلَد اللي بالنُّص.
I'm an only child.	ána waħīd.	أنا وَحيد.
twin	táwʔam tōm	تَوْأُم تُوْم
Are you twins?	íntu tōm? íntu táwʔam?	إنْتو تُوْم؟ إنْتو تَوْأُم؟
I have a twin brother.	3índi áxu táwʔam.	عِنْدي أخُو تَوْأُم.
half-brother	áxu min ilʔábu	أخُو مِن الأبُو
half-sister	úxut min ilʔámm	أُخُت مِن الأمّ
He's my half-brother.	hāda axūwi min abūwi.	هادا أخُوي مِن أبُوي

husband	*jōz* *zōj*	جوْز زوْج
wife	*mára*	مرا
__'s wife	*mart __*	مرْت__
His wife came with him.	*ájat mártu má3u.*	أجت مرْتو معو.

stepfather	*jōz ilʔámm*	جوْز الأمّ
stepmother	*mart ilʔábu*	مرْت الأبو
stepbrother	*axūwi min mart abūwi*	أخوي مِن مرْت أبوي
stepsister	*úxut min mart abūwi*	أُخْت مِن مرْت أبوي
stepson	*íbin jōz* *íbin mart__*	اِبن جوْز اِبن مرْت__
stepdaughter	*bint zōj* *bint mart__*	بِنْت جوْز بِنْت مرْت__
grandfather	*sīd (syād)*	سيد (سْياد)
grandmother	*sitt*	سِتّ

grandma and grandpa	*sítti w sīdi*	سِتّي وسيدي
great-grandfather	*ábu sīd*	أبو سيد
grandson	*ḥafīd (aḥfād)*	حفيد (أحْفاد)
granddaughter	*ḥafīda*	حفيدة
grandchildren	*aḥfād [pl.]*	أحْفاد
uncle (father's brother)	*3amm (3mām)*	عمّ (عْمام)
aunt (father's brother's wife)	*mart 3amm*	مرْت عمّ

aunt (father's sister)	*3ámma*	عمّة
uncle (father's sister's husband)	*jōz 3ámma*	جوْز عمّة
uncle (mother's brother)	*xāl (xwāl)*	خال (خْوال)
aunt (mother's brother's wife)	*mart xāl*	مرْت خال
aunt (mother's sister)	*xāla*	خالة
uncle (mother's sister's husband)	*jōz xāla*	جوْز خالة
cousin (father's brother's son)	*íbin 3amm*	اِبن عمّ
cousin (father's brother's daughter)	*bint 3amm*	بِنْت عمّ
cousin (father's sister's son)	*íbin 3ámma*	اِبن عمّة
cousin (father's sister's daughter)	*bint 3ámma*	بِنْت عمّة
cousin (mother's brother's son)	*íbin xāl*	اِبن خال
cousin (mother's brother's daughter)	*bint xāl*	بِنْت خال
cousin (mother's sister's son)	*íbin xāla*	اِبن خالة
cousin (mother's sister's daughter)	*bint xāla*	بِنْت خالة
We're cousins.	*íḥna wlād 3amm.*	إحْنا وْلاد عمّ.

The above example refers to two or more men/boys whose fathers are brothers.

orphan	*yatīm (aytām)*	يَتيم (أَيْتام)
orphanage	*dār ilʔaytām*	دار الأَيْتام
to adopt	*(i)tbánna, yitbánna*	اِتْبنّى، بِتْبنّى
adoption	*tabánni*	تبنّي
I was adopted.	*ána -tbannūni.* [lit. they adopted me]	أنا اتْبنّوني.

an adopted son	*íbin bi-ttabánni*	اِبِن بِالتَّبنّي
adoptive parents	*áhil bi-ttabánni*	أهِل بِالتَّبنّي
ancestors, forefathers	*syād* [pl.]	سْياد

Some people say جُداد *jdād* 'ancestors.'

| descendents | *aḥfād* [pl.] | أحْفاد |

to love, be in love	*ḥabb, yḥibb*	حبّ، يْحِبّ
love	*ḥubb*	حُبّ
I love you!	*baḥíbbak!*	بحِبّك!
darling	*ḥabībi*	حبيبي
romance	*rōmānsíyya*	رُوْمانْسية
to love passionately	*3íšig, yí3šag*	عِشِق، يِعْشق
passion	*3íšig*	عِشِق
lover	*3āšig (3uššāg)*	عاشِق (عُشّاق)
date (romantic)	*ṭál3a rōmānsíyya*	طلْعة رُوْمانْسية
to go on a date with __	*ṭíli3 [55] ṭál3a rōmānsíyya ma3*	طِلع طلْعة رُوْمانْسية مع
dating, in a relationship	*biḥíbbu bá3aḍ* *bēnhum 3alāqa*	بيحِبّوا بعض بيْنْهُم علاقة
a couple	*ḥabbība*	حبّيبة
going out, dating	*ṭāl3īn ma3 bá3aḍ*	طالْعين مع بعض
boyfriend	*ḥabīb (ḥabāyib)*	حبيب (حبايِب)
girlfriend	*ḥabība*	حبيبة
to break up with, leave	*sāb, yˈsīb*	ساب، يْسيب
to break someone's heart	*kásar gálbu, yíksir gálbu* *járaḥ, yíjraḥ*	كسر قلْبو، يِكْسِر قلْبو جرح، يِجْرح
heartbroken	*maksūr gálbu* *majrūḥ*	مكْسور قلْبو مجْروح
engagement	*xúṭba*	خُطْبة
to get engaged	*inxáṭab, yinxíṭib*	اِنْخطب، يِنْخِطِب

to ask her father for her hand in marriage	ṭálab [55] īdha min abūha	طلب إيدْها مِن أبوها
fiancé	xaṭīb	خطيب
fiancée	xaṭība	خطية
Her fiancé works abroad.	xaṭībha bištíɣil bárra.	خطيبْها بيشْتِغِل برّا.
married (to)	midjáwwiz	مِتْجوّز
Are you married?	ínta midjáwwiz?	إنْتَ مِتْجوّز؟
single, unmarried	miš midjáwwiz á3zab	مِش مِتْجوّز أعْزب
to get married, marry, wed	idzáwwaj, yidzáwwaj	إتْجوّز، يِتْجوّز
marriage	jawāz	جَواز
They got married last year.	idjáwwazu -ssána -lli fātat.	إتْجوّزوا السّنة اللي فاتت.
wedding	3úrus	عُرُس
groom	3arīs (3irsān)	عريس (عِرْسان)
bride	3arūs (3arāyis)	عروس (عرايِس)
honeymoon	šahr il3ásal	شهْر العسل
(wedding) anniversary	3īd jawāz	عيد جَواز
They celebrated their tenth anniversary.	iḥtáfalu bi-3āšir sána jawāz.	اِحْتفلوا بِعاشِر سنة جَواز.
divorce	ṭalāg	طلاق
to get divorced	iṭṭállag, yiṭṭállag	إِتْطلّق، يِتْطلّق
divorced; divorcee	mṭállag	مْطلّق
to remarry	ríji3 [55] idjáwwaz	رِجع اِتْجوّز
My father remarried last year.	abūwi ríji3 idzáwwaj issána -lli fātat.	أبوي رِجِع اِتجوّز السّنة اللي فاتت.
widower	ármal (arāmil)	أرْمل (أرامِل)

widow	*ármala*	أَرْملة
to cheat on __ (with), have an affair (with)	*xān __, yxūn __ (ma3)*	خان ___، يْخون ___ مع
He is cheating on his wife with his secretary.	*bixūn mártu ma3 sikirtērtu.*	بيخون مرْتو مع سِكِرْتيْرْتو.
kiss	*bōsa*	بوْسة
to kiss	*bās, ybūs*	باس، يْبوس
Kiss me!	*būsni!*	بوسْني!
sex	*jins*	جِنْس
to have sex	*māras ijjíns, ymāris ijjíns*	مارس الجِّنْس، يْمارِس الجِّنْس
to sleep with	*nām, ynām ma3*	نامر، يْنام مع
to sleep together	*nāmu ma3 bá3aḍ, ynāmu ma3 bá3aḍ*	ناموا مع بعض، يْناموا مع بعض
to fuck	*nāk, ynīk**	ناك، يْنيك

*See page 25 for notes on vulgar words.

4 Names and Addressing People

name; first name	*ísim (asmāʔ, asāmi)*	اِسِم (أَسْماء، أَسامي)
What's your name?	*šū ísmak?*	شو اِسْمك؟
My name is __.	*ána ísmi __.*	أنا اِسْمي ___.
last name	*ísim il3ēla*	اِسْم العيْلة
full name	*ilʔísim kāmil*	الاِسِم كامِل
to name	*sámma, ysámmi*	سمّى، يْسمّي
to be called, named	*(i)tsámma, yitsámma*	اِتْسمّى، يِتْسمّى
to call	*nāda, ynādi*	نادى، يْنادي
How should I address you?	*kēf bitḥíbb anādīk?*	كيْف بِتْحِبّ أناديك؟
Just call me __.	*nādīni ___.*	ناديني.___
title; nickname	*láqab (alqāb)*	لقب (ألْقاب)
There's no need for titles.	*mā fī dā3i la-lʔalqāb.*	ما في داعي للألْقاب.
I don't have a nickname.	*malíš láqab.*	مليش لقب.
alias, pseudonym	*ism iššúhra*	اِسْم الشُّهْرة
teknonym	*kúnya*	كُنْية

A teknonym is an epithet used in Arab culture to show familiarity and respect. It conists of the word أبو *ábu* for a man and إمّ *imm* for a woman followed by the name of his or her eldest son, or, if there is no son, eldest daughter.

Abu Khaled	*ábu xālid*	أبو خالِد
Umm Ali	*amm 3áli*	أمّ علي
Sir!	*ustāz!*	أُسْتاذ!
Ma'am!	*madām!*	مدام!

| Miss! | *ānisa!* | آنِسة! |

The following are titles which precede someone's name. Unlike in English, titles often precede one's given name.

Mr. __	*ustāz* __	أُسْتاذ__
Mrs. __	*madām* __	مدام__
Miss __	*ānisa* __	آنسة__
Dr. __ (medical or Ph.D.)	*duktōr* __	دُكتوْر__

| **Yes?** (response to someone calling your name) | *ná3am?* | نعم؟ |

body	*jísim (ajsām)*	جِسِم (أَجْسام)
head	*rās (rūs)*	راس (روس)
brain, mind	*dmāɣ (ádmiɣa)* *3ágil (3gūl)*	دْماغ (أَدْمِغة) عقِل (عْقول)
skull	*júmjuma (jamājim)*	جُمْجُمة (جماجِم)
face	*wíjih (wjūh)*	وِجِهْ (وْجوهْ)
He has a **round** face.	*wíjhu mdáwwar*	وِجْهو مْدوّر.
She has a **oblong** face.	*wíjihha ṭawīl.*	وِجِهْها طَويل.
I have a **square** face.	*wíjhi mrábba3.*	وِجْهي مْربّع.
You have an **oval** face.	*wíjhak bayḍāwi.*	وِجْهك بَيْضاوي.
to wash one's face	*ɣásal [55] wíjhu*	غسل وِجْهو
forehead	*jbīn*	جْبين
He has a big forehead.	*jbīnu 3arīḍ.*	جْبينو عريض.
brow	*ḥawājib [pl.]*	حَواجِب
to frown, knit one's brow, scowl	*3ágad ḥwājbu,* *yí3gid ḥwājbu* *kášsar, ykáššir*	عقد حْواجْبو، يِعْقِد حْواجْبو كشّر، يْكشّر
cheek	*xadd (xdūd)*	خدّ (خْدود)
chin	*dágin (dgūn)*	دقِن (دْقون)
jaw	*fakk (fkūk)*	فكّ (فْكوك)
eye	*3ēn (3yūn)*	عين (عْيون)

The dual becomes عينيْ *3ēnē-* when taking a pronoun suffix. The singular, dual, or plural may be used when referring to a person's eyes.

My eyes itch.	*3ēnáyya bitḥúkkni.*	عينيّا بِتْحُكّني.

blue eyes	*3ēnēn zúrug*	عيْنيْن زُرُق
green eyes	*3ēnēn xúḍur*	عيْنيْن خُضُر
brown eyes	*3ēnēn binniyāt*	عيْنيْن بِنِّيات
She has beautiful brown eyes.	*3ēnēha binniyāt ḥilwāt.*	عيْنيْها بِنِّيات حِلْوات.
What color are his eyes?	*šū lōn 3ēnē?*	شو لوْن عيْنيْه؟
His eyes are green.	*3ēnē xúḍur.*	عيْنيْه خُضُر.
eyebrow	*ḥājib (ḥwājib)*	حاجِب (حْواجِب)
eyelid	*jífin (jfūn)*	جِفِن (جْفون)
eyelash	*rímiš (rmūš)*	رِمِش (رْموش)
She has long eyelashes.	*rmūšha ṭwāl.*	رْموشْها طْوال.
sclera, the white of one's eyes	*bayāḍ 3ēn*	بَياض عيْن
pupil	*bú?bu?*	بُؤْبُؤ
to blink	*rámaš 3ēnu, yírmiš 3ēnu*	رمش عيْنو، يِرْمِش عيْنو
to wink	*ɣámaz, yíɣmiz*	غمز، يِغْمِز
to close one's eyes	*ɣámmaḍ 3ēnē, yɣámmiḍ 3ēnē*	غمَّض عيْنيْه، يْغمِّض عيْنيْه
to open one's eyes	*fáttaḥ 3ēnē*	فتَّح عيْنيْه
dark circles under one's eyes	*sawād táḥit 3ēnē*	سَواد تحِت عيْنيْه
cross-eyed	*áḥwal, ḥōla (ḥíwil)*	أحْوَل، حوْلا (حِوِل)
blind	*á3ma, 3ámya (3imyān)*	أعْمى، عمْيا (عِمْيان)
to see	*šēf, yšūf*	شاف، يْشوف
I can't see the clock from here.	*miš gādir ašūf issā3a min hān.*	مِش قادِر أشوف السّاعة مِن هان.
eyesight, vision	*náẓar*	نظر
I have perfect eyesight.	*náẓari gáwi ktīr.*	نظري قَوي كْتير.
to wear glasses	*líbis [6] náḍḍarāt*	لِبِس نضّارات
I think you need glasses.	*šáklu bíddak náḍḍarāt.*	شكْلو بِدّك نضّارات.

to cry	ṣáyyaḥ, yṣáyyiḥ	صيّح، يْصيّح

English	Transliteration	Arabic
a tear	dám3a (dmū3)	دمْعة (دْموع)
Why are your eyes red? Have you been crying?	lēš 3ēnēk ḥúmur? kunt tṣáyyiḥ?	ليْش عيْنيْك حُمُر؟ كُنْت تْصيّح؟
nose	munxār (manaxīr) ánf (unūf)	مُنْخار (مناخير) أنْف (أُنوف)

English	Transliteration	Arabic
nostril	fátḥit munxār	فتْحِةْ مُنْخار
big/pronounced nose	munxār kbīr	مُنْخار كْبير
petite nose	munxār ṣyīr	مُنْخار صْغير
sharp/pointy nose	munxār 3ídil	مُنْخار عِدِل
hook/crooked nose	munxār ma3wūj	مُنْخار معْووج
to sneeze	3áṭas, yú3ṭus	عطس، يُعْطُس
snot	barābīr	برابير

English	Transliteration	Arabic
(to have) a runny nose	mrášših	مْرشّح
to blow one's nose	naff, yniff	نفّ، يْنِفّ

English	Transliteration	Arabic
to pick one's nose	lí3ib [55] b-munxāru	لِعِب بِمنْخارو
to smell	šamm, yšimm	شمّ، يْشِمّ
sense of smell	ḥāsit šamm	حاسِةْ شمّ
I don't have a very good sense of smell.	mā 3índi ḥāsit šamm gawíyya.	ما عِنْدي حاسِةْ شمّ قَوية.
I think I smell smoke.	šáklu fī rīḥit duxān.	شكْلو في ريحِةْ دُخان.
ear	dān [f.] (dīnēn)	دان (دينيْن)
earlobe	ḥálamit dān [lit. ear nipple]	حلِمِةْ دان

to cup one's ear	ḥaṭṭ [55] īdu wára dānu	حطّ إيدو وَرا دانو
to hear	sími3, yísma3	سِمِع، يِسْمَع
Do you hear that noise?	sāmi3 ha-ṣṣōt?	سامِع هالصّوْت؟
ringing in one's ear	ṣōt taṣfīr bi-ddān	صوْت تصْفير بِالدّان
to be hard of hearing	sáma3u tgīl	سمعو تْقيل
deaf	áṭraš, ṭárša (ṭuršān)	أطْرش، طرْشا (طرْشان)
to wear a hearing aid	líbis [6] sammā3a	لِبِس سمّاعة
pierced ears	dān maxzūga	دان مخزوقة
ear wax	wásax iddān [lit. ear filth]	وَسخ الدّان

mouth	timm (tmām)	تِمّ (تْمام)
to smile	ibtásam, yibtísim	إنْتسم، يِبْتِسِم
to open one's mouth	fátaḥ [55] tímmu	فتح تِمّو
to close one's mouth	sákkar tímmu, ysákkir tímmu	سكّر تِمّو، يْسكّر تِمّو
tongue	lsān	لْسان
to taste	dāg, ydūg	داق، يْدوق
Can you taste the mint in this dessert?	ḥāsis b-ṭá3im inná3na3 fi -lḥílu hād?	حاسِس بْطعِم النّعْنع في الحِلو هاد؟
lip	šíffa (šafāyif)	شِفّة (شفايِف)
upper lip	iššíffa -lli fōg	الشُّفّة اللي فوْق
lower lip	iššíffa -lli táḥit	الشُّفّة اللي تحِت
thin lips	šafāyif ṣyār	شفايِف صْغار
full lips	šafāyif kbār	شفايِف كْبار
chapped (dry) lips	šafāyif našfāt	شفايِف ناشْفات
tooth	sinn (snān)	سِنّ (سْنان)
gums	lítta	لِثّة

front teeth	snān guddamāníyya	سْنان قُدّمانية
to bite	3aḍḍ, y3aḍḍ	عضّ، يْعضّ
molar	ṭāḥūna (ṭawāḥīn)	طاحونة (طواحين)
to chew	máḍay, yúmḍuy	مضغ، يِمْضُغ
to spit	taff, ytiff	تفّ، يْتِفّ
spit, spittle	táffa	تفّة
saliva	riyāla	رِيالة
to yawn	(i)ttāwab, yittāwab	إِتّاوب، يِتّاوَب
to cough	qaḥḥ, yquḥḥ	قحّ، يْقُحّ

Some people say كحّ، يْكُحّ *kaḥḥ, ykuḥḥ* 'to cough.'

| to burp, belch | (i)ttárra3, yittárra3 | إِتّرّع، يترّع |

Some people say اِتْكرّع، يِتْكرّع *itkárra3, yitkárra3* 'to burp.'

| bad breath | rīḥit timm múgrifa | ريحِةْ تِمّ مُقْرِفة |
| tonsils | lúwaz [pl.] | لُوَز |

neck	rágaba (rgāb)	رقبة (رْقاب)
nape of the neck	gáfa	قفا
throat	zōr	زوْر

Some people use the more formal MSA حلق *ḥálaq* 'throat.'

larynx	ḥúnjura (ḥanājir)	حُنْجُرة (حناجِر)
to breathe	(i)tnáffas, yítnaffas	إِتْنفّس، يِتْنفّس
to take a deep breath	áxad [55] náfas 3amīq	أخد نفس عميق
breathing	tanáffus	تنفّس
to swallow	bála3, yíbla3	بلع، يِبْلع
to choke	šírig, yíšrag	شِرِق، يِشْرق
He started choking on a piece of food.	3állagat illúgma fi zōru.	علّقت اللُّقمة في زوْرو.

hair	šá3ar	شعر
dark brown hair	šá3ar bínni ɣāmiǧ	شعر بِنّي غامِق
light brown hair	šá3ar bínni fātiḥ	شعر بِنّي فاتح
blond hair	šá3ar ášgar	شعر أُشْقر
black hair	šá3ar áswad	شعر أُسْوَد
red hair	šá3ar áḥmar	شعر أحْمر
gray hair	šá3ar ramādi	شعر رمادي
white hair	šá3ar ábyaḍ	شعر أبْيَض
to dye one's hair	ṣábaɣ šá3ru, yúṣbuɣ šá3ru	صبغ شعْرو، يُصْبُغ شعْرو
She dyes her hair blond.	btúṣbuɣ šá3arha ášgar.	بْتصْبُغ شعرْها أشْقر.
She's a natural blond.	šá3arha ášgar ṭabī3i.	شعرْها أشْقر طبيعي.
long hair	šá3ar ṭawīl	شعر طَويل
short hair	šá3ar gaṣīr	شعر قصير
shoulder-length hair	ṭūl iššá3ar la-lkítif	طول الشَّعر للْكِتِف
straight hair	šá3ar nā3im	شعر ناعِم
curly hair	šá3ar mjá33ad	شعر مْجعّد

English	Transliteration	Arabic
wavy hair	šá3ar mmáwwaj	شعر مْموّج
She has long beautiful straight brown hair.	šá3arha ṭawīl w ḥílu w nā3im w bínni.	شعرْها طَويل وحِلو وناعِم وبنّي.
to comb/brush one's hair	máššaṭ šá3ru, ymášši̧ṭ šá3ru	مشّط شعْرو، يمْشِّط شعْرو
to get a haircut	gaṣṣ [55] šá3ru	قصّ شعْرو
bald	áṣla3	أضْلع
to go bald	ṣār [55] áṣla3	صار أضْلع
sideburns	sawālif [pl.]	سَوالِف
pony-tail	dēl liḥṣān	ديْل الِحْصان

braids	*jadāyil* [pl.]	جدايِل
She wears her hair in braids.	*btúrbuṭ šá3arha jadāyil.*	بْتُرْبُط شعرْها جدايِل.

bun	*ká3ka*	كعْكة
She usually wears her hair in a bun.	*bi-l3āda btúrbuṭ šá3arha ká3ka.*	بِالعادة بْتُرْبُط شعرْها كعْكة.
bangs	*ɣúrra*	غُرّة
You look good with bangs.	*šáklik ḥílu bi-lɣúrra.*	شكْلِك حِلو بِالغُرّة.
wig, toupee	*barūka*	بروكة
You can tell he wears a toupee.	*šáklu ḥāṭiṭ barūka.*	شكْلو حاطِط بروكة.
beard	*dágin* [f.] *(dgūn)*	دقِن (دْقون)
mustache	*šánab*	شنب
He has a beard and mustache.	*3āmil dágin w šánab.*	عامِل دقِن وشنب.
goatee	*saksūka*	سكْسوكة
to trim one's beard	*zábbaṭ dágnu, yzábbiṭ dágnu*	زبّط دقْنو، يْزبِّط دقْنو
to shave	*ḥálag, yíḥlig*	حلْق، يِحْلِق
He shaves every morning.	*bíḥlig kull yōm iṣṣúbiḥ.*	بيحْلِق كُلّ يوْم الصُّبِح.
clean-shaven	*mná33im* [lit. softened]	مْنعّم
stubble	*dágin xafīfa*	دقِن خفيفة
skin	*jílid* *bášra*	جِلِد بشْرة
pimple, blemish	*ḥábba*	حبّة
I have a huge pimple on my chin!	*3índi ḥábba kbīra b-dágni.*	عِنْدي حبّة كْبيرة بْدقْني.
acne	*ḥabb iššabāb*	حبّ الشّباب

As a teenager, he had a lot of acne.	kān 3índu ḥabb šabāb lámma kān b-3úmur ilmurāhaqa.	كان عِنْدو حبّ شباب لمّا كان بُعْمُر المُراهقة.
bad (blemished) skin	bášra ta3bāna	بشْرة تعبانة
a good complexion	bášra ṣāfya	بشْرة صافْية
fair-skinned	ábyaḍ, báyḍa (bīḍ)	أَبْيَض، بيْضا (بيض)
dark-skinned	ásmar, sámra (súmur)	أَسْمر، سمْرا (سُمُر)
oily skin	bášra dúhníyya	بشْرة دُهْنية
dry skin	bášra jāffa	بشْرة جافّة
to put on lotion	ḥaṭṭ [55] krēm	حطّ كْريم
to put on sunscreen	ḥaṭṭ [55] wāqi šámis	حطّ واقي شمِس
freckles	námaš	نمش
She has a lot of freckles.	3índha námaš ktīr.	عِنْدها نمش كْتير.
mole, birthmark	wáḥma	وَحْمة
wrinkles	tajā3īd [pl.]	تجاعيد
You get wrinkles as you get older.	kull ma tíkbar biṣīr 3índak tajā3īd áktar.	كُلّ ما تِكْبر بيصير عِنْدك تجاعيد أكْتر.
scar	3alāma	علامة
tattoo	wášim	وَشِم
He has a tattoo on his left arm.	ḥāṭiṭ wášim 3a ʔīdu lišmāl.	حاطِط وَشِم عَ إيدو الشْمال.
Do you have any tattoos?	ḥāṭiṭ wášim?	حاطِط وَشِم؟
arm; hand	īd (īdēn)	إيد (إيديْن)
What's in your hand?	šū fī b-ʔīdak?	شو في بْإيدك؟
They're all wearing watches on their wrists.	kúllhum lābsīn sā3āt fi ʔīdēhum.	كُلّهُم لابْسين ساعات في إيديْهُم.
elbow	kū3	كوع
armpit	abāṭ	أباط

to sweat	3írig, yí3rag	عِرِق، يِعْرق
sweaty	3argān	عرْقان
He was very sweaty after playing soccer.	kān 3argān ktīr bá3id la3b ilkōra.	كان عرْقان كْتير بعِد لِعْب الكوْرة.
finger	íşba3 (aşābi3)	إصْبع (أصابِع)
finger print	báşma	بصْمة
thumb	il?íşba3 likbīr	الإصْبع الكِبير
index finger	issabbāba	السّبّابة
middle finger	il?íşba3 ílli fi -nnuşş	الإصْبع اللي في النُّصّ
ring finger	íşba3 ilxātim	إصْبع الخاتِم
little finger, pinky	xúnşur	الإصْبع الصْغير
finger nail	íḑfar	إضْفر
palm	kaff	كفّ
back of the hand	gáfa -l?īd	قفا الإيد
ball of the hand	bátin il?īd	بطِن الإيد
joint; knuckles; wrist	máfşal	مفْصل
to make a fist	3ámal [55] īdu bōks	عمّل إيدو بوكْس
to extend one's fingers	madd aşābī3u, ymidd aşābī3u	مدّ أصابيعو، يمِدّ أصابيعو
to hold, grip	másak, yímsik	مسك، يمْسِك
to point to	áššar 3a, ygáššir 3a	أشّر عَ، يْأشِّر عَ
He pointed at the clock.	áššar 3a-ssā3a.	أشّر عَ السّاعة.
leg, foot	ríjil (rijlēn) [f.]	رِجِل (رِجْلين)
thigh	fáxda (fxād)	فخْدة (فْخاد)
shin	gáşabit ríjil	قصبِة رِجِل
calf	báttit ríjil	بطّة رِجِل

knee	rúkba (rúkab)	رُكْبة (رُكَب)
ankle	kāḥil (kḥūl)	كاحِل (كْحول)
sole	bāṭin ríjil	بطِن رِجِل
heel	ká3ib (k3ūb)	كعِب (كْعوب)
toe	íṣba3 ríjil	إصْبع رِجِل

shoulder	kítif (ktāf)	كتِف (كْتاف)
broad shoulders	ktāf 3rāḍ	كْتاف عْراض
chest, bosom	ṣídir (ṣdūr)	صِدِر (صْدور)
breast, boob	bizz (bzāz)*	بِزّ (بْزاز)
nipple	ḥálama*	حلمة
flat chested	ṣídir msáṭṭaḥ	صِدِر مْسطّح
abdomen, belly	báṭin (bṭūn)	بطِن (بْطون)
back	ḍáhir (ḍhūr)	ضهِر (ضْهور)
waist, hips	xáṣir (xṣūr)	خصِر (خْصور)
navel, belly button	ṣúrra	صُرّة
internal organs	il3úḍu -ddāxili (ilʔa3ḍāg ildāxilíyya)	العُضو الدّاخِلي (الأعْضاء الدّاخِلية)
stomach	mí3da	مِعْدة
intestines, bowels	muṣrān (maṣārīn)	مُصْران (مصارين)
lung	ríʔa	رِئة
heart	galb (glūb)	قلْب (قْلوب)
to beat, palpitate	dagg, ydugg nábaḍ, yúnbuḍ	دقّ، يْدُقّ نبِض، يِنْبُض
heart beat, pulse	dággit ilgálb	دقّة القلْب
liver	kíbid (akbād)	كبِد (أكْباد)
kidney	kílya (kalāwi)	كِلْية (كلاوي)

bladder	*maṯāna*	مثانة
gallbladder	*marāra*	مرارة
gland	*ɣúdda (ɣúdad)*	غُدَّة (غُدد)
thyroid gland	*ɣúdda daraqíyya*	غُدَّة درقية
bone	*3áḍma (3ḍām)*	عضْمة (عُضام)
skeleton	*hēkal 3áḍmi (hayākil 3aḍmíyya)*	هيْكل عضْمي (هَياكِل عضْمية)
spine	*3āmūd fáqari (3awāmīd fiqaríyya)*	عامود فقري (عواميد فقرية)
rib	*ḍíli3 (ḍlā3)*	ضِلع (ضْلاع)
muscle	*3áḍala*	عضلة
vein	*warīd (áwrida)*	وَريد (أوْرِدة)
artery	*širyān (šarāyīn)* *3írig (3rūg)*	شِرْيان (شرايين) عِرِق (عْروق)
blood	*damm*	دمّ
nerve	*3áṣab (a3ṣāb)*	عصب (أعْصاب)

Needless to say, caution should be exercised when talking about 'private parts'. There are numerous synynoms (and euphemisms) for these, but each is appropriate only in certain social contexts. There are medical terms which can be used when necessary to mention 'private parts', such as when speaking to a doctor. There are also euphemisms used with small children. And of course, there are vulgar terms which should only be used among close friends who are not offended by such vulgarities. As a non-native speaker, you are advised to avoid using vulgar terms altogether, as they will tend to get you into trouble; nonetheless, they have been included here for recognition purposes. However, due to their sensitive nature, they (and similarly sensitive words) do not appear on the MP3s and are marked with an asterisk.

sexual organs, private parts	*a3ḍāʔ tanāsulíyya* [pl.]	أعْضاء تناسُلية
penis	*gaḍīb (guḍbān)**	قضيب (قُضْبان)

dick, cock	zibb (zbāb) zúbur (zbār)*	زِبّ (زْباب) زُبُر (زْبار)
to get an erection/boner	zíbbu wígif*	زِبّو قام
boner, hard-on	zibb gāgim*	زِبّ قايِم
testicle	bēḍa*	بيْضة
scrotum, testicles	kīs ṣáfan (akyās aṣfān)*	كيس صفن) أُكْياس صفن)
balls, nuts (scrotum)	bēḍāt* [pl.]	بيْضات
vagina	máhbal (mahābil)*	مهْبل (مهابِل)
'girl parts'	ilmanāṭig ilHassāsa la-lbínit*	المناطِق الحسّاسة للْبِنِت
pussy	kuss (ksās)*	كُسّ (كْساس)
naked, bare	miš lābis íši 3iryān	مِش لابِس إشي عِرْيان
buttocks, bottom, posterior	xalfíyya	خلْفية
bottom	táħit	تحِت
ass, butt	ṭīz (ṭyāz)*	طيز (طْياز)
anus	šarj*	شرْج
ass hole	fáthit ṭīz*	فتْحِةْ طيْز
to urinate	tbáwwal, yitbáwwal	اِتْبوّل، يِتْبوّل
urine	bōl	بوْل
to pee	fann, yfinn	فنّ، يْفِنّ
to piss, take a piss	šaxx, yšuxx*	شخّ، يْشُخّ
to defecate	(i)tbárraz, yitbárraz	اِتْبرّز، يِتْبرّز
excrement, feces	burāz	بُراز
to poo, poop	3ámal [55] kákka	عمل ككّة
shit	xára*	خرا

to go to the bathroom	rāḥ [55] 3a -lḥammām	راح عَ الحمّام
I need to go to the bathroom.	bíddi ʔarūḥ 3a -lḥammām.	بِدّي أروح عَ الحمّام.
to pass gas, break wind	ṭálla3 [55] rīḥ	طلّع ريح
to fart	fáṣṣaṣ, yfáṣṣiṣ*	فصّص، يْفصّص

Some people say **ضرّط، يْضرّط** ḍárraṭ, yḍárriṭ 'to fart.'

fart	faṣṣ*	فصّ
height	ṭūl	طول
tall	ṭawīl (ṭwāl)	طَويل (طْوال)
average height	ṭūlu 3ādi	طولو عادي
short	gaṣīr (gṣār)	قصير (قْصار)
How tall are you?	gaddēš ṭūlak?	قدّيْش طولك؟
I'm 1.75 meters tall.	ṭūli míyya w xámsa w sab3īn sánti.	طولي ميّة وخمْسة وسبْعين سانْتي.
weight	wázin (awzān)	وَزِن (أوْزان)
How much do you weigh?	gaddēš wáznak?	قدّيْش وَزْنك؟
I weigh 70 kg.	wázni sab3īn kēlu.	وَزْني سبْعين كيْلو.
one's build, body shape	šíkil jísim	شِكِل جِسِم
fat, overweight	nāṣiḥ (nāṣḥīn) ṭxīn (ṭxān) smīn (smān)	ناصِح (ناصْحين) تْخين (تْخان) سْمين (سْمان)
to get fat	níṣiḥ, yínṣaḥ tíxin, yítxan símin, yísman	نِصِح، يِنْصح تِخِن، يِتْخن سِمِن، يِسْمَن
Don't overeat so you don't get fat.	tākílš ktīr 3ašān mā tínṣaḥiš.	تاكِلْش كْتير عشان ما تِنْصحِش.

chubby, plump, stout	malyān mkálbiz	مَلْيان مْكَلْبِز
average weight	wázin 3ādi	وَزِن عادي
thin	ḍ3īf (ḍ3āf) rfī3 (rfā3)	ضْعيف (ضْعاف) رْفيع (رْفاع)
skinny	m3áḍḍam	مْعضَّم
one's looks	šáklu	شكْلو

good-looking;
  handsome; beautiful,
  pretty
	ḥílu
	mráttab
		حِلو
		مْرتَّب

cute	nā3im	ناعِم

My God, those girls are
  so cute!
	ya-llāh, hadōl ilbanāt
	  nā3mīn ktīr!
		يا الله، هدوْل البنات ناعْمين كْتير!

ugly	bíši3 miš ḥílu	بِشِع مِش حِلو
average-looking	jamāl 3ādi	جمال عادي

Clothing, Jewelry, and Accessories

clothing	*awā3i* [pl.]	أواعي
men's clothing	*awā3i rijjāli*	أواعي رِجّالي
women's clothing	*awā3i sittāti*	أواعي سِتّاتي
undergarments	*awā3i dāxilíyya*	أواعي داخِلية
underwear; panties	*klōt*	كْلوْت
panty hose, tights	*kōlōn*	كوْلوْن
bra	*sintyāna*	سِنتْيانة
(button-up) shirt	*gamīṣ (gumṣān)*	قميص (قُمْصان)
t-shirt, polo shirt; blouse	*blūza (balāyiz)*	بْلوزة (بلايِز)

بْلوزة *blūza* is a cognate of the English word 'blouse,' but it is, in fact, used for men's clothing, as well.

collar	*gábba*	قبّة
sleeve	*kumm*	كُمّ
long-sleeved shirt	*gamīṣ kumm*	قميص كُمّ
short-sleeved shirt	*gamīṣ nuṣṣ kumm*	قميص نُصّ كُمّ
(pair of) pants	*bānṭalōn*	بنْطلوْن
pant leg	*ríjil bānṭalōn*	رِجِل بنْطلوْن
jeans	*jīnz* *kabōy* [from English 'cowboy']	جينْز كبوْي
shorts	*šurt*	شُرْط
belt	*gšāṭ* *ḥzām* *sēr*	قْشاط حْزام سير

(belt) buckle	rās ligšāṭ	راس القْشاط
suit	bádla	بدْلة
suit jacket	jākētt ilbádla	جاكيْتّ البدْلة
uniform	ziyy	زِيّ
abaya (traditional full-length garment)	3abāya	عبايَة
neck tie	grāfa garafáṭṭa	قْرافة قرفطّة
to tie one's neck tie	rábaṭ [55] grāftu	ربط قْرافْتو
watch	sā3a	ساعة
wallet	máḥfaẓa ḍuzdān	محْفظة ضُزْدان
bag, briefcase	šánta (šúnat)	شنْطة (شُنط)

Notice that ط is commonly written, preserving the spelling from MSA in this word even though it is pronounced ت in Palestinian Arabic.

courier bag	šánta rijjāli	شنْطة رِجّالي
handbag, purse	šántit ʔīd	شنْطِةّ إيد
dress	fustān (fasātīn)	فُسْتان (فساتين)
skirt	tannūra (tananīr)	تنّورة (تنانير)
hijab, headscarf	ḥijāb šāla šēla	حِجاب شالة شيْلة
niqab	niqāb	نِقاب
(women's) scarf	išárb mandīl (manādīl)	إشرْب منْديل (مناديل)
hair ribbon	rábṭit šá3ar	رِبْطِة شعر

barrette, hair clip	*klīps* *málgaṭ šá3ar*	كُليبْس مَلْقط شعر
hat (also: **cap, beanie,** etc.)	*ṭāgíyya (ṭawāgi)*	طاقية (طَواقي)
turban	*turbān*	تُرْبان
jacket	*jākētt*	جاكيتّ
coat	*bālṭō* *kōt*	بالْطوْ كوْت
sweater	*blūza ṣūf*	بْلوزة صوف
zip-up sweater	*blūza ṣūf b-saḥḥāb*	بْلوزة صوف بْسحّاب
scarf	*láfḥa*	لفْحة
gloves	*kaffāt* [pl.] *kfūf* [pl.]	كفّات كُفوف
bathrobe	*rōb ḥammām*	روْب حمّام
pajamas	*bajāma*	بجامة
nightgown	*gamīṣ nōm*	قميص نوْم
swimsuit, bathing suit	*mayō*	مَيوْه
bikini	*bīkīni*	بيكيني
pocket	*jēba*	جيْبة
to put __ in one's pocket	*ḥaṭṭ* [55] __ *b-jēbtu*	حطّ ــ بْجيْبْتو
to take __ out of one's pocket	*ṭálla3* [55] __ *min jēbtu*	طلّع ــ مِن جيْبْتو
button	*zirr (zrār)*	زِرّ (زْرار)
to button up	*sákkar lizrār, ysákkir lizrār*	سكّر الزِرار، يْسكّر الزِرار

to unbutton	*fakk lizrār, yfikk lizrār*	فكّ الزِرار، يْفِكّ الزِرار
zipper	*saḥḥāb*	سحّاب
to zip up	*sákkar issaḥḥāb*	سكّر السّحّاب
to unzip	*fátaḥ [55] issaḥḥāb*	فتح السّحّاب
(pair of) shoes	*jázma (jízam)* *kúndara (kanādir)* *bōt (bwāt)*	جزْمة (جزم) كُنْدرة (كنادِر) بوْت (بْوات)
shoe	*fárdit bōt* *fárdit kúndara*	فرْدِةْ بوْت فرْدِةْ كُنْدرة
boots	*bōt*	بوْت
بوْت *bōt* can means 'boots' or, more broadly, any kind of shoes.		
sandals	*ṣándal*	صنْدل
high heels	*ká3ib 3āli*	كعِب عالي
(pair of) slippers	*šíbšib* *zannūba* *ḥaffāya*	شِبْشِب زنّوبة حفّايَة
shoelaces	*rabbāṭ ilbōt*	ربّاط البوْت
to tie one's shoes	*rábaṭ [55] bōtu*	ربط بوْتو
to untie one's shoes	*fakk rabbāṭ bōtu*	فكّ ربّاط بوْتو
Your shoelaces have come undone.	*rabbāṭ bōtak fālit.*	ربّاط بوْتك فالِت.
shoe polish	*bōyit jízam*	بوْيِةْ جِزم
to polish one's shoes	*dáhan jázmitu, yídhan jázmitu*	دهن جزْمِتو، يِدهن جزْمِتو
shoe size	*magās ríjil*	مقاس رِجِل
What size shoes do you wear?	*šū magās ríjlak?*	شو مقاس رِجْلك؟
I wear size 40.	*ána bálbis nímra arb3īn.*	أنا بلْبِس نمْرة أرْبعين.

I'm not sure about my size.	*miš mitʔákkid gaddēš nímrit ríjli.*	مِش مِتْأكّد قَدّيْش نِمْرِةْ رِجْلي.
(pair of) socks	*jarābīn*	جرابين
to wear, to get dressed, to put on	*líbis, yílbis*	لِبِس، يِلْبِس
What are you going to wear today?	*šū ḥatílbis ilyōm?*	شو حتِلْبِس اليوْم؟
He took a shower, got dressed, and left for work.	*(i)tḥámmam, w líbis, w rāḥ 3a šúɣlu.*	اِتْحمّم ولِبِس وراح عَ شُغْلو.

Like the English verbs 'put on' and 'wear', لِبِس *líbis* can take a variety of complements: shirt, pants, hat, belt, shoes, glasses, jewelry, etc. But it is not used with perfume, lotion, etc.

to take off	*šálaḥ, yíšlaḥ*	شلح، بِشْلح
to get undressed	*šálaḥ awā3ī*	شلح أواعيه
I took off my jacket.	*šaláḥit jākētti.*	شلحِت جاكيتّي.
to change one's clothes	*ɣáyyar [55] awā3ī*	غيّر أواعيه
(clothing) size	*magās*	مقاس
small (S)	*smōl*	سْمولْ
medium (M)	*mīdyam*	ميدْيَم
large (L)	*lārj*	لارْج
extra-large (XL)	*iks lārj*	إِكْس لارْج
loose	*wāsi3*	واسِع
tight	*ḍíyyig*	ضِيّق
just right (not too loose or tight)	*3a -lgadd*	عَ القدّ
Does the shirt fit you?	*jāy 3alēk ilgamīṣ?*	جاي عليْك القميص؟
Yes, it fits just right.	*ā, jāy 3a -lgadd.*	آه، جاي عَ القدّ.
It doesn't fit.	*miš jāy 3a gáddi.*	مِش جاي ع قدّي.
It's a bit big.	*kbīr šwáyya.*	كْبير شْوَيّة.

| It's too tight. | *ḍíyyig šwáyya.* | ضَيِّق شْوَيَّة. |

to do the laundry	*ɣásal [55] ilɣasīl*	غسل الغسيل
to hang out the laundry	*nášar ilɣasīl, yúnšur ilɣasīl*	نشر الغسيل، يْنْشُر الغسيل
to dry the laundry	*náššaf ilɣasīl, ynáššif ilɣasīl*	نشِّف الغسيل، يْنشِّف الغسيل
washing machine	*ɣassāla*	غسّالة
(clothes) dryer	*mujáffifit ilɣasīl*	مُجفِّفِة الغسيل
clothes line	*ḥábil ɣasīl*	حبِل غسيل
laundry basket	*sállit ɣasīl*	سلِّة غسيل
to iron	*káwa, yíkwi*	كَوى، يِكْوي
iron	*mákwa*	مكْوى
ironing board	*ṭāwlit káwi*	طاوْلِة كَوي
wrinkled	*mjá3lak*	مْجعْلك
This shirt is wrinkled. I need to iron it.	*ilgamīṣ hād mjá3lak. bíddi akwī.*	القميص هاد مْجعْلك. بِدّي أكْويه.

cloth, fabric	*gmāš*	قْماش
cotton	*gúṭun*	قُطْن
wool	*ṣūf*	صوف
silk	*ḥarīr*	حرير
nylon	*nāylūn*	نايْلون
linen	*kittān*	كِتّان
Is this t-shirt cotton?	*hādi liblūza gúṭun?*	هادي البْلوزة قُطْن؟
This shirt is silk.	*hāda -gamīṣ ḥarīr.*	هادا القميص حرير.
leather	*jílid*	جِلِد

English	Transliteration	Arabic
glasses	*naḍḍārāt* [pl.]	نظّارات

English	Transliteration	Arabic
contact lenses	*3adasāt* [pl.]	عدسات
Do you wear glasses?	*ínta btílbis naḍḍārāt?*	إنْت بْتِلْبِس نظّارات؟
Oh, you're wearing glasses today!	*šū hāda! lābis naḍḍārāt ilyōm?*	شو هاد! لابِس نظّارات اليوْم؟
I usually wear contacts.	*ána bi-l3āda bálbis 3adasāt.*	أنا بِالعادة بلْبِس عدسات.
sunglasses	*naḍḍārāt šámis*	نظّارات شمِس

English	Transliteration	Arabic
reading glasses	*naḍḍārāt la-ligrāya*	نظّارات للِقْرايَة
I can't find my glasses.	*miš lāgi naḍḍārāti.*	مِش لاقي نظّاراتي.
jewelry	*mujawharāt*	مُجَوْهرات
ring	*xātim (xawātim)*	خاتِم (خواتِم)
wedding ring	*máḥbas*	محْبس
engagement ring	*xātim xúṭūba*	خاتِم خُطوبة
bracelet	*iswāra (asāwir)*	إسْوارة (أساوِر)
earring	*ḥálag (ḥlūg)*	حلق (حْلوق)
I lost my earring.	*ḍayyá3it ḥálagi.*	ضيّعِت حلقي.
necklace	*sinsāl (sanāsīl)*	سِنْسال (سناسيل)
brooch	*dabbūs* *3allāga*	دبّوس علّاقة
diamonds	*almās*	ألْماس
ruby	*yāqūt*	ياقوت
topaz	*yāqūt áṣfar*	ياقوت أصْفر
emeralds	*zumúrrud*	زُمُرّد
gold	*dáhab*	دهب

| silver | *fídḍa* | فِضّة |
| a diamond ring, gold bracelet, and silver necklace | *xātim almās, w iswāra dáhab, w sinsāl fídḍa* | خاتِم أَلْماس وإسْوارة دهب وسِنْسال فِضّة |

7 | The House

house	dār (dūr) bēt (byūt)	دار (دور) بيْت (بْيوت)
apartment	šágga (šúgag)	شقَّة (شُقق)
two-story apartment	vílla (vílal)	فيْلَّا (فِلل)
penthouse apartment	šágga rūf	شقَّة روف
story, floor	ṭābig (ṭawābig)	طابِق (طَوابِق)
The apartment is on the fourth floor.	iššágga bi-ṭṭābig irrābi3.	الشّقة بِالطّابِق الرّابِع.
to rent an apartment	(i)tʔájjar šágga, yitʔájjar šágga	اِتْأجَّر شقَّة، بِتْأجَّر شقَّة
rent	ajār	أجار
How much is the rent?	gaddēš ilʔajār?	قدّيْش الأجار؟
How much do you pay in rent?	gaddēš btídfa3 ajār?	قدّيْش بْتِدْفع أجار؟
tenant, renter	mistáʔjir	مِسْتأجِّر
landlord	ṣāḥib ilmakān	صاحِب المكان
landlady	ṣāḥbit ilmakān	صاحْبِة المكان

المكان *ilmakān* 'the place' can be substituted with a more specific word depending on the kind of property, for example صاحِب الشّقَّة *ṣāḥib iššágga* 'the landlord of the apartment.'

to rent an apartment (to)	ájjar šágga, yʔájjir šágga	أجّر شقَّة، يْأجِّر شقَّة
roof	súṭuḥ (sṭūḥ) rūf	سُطُح (سْطوح) روف
fence	sūr (aswār) syāj	سور (أسْوار) سْياج

gate	bawwāba	بوّابة
gardener	janāyni	جنايْني
The gardener comes once a week.	ijjanāyni bīji márra bi-lʔisbū3.	الجّنايْني بيجي مرّة بِالإسْبوع.
housekeeper, maid	xaddāma	خدّامة
doorman	bawwāb naṭūr (nawaṭīr)	بوّاب ناطور (نَواطير)
Ask the doorman to wash our car this afternoon.	gul la-lbawwāb yíɣsil issayyāra ba3d iḍḍúhur.	قُل للبوّاب يِغْسِل السّيّارة بعْد الضُّهُر.
room	ɣúrfa (ɣúraf)	غُرْفة (غُرف)
furniture	3áfiš	عفِش
furnished	mafrūš	مفْروش
chair	kúrsi (karāsi)	كُرْسي (كراسي)
table	ṭáwla	طاوْلة
door	bāb (bwāb)	باب (بْواب)
front door	bāb amāmi	باب أمامي
key	muftāḥ (mafatīḥ)	مُفْتاح (مفاتيح)
floor	arḍ	أرْض (أراضي)
ceiling	ságif (sgūf)	سقِف (سْقوف)
carpet	sijjāda (sijjād)	سِجّادة (سِجّاد)
tiles	balāṭ	بلاط
hardwood floor	arḍ xášab	أرْض خشب
window	šubbāk (šababīk)	شُبّاك (شبابيك)
curtain, blinds	stāra (satāyir)	سْتارة (ستايِر)
shutters	abājōr šīš	أباجْور شيش

shelf	*raff (rfūf)*	رفّ (رْفوف)
wall	*ḥēṭ (ḥēṭān)*	حيْط (حيْطان)
wall clock	*sā3it ḥēṭ*	ساعِةْ حيْط
painting, picture	*ṣūra (ṣúwar)* *láwḥa*	صورة (صُوَر) لَوْحة
to hang a picture on the wall	*3állag ṣūra 3a -lḥēṭ, y3állig ṣūra 3a -lḥēṭ*	علّق صورة عَ الحيْط، يْعلّق صورة عَ الحيْط
I love that painting hanging over the sofa.	*3ājbāni -lláwḥa -lim3állga fōg ilkánaba.*	عاجْباني اللَوْحة المْعلّقة فوْق الكنبة.
poster	*yāfṭa* *pōstar*	يافْطة بوْسْتر
to do housework	*ištáɣal šuɣl iddār, yištíɣil šuɣl iddār*	إِشْتغل شُغْل الدّار، يِشْتِغِل شُغْل الدّار
to clean	*náḍḍaf, ynáḍḍif*	نضّف، يْنضّف
to tidy up	*ráttab, yráttib*	رتّب، يْرتّب
to wash the windows	*ɣásal [55] iššabābīk*	غسل الشّبابيك
broom	*múknisa*	مُكْنِسة
to sweep	*kánnas, ykánnis*	كنّس، يْكنّس
mop	*mámsḥa*	مِمْسَحة
to mop, wipe	*másaḥ, yímsaḥ*	مسح، يِمْسح
vacuum cleaner	*múknisit káhrab*	مُكْنِسِةْ كَهْرب
to vacuum the carpet	*šáffaṭ issijjāda, yšáffiṭ issijjāda*	شفّط السِّجّادة، يْشفّط السِّجّادة
dust	*ɣábara*	غبرة
to dust	*másaḥ ilɣábara*	مسح الغبرة

dusty	myábbir	مْغبّر
to beat the dust out of a carpet	náffaḍ issijjāda min ilɣábara, ynáffiḍ issijjāda min ilɣábara	نْقّض السَّجّادة مِن الغبرة، يْنفّض السَّجّادة مِن الغبرة
light	ḍaww (ḍwāw)	ضوّ (ضْواوْ)
lamp	lámba	لمْبة
to turn on the light	ḍáwa -ḍḍaww, yíḍwi -ḍḍaww	ضَوى الضّوّ، يِضْوي الضّوّ
to turn off the light	ṭáfa [55] -ḍḍaww	طفى الضّوّ، يِطْفي الضّوّ
Could you turn off the light in the kitchen, please?	múmkin tíṭfi ḍaww ilmáṭbax bá3id íznak?	مُمْكِن تِطْفي ضوّ المطْبخ بعِد إذْنك؟
light switch	kábsit ḍaww	كبْسِةْ ضوّ
electrical outlet, socket	brīz	بْريز
plug	fīša	فيشة
to plug in	ḥaṭṭ [55] ilfīša	حطّ الفيشة
to unplug	šāl ilfīša, yšīl ilfīša	شال الفيشة، يْشيل الفيشة
extension cord, adapter	mutállat štíkar	مُتلّت شْتِكر

مُتلّت *mutállat,* which literally means 'triangled' or 'three-pronged,' is used because most extension cords have three outlets.

fuse box	tāblōn káhraba	طبْلوْن كهْربا
fuse	fyūz	فْيوز
A fuse has blown.	inḥárag fyūz.	انْحرق فْيوز.
the power went out	gáṭ3at ilkáhraba	قطْعت الكهْربا
The power went out for an hour this afternoon.	ilkáhraba gáṭ3at sā3a -lyōm ba3d iḍḍúhur.	الكهْربا قطْعت ساعة اليوْم بعْد الضُّهُر.
candle	šám3a	شمْعة
heater	daffāya	دفّايَة

air-conditioner	mukáyyif	مُكَيِّف
living room	ṣālōn ṣāla	صالوْن صالة
formal sitting room (for entertaining guests)	ɣúrfit ḍyūf	غُرْفِةْ ضْيوف
sofa, couch	kánaba	كنبة
television	tilfizyōn	تِلْفِزْيوْن
to watch TV	ḥíḍir [55] tilfizyōn	حِضِر تِلْفِزْيوْن
The only thing I want to do this evening is watch TV.	ilʔ íši -lwaḥīd ílli bíddi á3malu -llēla húwwa ʔínni áḥḍar tilfizyōn.	الإشي الوَحيد اللي بِدّي أعْملو اللّيْلة هُوّ إنّ إنّي أحْضر تِلْفِزْيوْن.
dining room	ɣúrfit ilʔákil	غُرْفِةْ الأكِل
dining table	ṭāwlit ilʔákil	طاوْلِةْ الأكِل
to set the table	jáhhaz iṭṭāwla, yjáhhiz iṭṭāwla	جهّز الطّاوْلة، يْجهّز الطّاوْلة
to clear the table	náḍḍaf iṭṭāwla	نضّف الطّاوْلة
to sit at the table	gá3ad [55] 3a -ṭṭāwla	قعد عَ الطّاوْلة
Dinner's ready! Come to the table!	il3áša jāhiz! itfáḍḍlu 3a -ṭṭāwla!	العشا جاهِز! اِتْفضّلوا عَ الطّاوْلة!
(flower) vase	fāza	فازة
plate, dish	ṣáḥin (ṣḥūn)	صحِن (صْحون)
spoon	má3lga (m3ālig)	معْلقة (معالِق)
fork	šōka (šúwak)	شوْكة (شُوَك)
knife	sikkīna (sakakīn)	سِكّينة (سكاكين)
bowl	jāṭ	جاط
napkin	mandīl (manadīl) máḥrama (maḥārim)	مِنْديل (مناديل) مخْرمة (محارِم)

kitchen	máṭbax (maṭābix)	مطْبخ (مطابِخ)
cupboard, cabinet	xzāna	خْزانة
refrigerator	tallāja	تلّاجة
freezer	frēzar	فْرِيزر
stove	ɣāz	غاز
oven	fúrun (frān)	فُرُن (فْران)
microwave (oven)	māykrōwēv	مايْكْرْوْويْف
to microwave	ḥaṭṭ [55] fi -lmāykrōwēv	حطّ في المايْكْرْوْويْف
Just put it in the microwave for two minutes.	bass ḥúṭṭu dagigtēn fi -lmāykrōwēv.	بسّ حُطّو دقيقْتيْن في المايْكْرْوْويْف.
to heat up	sáxxan, ysáxxin	سخّن، يْسخّن
I heated up the soup in the microwave.	ána saxxánit iššōraba bi-lmāykrōwēv.	أنا سخّنِت الشّوْربة بِالمايْكْرْوْويْف.
cooking	ṭábix	طبِخ
to make dinner	3ámal [55] il3áša	عمل العشا
to cut	ɡáṭṭa3, yɡáṭṭi3	قطّع، يْقطّع
to dice	ɡáṭṭa3 ɡíṭ3a ṣɣīra	قطّع قِطع صْغيرة
to slice	ɡáṭṭa3 šarāyiḥ	قطّع شرايِح
to cut up, chop (up)	xárraṭ, yxárriṭ	خرّط، يْخرّط
to cut in half	ɡáṭṭa3 bi-nnúṣṣ	قطّع بالنُّصّ
to cook (on the stove)	ṭábax, yúṭbux	طبخ، يُطبُخ
to bake (bread)	xábaz, yúxbuz	خبز، يُخْبُز
to boil	sálag, yúslug	سلق، يُسْلُق
to fry	ɡála, yíɡli	قلى، يِقْلي
pot	ṭínjara	طِنْجرة
pan	gallāya ṭāwa	قلّايَة طاوَة

tray, casserole dish	ṣiníyya (ṣawāni)	صينية (صَواني)
recipe	wáṣfa	وَصْفة
to follow a recipe	tábba3 wáṣfa, ytábbi3 wáṣfa	تبَّع وَصْفة، يتبَّع وَصْفة
cook book	ktāb ṭábix	كْتاب طبِخ
blender; mixer	xallāṭ	خلَّاط
toaster	tōst	توْسْت
sink	máɣsala (maɣāsil)	مغْسلة (مغاسِل)
faucet	ħanafíyya	حنفية
to do the dishes	jála -jjáli, yíjli -jjáli	جلى الجَّلي، يِجْلي الجَّلي
dishwashing liquid	sāʔil jáli	سائِل جلي
to make tea	3ámal [55] šāy	عمل شاي
kettle	bōylar kúmkum	بوْيْلر كُمْكُم
to make coffee	3ámal [55] gáhwa	عمل قهْوَة
coffee maker	mākīnit gáhwa	ماكينِةْ قهْوَة
garbage	zbāla	زْبالة
garbage can	sáṭil zbāla sállit zbāla	سطِل زْبالة سلَّةْ زْبالة
to throw away	ráma [55] zatt, yzitt	رمى زتَّ، يْزِتَّ
to take out the garbage	ṭálla3 [55] lizbāla	طلَّع الزِبالة
bedroom	ɣúrfit nōm	غُرْفِةْ نوْم
bed	táxit (txūt)	تخِت (تْخوت)

single bed, twin bed	táxit mífrid	تْخِت مِفْرِد
double bed, queen bed, king bed	táxit míjwiz	تْخِت مِجْوِز
headboard	rūsíyyit táxit	روسِيّةْ تْخِت
mattress	fáršit srīr	فَرْشِةْ سْرير
blanket	ħrām baṭṭāníyya	حْرام بطّانية
bedsheet	šáršaf	شَرْشف
pillow, cushion	mxádda	مْخدّة
pillow case	wíjih mxádda	وِجِهْ مْخدّة
to make one's bed	ráttab ittáxit, yráttib ittáxit	رتّب التّخِت، يْرتّب التّخِت
sleep	nōm	نوْم
to sleep, fall asleep, go to sleep, go to bed	nām, ynām	نام، يْنام
I only got four or five hours' sleep last night.	imbāriħ nímit tagrīban árba3 aw xámas sā3āt.	إمْبارِح نِمِت تقْريباً أرْبع أوْ خمس ساعات بس.
What time did you go to bed?	3a -l?ákam nímit?	عَ الأكم نِمِت؟
asleep	nāyim	نايِم
sleepy, drowsy	na3sān mdárwax	نعْسان مْدرْوَخ
to be sleepy	miš gādir yfáttiħ 3ēnē	مِش قادِر يْفتّح عيْنه
to doze off	ɣífi, yíɣfa	غِفي، يِغْفى
to take a nap	ɣáffa, yɣáffi áxad [55] ɣáfwa	غفّى، يْغفّي أخد غفْوة
I was feeling sleepy, so I took a short nap.	kúnit na3sān, rúħit ɣaffētli šwáyya.	كُنِت نعْسان، رُحِت غفّيْتلي شْوَيّة.
to dream	ħílim, yíħlam	حِلِم، يِحْلم

a dream	ḥílim (aḥlām)	حِلِم، (أَحْلام)
a nightmare	kābūs (kawabīs)	كابوس (كَوابيس)
to have a nightmare	ḥílim b-kābūs kōbas, ykōbas	حِلِم بُكابوس كوْبِس، يُكوْبِس
to snore	šáxxar, yšáxxir	شخّر، يْشخّر
to talk in one's sleep	ḥáka [55] w húwwa nāyim	حكى وهُوّ نايِم
to sleepwalk	máša [55] w húwwa nāyim	مشى وهُوّ نايِم
unable to get to sleep, have a restless night's sleep	galgān miš 3ārif ynām	قلْقان مِش عارِف يْنام
You don't look like you slept well.	šáklak miš nāyim mnīḥ.	شكْلك مِش نايِم مْنيح.
to have insomnia	3índu ʔárag 3índu gálag	عِندو أرق عِنْدو قلق
to be a light sleeper	nōmu xafīf	نوْمو خفيف
in a deep sleep	b-sābi3 nōma	بْسابِع نوْمة
to be a deep sleeper	nōmu tgīl	نوْمو تْقيل
to stay up late	síhir illēl, yíshar illēl	سِهِر اللّيْل، يِسْهر اللّيْل
to stay up all night	síhir ṭūl illēl	سِهِر طول اللّيْل
to wake (up), rouse	ṣáḥḥa, yṣáḥḥi	صحّى، يْصحّي
My mom woke me up.	ámmi ṣáḥḥatni (min innōm).	أمّي صحّتْني (مِن النّوْم.)
to wake up	ṣíḥi, yíṣḥa	صِحي، يِصْحى
I woke up at six o'clock in the morning.	ṣḥīt issā3a sítta -ṣṣúbiḥ.	صْحيت السّاعة سِتّة الصُّبِح.
A loud noise woke me up.	ṣḥīt 3a ṣōt dáwša.	صْحيت عَ صوْت دوْشة.
to get up, get out of bed	gām min ittáxit, ygūm min ittáxit	قامِ مِن التّخِت، يْقوم مِن التّخِت

wardrobe	*xzāna*	خْزانة
hanger	*3allāga*	علّاقة
dresser, vanity	*tasrīḥa*	تسْريحة
drawer	*dúruj (drāj)* *jarrār*	دُرْج (دْراج) جرّار
bedside table	*kōmīdīna*	كوْميدينة
alarm clock	*munábbih*	مُنبّه
I set my alarm for six in the morning.	*ḥaṭṭēt ilmunábbih 3a -ssā3a sítta -ṣṣúbiḥ.* *zabbáṭit ilmunábbih 3a -ssítta -ṣṣúbiḥ.*	حطّيْت المُنبّهْ عَ السّاعة ستّة الصُّبِح. زبّطِت المُنبّهْ عَ السِّتّة الصُّبِح.
bookcase	*máktaba*	مكْتبة
desk	*máktab (makātib)* *ṭāwlit máktab*	مكْتب (مكاتِب) طاوْلِة مكْتب
bathroom	*ḥammām*	حمّام
bath tub	*bānyō (bānyōhāt)*	بانْيوْ (بانْيوهات)
to take a bath	*(i)tḥámmam, yítḥammam*	اِتْحمّم، يِتْحمّم
shower	*dušš*	دُشّ
to take a shower	*áxad [55] dušš*	أخد دُشّ
sponge, loofah	*līfa*	ليفة
shampoo	*šāmbō*	شامْبوْ
to dry off, towel oneself off	*náššaf [6] ḥālu*	نشّف حالو
towel	*mánšafa (manāšif)* *baškīr (bašākīr)*	منْشفة (مناشِف) بشْكير (بشاكير)
towel rack	*3allāgit ilmánšafa* *3allāgit ilbaškīr*	علّاقِة المنْشفة علّاقِة البشْكير
hair dryer	*siušwār*	سِشْوار

toilet (bowl)	kabanē	كبنيّه
toilet seat	kúrsi -lkabanē	كُرسي الكبنيّه
to flush the toilet	šadd issīfōn, yšidd issīfōn	شدّ السّيفوْن، يْشِدّ السّيفوْن
toilet paper	wárag ḥammām wárag twālētt	وَرق حمّام وَرق تْواليْتّ
sink	máɣsala (maɣāsil)	مغْسلة (مغاسِل)
hot water	máyya súxna	ميّة سُخْنة
cold water	máyya sāg3a	ميّة ساقْعة
(gas) water heater	saxxān máyya 3a -lɣāz	سخّان مية عَ الغاز
mirror	mrāya	مْرايَة
to brush one's teeth	fárša snānu, yfárši snānu	فرْشى سْنانو، يْفرْشي سْنانو
toothbrush	furšāyit snān	فُرْشايِةْ سْنان
tooth paste	ma3jūn snān	معْجون سْنان
dental floss	xēṭ snān	خيْط سْنان
to floss one's teeth	náḍḍaf [7] snānu bi-lxēṭ	نضّف سْنانو بِالخيْط
to wash one's face	ɣásal [55] wíjhu	غسل وِجْهو
(bar of) soap	ṣābūna	صابونة
to shave	ḥálag, yíḥlig	حلق، يِحْلِق
razor (blade)	šáfra	شفْرة
electric razor	mākīnit ḥlāga	ماكينِةْ حْلاقة
shaving cream	ma3jūn ḥlāga	معْجون حْلاقة
lawn	ḥašīš	حشيش
to mow the lawn	gaṣṣ [55] ilḥašīš	قصّ الحشيش
courtyard	sāḥa	ساحة

garden, yard	ḥadīqa jnēna	حديقة جُنّيْنة
to garden	zára3, yízra3	زرع، يِزرع
shovel	krēk	كُريْك
to dig	ḥáfar, yúḥfur	حفر، يُحْفُر
(garden) hose	barbīš	برْبيش
tool	3ídda (3ídad)	عِدّة (عِدد)
saw	munšār (manāšīr)	مُنْشار (مناشير)
to saw	gaṣṣ [55] bi-lmunšār	قصّ بِالمنُشار
hammer	šākūš (šawākīš)	شاكوش (شَواكيش)
to hammer	dagg [5] bi-ššākūš	دقّ بِالشّاكوش
nail, screw	musmār (masamīr)	مُسْمار (مسامير)
screwdriver	mafákk	مفكّ
axe	bálṭa	بلْطة
to chop wood	gaṣṣ [55] ilxášab	قصّ الخشب
wrench (UK: spanner)	muftāḥ inglīzi	مُفْتاح إنْجْليزي

8 Food and Drink

to eat	*ákal, yākul*	أكَل، ياكُل
What do you feel like eating?	*šū bíddak tākul?*	شو بِدّك تاكُل؟
food	*ákil*	أكِل
to drink	*šírib, yíšrab*	شِرِب، يِشْرب
drink, beverage	*mašrūb*	مشْروب
a bite, a sip, a mouthful	*bugg*	بُقّ
a bite	*lúgma*	لُقْمة
to take a bite of	*áxad [55] lúgma min* *áxad [55] bugg min*	أخد لُقْمة مِن أخد بُقّ مِن
He took a bite of the hamburger and put it down.	*áxad lúgma min sándwiš ilhāmburgar w sābu.*	أخد لُقْمة مِن سنْدْوِش الهامْبرْجر وسابو.
a sip	*šáfṭa*	شفْطة
to take a drink/sip (of)	*šírib šáfṭa min* *āxad [55] bugg min*	شِرِب شفْطة مِن أخد بُقْ مِن
She took a sip of water and put the glass down.	*áxdat šáfṭit máyya w ḥáṭṭat ilkubbāya.*	أخْدت شفْطةْ مِيّة وحطّت الكُبّايَة.
to chew	*mádaɣ, yúmduɣ*	مدغ، يمّْدُغ
to swallow	*bála3, yíbla3*	بلع، يِبْلع
to choke on	*šírig, yíšrag*	شِرِق، يِشْرق
hungry	*ja3ān*	جعان
to get hungry	*jā3, yjū3*	جاع، يْجوع
hunger	*jū3*	جوع
thirsty	*3aṭšān*	عطْشان

I'm so thirsty. Could I have some water?	ána 3aṭšān. múmkin ášrab máyya?	أنا عطْشان. مُمْكِن أشْرب ميّة؟
to become thirsty	3íṭiš, yí3ṭaš	عِطِش، يِعْطش
thirst	3áṭaš	عطش
full, satiated	šab3ān	شبْعان
to become full	šíbi3, yíšba3	شِبِع، يِشْبع
Thanks, I'm full.	šúkran, šbí3it.	شُكْراً، شْبِعِت.
to taste	dāg, ydūg	داق، يْدوق
Taste the soup. Does it need salt?	dūg iššōraba, bíddha máliḥ?	دوق الشّوْربة، بِدْها ملح؟
delicious, tasty	zāki lazīz	زاكي لزيز
taste	ṭá3im	طعِم
I don't like how it tastes.	mā 3ájabni ṭá3mu.	ما عجبْني طعْمو
The milk tastes funny.	illában ṭá3mu yarīb.	اللّبن طعْمو غريب.
to go bad	xírib, yíxrab	خِرِب، يِخْرب
The milk has gone bad.	illában xírib.	اللّبن خِرِب.
to expire, be past its expiration date	íntahat ṣalāḥītu	إنْتهت صلاحيتو
The milk is past its expiration date.	íntahat ṣalāḥīt ilḥalīb.	اِنْتهت صلاحيةْ الحليب.
to rot	3áffan, y3áffin	عفّن، يْعفّن
fresh	ṭāza	طازة
stale	bāyit	بايِت
bland	xafīf māsix	خفيف ماسِخ
salty	māliḥ	مالح

How does the soup taste? It's a little salty.	*kēf ṭa3m iššōraba? mālḥa šwáyya.*	كَيْف طَعْم الشّوْربة؟ مالْحة شْوَيّة.
sweet	*ḥílu*	حِلو
sour	*ḥāmiḍ*	حامِض
bitter	*murr*	مُرّ
spicy	*ḥarrāg* *bíḥrig*	حرّاق بيحْرِق
I don't like spicy food.	*baḥíbbiš ilʔákil ilḥarrāg.* *baḥíbbiš ilʔákil ílli bíḥrig.*	بحبِّش الأكِل الحرّاق. بحبِّش الأكِل اللي بيحْرِق.
pungent	*nákhitu ʔawíyya* *bílda3*	نكْهِتو قَوِية بِلْدع
healthy, healthful	*ṣíḥḥi*	صِحّي
good for you	*kwáyyis la-ṣíḥḥtak*	كْوَيِّس لصِحْتك
unhealthy	*miš ṣíḥḥi*	مِش صِحّي
bad for you	*muḍírr la-ṣíḥḥtak*	مُضِرّ بْصِحْتك
Potato chips are really bad for you.	*iššíbs muḍírr la-ṣíḥḥtak.*	الشِّبْس مُضِرّ بْصِحْتك.
meal	*wájba*	وَجْبة
breakfast	*fṭūr*	فْطور
to have breakfast	*áfṭar, yífṭar*	أفْطر، يِفْطر
lunch	*ɣáda*	غدا
to have lunch	*(i)tɣádda, yitɣádda*	إِتْغدّى، يِتْغدّى
dinner	*3áša*	عشا
to have dinner	*(i)t3ášša, yit3ášša*	إِتْعشّى، يِتْعشّى
a snack	*wájba xafīfa* *snāk*	وَجْبة خفيفة سْناك

to have a snack	*ákal wájba xafīfa* *ákal snāk*	أكّل وَجْبة خفيفة أكّل سْناك
If I feel hungry, I just have a small snack.	*lámma ʔajū3 bākul wájba xafīfa.*	لمّا أجوع باكُل وَجْبة خفيفة.
water	*máyya*	ميّة
ice	*tálij*	تلج
Can I have a glass of water, please?	*múmkin āxud kubbāyit máyya, law samáḥit?*	مُمْكِن آخُد كُبّايِةْ ميّة لَو سمحِت؟
mineral water	*máyya ma3daníyya*	ميّة معْدنية
juice	*3aṣīr*	عصير
orange juice	*3aṣīr lāmūn*	عصير لمون
soda, carbonated drink	*mašrūb ɣāzi*	مشْروب غازي
cola; soda	*kōla*	كوْلا
Would you like some cola?	*bíddak kōla?*	بِدّك كوْلا؟
Pepsi	*bépsi*	بيبْسي
Diet Pepsi	*bépsi dāyt*	بيبْسي دايْت
Coke, Coca Cola	*kōka kōla*	كوْكا كوْلا
Diet Coke	*kōka kōla dāyt*	كوْكا كوْلا دايْت
can	*3ílba* *tánaka*	عِلْبة تنكة
There's a can of cola in the fridge.	*fī 3ílbit kōla bi-ttallāga.*	في عِلْبِةْ كوْلا في التلّاجة.
bottle	*gzāza* *giníyya*	قْزازة قنية
glass	*kubbāya*	كُبّاية
cup	*finjān (fanajīn)*	فِنْجان (فناجين)

mug	*mag*	ماغ
coffee	*gáhwa*	قَهْوة
espresso	*isprésso*	إسْبْرِسّو
Turkish coffee	*gáhwa turkíyya*	قَهْوَة تُرْكية
How would you like your coffee?	*kēf gáhwitak?*	كيْف قَهْوِتك؟
without sugar	*sāda* [lit. plain]	سادة
with little sugar	*súkkar xafīf* *3a -rrīḥa*	سُكّر خفيف عَ الرّيحة
medium-sweet	*wásaṭ*	وَسط
sweet	*ḥílwa*	حِلْوَة
coffee beans	*bunn* *ḥabbāt ilbúnn*	بْنّ حبّات البْنّ
instant coffee	*neskafē*	نِسْكافيْه
tea	*šāy*	شاي
alcohol	*kuḥūl*	كُحول
beer	*bīra*	بيرة
wine	*nabīd*	نبيذ
red wine	*nabīd áḥmar*	نبيذ أحْمر
white wine	*nabīd ábyaḍ*	نبيذ أبْيَض
drunk	*sakrān*	سكْران
to get drunk	*síkir, yískar*	سِكِر، يِسْكر
tipsy	*sakrān šwáyya*	سكْران شْوَيّة
to drink and drive	*sāg* [13] *w húwwa sakrān*	ساق وهُوّ سكْران
Cheers!	*bṣíḥḥtak!*	بْصِحْتك!

dairy products	muntajāt ilḥalīb	مُنْتجات الحليب
milk	ḥalīb	حليب
yoghurt	lában	لبن
butter	zíbda	زِبْدة
ice cream	áskimo būẓa	أُسْكِمو بوظة

English	Transliteration	Arabic
Eat your ice cream before it melts.	kūl ilʔáskimo gábil ma tdūb.	كوْل الأسْكِمو قبِل ما تْدوب.
cream	krēma	كُريْمة
margarine	mangarīna zíbda	منْغرينا زِبْدة
cheese	jíbna	جِبْنة
Areesh cheese (similar to cottage cheese or Ricotta)	jíbna garīš	جِبْنة قريش
Cheddar cheese (semi-hard, sharp, yellow cheese)	jíbnit tšīdar	جِبْنِةْ شيدر
Domiati cheese (soft, white, salty cheese)	jíbna bēḍa	جِبْنة بيْضة
Halloumi cheese (semi-hard, unripened cheese made from goat milk)	jíbna ḥallūm	جِبْنة حلّوم
Istanbuli cheese (feta cheese)	jíbna sṭanbūli	جِبْنة اسطنْبولي
Romy cheese (a sharp, pungent, hard cheese)	jíbna rūmi	جِبْنة رومي
junk food, fast food	ákil jāhiz wájba sarī3a	أكِل جاهِز وَجْبة سريعة
pizza	bīdza	بيتْزا

hamburger	*hambúrgar*	همْبُرجر
chewing gum	*lēdan*	لِيْدن
Some people say علْكة *3ílka* 'chewing gum.'		
to chew gum	*máday lēdan, yúmduɣ lēdan*	مدغ لِيْدن، يمّْدُغ لِيْدن
chocolate	*šokolāta*	شوكُوْلاطة
Dark chocolate is better for you than milk chocolate.	*iššokolāta -lmúrra ʔaḥsánlak min iššokolāta -lli bi-lḥalīb.*	الشّوكُوْلاطة المرّة أحْسنْلك مِن الشّوكُوْلاطة اللي بِالحليب.
potato chips	*šibs*	شِبْس
candy, sweets, pastries	*ḥílu*	حِلو
pastries	*ḥála*	حلا
candy, sweets	*ḥalawiyyāt*	حلَوِيّات
cotton candy	*šá3ar ilbanāt* *ɣázl ilbanāt*	شعر البنات غزْل البنات
cookie, wafer, cracker	*baskōt*	بسْكوْت
cake	*kēk*	كيْك
pie	*fṭīra (faṭāyir)*	فْطيرة (فطايِر)
baklava (syrupy layers of phyllo pastry)	*baglāwa*	بقْلاوَة
basboosa (syrupy semolina cake)	*basbūsa*	بسْبوسة
kunafeh (syrupy fried cheese pastry)	*knāfia*	كْنافة
luqmat al-qadi (syrupy deep-fried dough balls)	*lúgmit ilgāḍi*	لُقْمِةْ القاضي
qatayef (sweet dumpling with nuts and cream)	*gṭāyif*	قْطايِف
rice pudding	*ruzz w ḥalīb* *ruzz b-ḥalīb*	رُزّ وحليب رُزّ بْحليب
vegetable	*xúḍra (xuḍār)*	خُضْرة (خُضار)

asparagus	halyōn	هَلْيوْن
bean, green bean	fāṣūlya	فاصوُلْيا
beet(root)	bánjar	بنْجر
broad bean, fava bean	fūl áxḍar	فول أَخْضر
broccoli	brōklī	بْروكْلي
cabbage	malfūf	ملْفوف
capsicum, sweet pepper, bell pepper	flēfla	فْلَيْفْلة
carrot	jázar	جزر
cauliflower	záhra gambūṭa	زهْرة قمْبوطة
celery	karāfs	كرفْس
chickpea	ḥúmmuṣ	حُمْص
chili pepper	fílfil	فِلْفِل
cucumber	xyār	خْيار
eggplant, aubergine	bitinjān	بِتِنْجان
garlic	tōma	توْمة
green onion	báṣal áxḍar	بصل أَخْضر
mushroom	fíṭir	فِطِر
okra	bāmya	بامْيَة
olive	zatūn	زتون
onion	báṣal	بصل
pea	bāzēlla	بازيْلّا
potato	baṭāṭa	بطاطا
radish	fíjil	فِجِل
spinach	sabāniy	سبانخ
sweet potato	baṭāṭa ḥílwa	بطاطا حِلْوَة

tomato	*bandōra*	بنْدوْرة
turnip	*lífit*	لِفِت
zucchini, courgette	*kūsa*	كوسا

salad	*sálaṭa*	سلطة
salad dressing	*ṣōṣ* *xálṭa*	صوْص خلْطة
Caesar salad	*sálaṭit sīzar*	سلطِةْ سيزر
chickpea salad	*sálaṭit ḥúmmuṣ*	سلطِةْ حُمُّص
green salad	*sálaṭit xuḍār*	سلطِةْ خُضار
potato salad	*sálaṭit baṭāṭa*	سلطِةْ بطاطا
tahini salad	*sálaṭit ṭḥīna*	سلطِةْ طْحينة

Some people say طحينية *ṭaḥīníyya.*

fattoush	*fattūš*	فتّوش
tabouli	*tabbūla*	تبّولة
fruit	*fākha (fawākih)*	فاكْهة (فَواكِهْ)
apples	*tuffāḥ*	تُفّاح
apricots	*míšmiš*	مِشْمِش
bananas	*mōz*	موْز
berries	*tūt*	توت
blueberries	*tūt ázrag* *blūberi*	توت أزْرق بْلوبري
cherries	*káraz*	كرز
dates	*bálaḥ*	بلح
figs	*tīn*	تين
grapes	*3ínab*	عِنب
grapefruit	*grēp frūt*	غْرِيب فْروت

lemons	*lāmūn*	لمون
mango	*mánga*	مانْجا
oranges	*burtgān* *burtuqāl*	بُرْتْقان بُرْتُقال
peaches; plums	*xōx*	خوْخ
pears	*injāṣ*	إنْجاص
pineapples	*anānās*	أناناس
pomegranates	*rumān*	رُمان
raspberries	*tūt áḩmar*	توت أُحْمر
strawberry	*farāwla*	فراوْلة
tangerine	*yūsfi*	يوسْفي

nuts, hazelnuts	*búndug*	بُنْدُق
almonds	*lōz*	لوْز
coconut	*jōz ilhínid*	جوْز الهِنْد
peanut	*fūl sūdāni*	فول سوداني
peanut butter	*zíbdit fūl sūdāni*	زِبْدِةْ فول سوداني
walnut	*3ēn iljámal*	عيْن الجمل
mixed nuts	*mukassarāt mšákkala*	مُكسَّرات مْشكَّلة

fresh herbs	*a3šāb*	أعْشاب
dry herbs, spices, condiments	*bahārāt*	بْهارات
aniseed	*yansūn*	يَنْسون
basil	*rīḩān*	ريحان
black pepper	*fílfil áswad*	فِلْفِل أسْوَد
chives	*tōm m3ámmir*	توْم مْعمَّر
cinnamon	*gírfa*	قِرْفة

cumin	*kamūn*	كَمّون
curry (powder)	*kāri*	كاري
ginger	*zanjabīl*	زَنْجبيل
nutmeg	*jōzt ițțīb*	جوْزْةْ الطّيب
parsley	*bagdūnis*	بقْدونِس
peppermint, spearmint	*ná3na3*	نعْنع
rosemary	*iklīl iljábal*	إكْليل الجّبل
salt	*máliħ*	ملح
sugar	*súkkar*	سُكّر
thyme	*zá3tar*	زعْتر
vanilla	*vānílla*	فانيلّا
sauce	*șōș*	صوْص
gravy	*máraga*	مرقة
ketchup	*kātšab*	كتْشب
mayonnaise	*māyōnēz*	مايوْنيْز
mustard	*xárdal* *mastárda*	خرْدل مسْترْدة
tomato sauce, tomato puree, salsa	*șálșa*	صلْصة
soy sauce	*șōș ișșōya*	صوْص الصّوْيا
vinegar	*xall*	خلّ
rice	*ruzz*	رُزّ
pasta	*ma3karōna*	معْكروْنة
(pita) bread	*xúbiz*	خُبِز
loaf of bread	*ryīf*	رْغيف
slice of bread	*xúbza*	خُبْزة

piece of bread	*šăgfit xúbiz*	شقْفِةْ خُبِز
sliced bread; toast	*tōst*	توْسْت
baguette, sandwich roll	*xúbiz faránsi* *bāgit*	خُبِز فرنْسي باغِت
yeast	*xamīra*	خميرة
flour	*ṭḥīn*	طْحين
jam	*murábba*	مُربّ
honey	*3ásal*	عسل
protein	*brōtīn*	بْروْتين
egg	*bēḍ*	بيْض
yolk	*ṣafār bēḍ*	صفار بيْض
egg white	*bayāḍ bēḍ*	بَياض بيْض
fried egg	*bēḍ mágli*	بيْض مقْلي
boiled egg	*bēḍ maslūg*	بيْض مسْلوق
scrambled egg	*bēḍ maxfūg*	بيْض مخْفوق
omelet	*ōmlēt*	أوْملِيْت
meat	*láḥim* *láḥma*	لحِم لحْمة
beef	*láḥmit 3íjil*	لحْمِةْ عِجِل
I don't feel like chicken. Let's have beef.	*miš jāy 3a bāli jāj; ta3āl nāxud láḥma.*	مِش جاي عَ بالي جاج. تعال ناخُد لحْمة.
(beef) steak	*stēk láḥma*	سْتيْك لحْمة
pastrami	*basṭírma*	بسْطِرْمة
minced meat	*láḥma mafrūma*	لحْمة مفْرومة

chicken	*jāj* *frāx*	جاج فْراخ
chicken filet	*fīlē jāj*	فيليْه الجّاج
whole chicken	*jāja* *frāxa*	جاجة فرْخة
lamb	*láḥim ḏāni* *láḥim xarūf*	لحِم ضاني لحِم خروف
pork	*láḥim xanzīr*	لحِم خنْزير
sausage	*nagānig* *sguʔʔ*	نقانِق سْجّقّ
fish	*sámak*	سمك
fish bone	*saffīr*	سفّير
salmon	*sálamun*	سلمُن
shark	*girš*	قِرْش
tuna	*tūna*	تونا
seafood	*maʔkūlāt baḥríyya* *ákil báḥri*	مأكُولات بحْرية أكِل بحْري
crab, lobster, crustaceans	*salṭa3ūn*	سلْطعون
mussel, shellfish	*maḥār*	محار
octopus	*uxṭubūṭ*	أخْطُبوط
oyster	*ṣádaf*	صدف
shrimp	*jámabri*	جمْبري
squid, cuttlefish	*ḥabbār*	حبّار
fat	*díhna (duhūn)*	دِهْنة (دُهون)

This meat has a lot of fat on it.	hādi -lláḥma malyāna díhna.	هادي اللّحْمة ملْيانة دِهْنة.
greasy, oily	mzáyyit mídhin	مْزيَّت مِدْهِن
This dish is quite greasy.	hāda -ṣṣáḥin mzáyyit šwáyya.	هادا الصّحِن مْزيِّت شْوَيّة.
soup	šōraba	شوْربة
to eat soup	šírib šōraba	شِرِب شوْربة
cream soup	šōrabit krāma	شوْربِةْ كْريمة
Jew's mallow (slimy green soup)	mlūxxíyya	مْلوخِّية
orzo soup	šōrabit lsān 3aṣfūr	شوْربِةْ لْسان عصْفور
tomato soup	šōrabit bandōra	شوْربِةْ بنْدوْرة
vegetable soup	šōrabit xuḍār	شوْربِةْ خُضار
fried	mágli	مقْلي
vegetable oil	(zēt) sīrij	(زيْت) سيرج
baked (bread)	maxbūz	مخْبوز
baked, roast	mḥámmar	مْحمَّر
boiled	maslūg	مسْلوق
grilled, roast	mášwi	مشْوي
carton	kartōna	كرْتوْنة
bag	kīs (kyās)	كيس (كْياس)
jar	martabān	مرْتِبان
spleen sandwich	sándwiš ṭúḥal	سنْدْوِش طُحل
falafel	falāfil	فلافِل
flatbread pizza	mangūša (manāgīš)	منْقوشة (مناقيش)
ful (refried fava beans)	fūl	فول

ful medames (boiled fava beans)	*fūl mdámmas*	فول مْدمَّس
koshari (lentils, rice and macaroni)	*kúšari*	كُشري
liver sandwich	*sándwiš kíbda*	سنْدوِش كِبْدة
pickled vegetables	*mxallalāt*	مْخلّلات
table manners	*ādāb ilʔákil*	آداب الأكِل
Thank you for the meal! (said to host(ess) after having tried the food)	*šúkran 3a -lʔákil!*	شُكْراً عَ الأكِل.
to talk with one's mouth full	*ħáka [55] w fī b-tímmu ákil*	حكى وفي بْتِمّو أكِل
Don't talk with your mouth full!	*tiħkīš w tímmak malyān!*	تِحْكيش وتِمَّك مِلْيان.
Excuse me for a moment. (when excusing oneself from the table)	*3an íznak.*	عن إذْنك.
Thank you for the meal. (said after finishing a meal in someone's home)	*dāyma.* *bētak 3āmir.*	دايْمة. بيْتك عامِر.
You're welcome. (response)	*şáħħa w 3āfya.* *áhla w sáhla.*	صحّة وعافْيَة. أهْلا وسهْلا.

9 **Work**

work, job, career	*šúɣul (ašɣāl)*	شُغُل (أَشْغال)
to work, be employed	*ištáɣal, yištíɣil*	إِشْتَغِل، يِشْتِغِل
She works as a teacher.	*híyya btištíɣil fi -lmádrasa.*	هِيَّ بْتِشْتِغِل في المدْرسة.
I work five days a week.	*ána baštíɣil xámas tiyyām bi-lʔisbū3.*	أنا بِشْتِغِل خمس تِيّام بِالإسْبوع.
job, task	*waẓīfa*	وَظيفة
full-time	*dawām kāmil*	دَوام كامِل
I work full-time.	*baštíɣil dawām kāmil.*	بِشْتِغِل دَوام كامِل.
part-time	*nuṣṣ dawām* *dawām júzʔi*	نُصّ دَوام دوام جُزْئي
I want a part-time job.	*bíddi šúɣul b-nuṣṣ dawām.*	بِدّي شُغُل بْنُصّ دَوام.
the private sector	*ilxāṣṣ*	الخاصّ
the public sector	*ilḥukūma* *issúlṭa*	الحُكومة السُلْطة
civil servant	*muwáẓẓaf ḥukūmi*	مُوَظَّف حُكومي
to look for a job	*dáwwar 3ála šúɣul, ydáwwir 3ála šúɣul*	دوَّر على شُغُل، يْدوّر على شُغُل
to apply for a job	*gáddam 3ála šúɣul, ygáddim 3ála šúɣul*	قدَّم على شُغُل، يْقدَّم على شُغُل
applicant, candidate	*mgáddim 3ála šúɣul*	مُقدَّم على شُغُل
experience	*xíbra*	خِبْرة
to have a job interview	*3índu mugābalit šúɣul*	عِنْدو مُقابلِة شُغُل
to interview	*gābal, ygābil*	قابل، يْقابِل

to find a job	*lāga [55] šúɣul*	لقى شُغُل
Have you found a job yet?	*lāgēt šúɣul wálla líssa?*	لقيْت شُغُل وَلّا لِسّا؟
to obtain employment	*(i)twáẓẓaf, yitwáẓẓaf*	اِتْوَظَّف، يِتْوَظَّف
to employ	*wáẓẓaf, ywáẓẓif*	وَظَّف، يْوَظِّف
employee	*muwáẓẓaf*	مُوَظَّف
employer	*ṣāḥib šúɣul (ṣḥāb šúɣul)*	صاحِب شُغُل (صْحاب شُغُل)
boss, manager	*mudīr*	مُدير
colleague, coworker	*zamīl (zúmala)*	زميل (زُملا)
company	*šírka*	شِركة
to start work	*báda [55] šúɣul*	بدا شُغُل
to take a break	*áxad [55] brēk* *áxad [55] rāḥa*	أخد بريْك أخد راحة
lunch break	*brēk ilɣáda*	بُريْك الغدا
to finish work, get off work	*xállaṣ šúɣul, yxálliṣ šúɣul*	خلَّص شُغُل، يْخلِّص شُغُل
to work overtime	*ištáɣal ōvar tāym*	اِشْتِغل أوْفر تايْم
working hours	*dawām*	دَوام
I work eight hours a day.	*ána baštíɣil dawām táman sā3āt fi -lyōm.*	أنا بشْتِغِل دَوام تمن ساعات في اليوْم.
day shift	*dawām bi-linhār*	دَوام بِالنْهار
night shift, graveyard shift	*dawām lēli* *dawām bi-llēl*	دَوام لَيْلي دَوام بِاللّيْل
I work the night shift.	*ána baštíɣil dawām lēli.*	أنا بشْتِغِل دَوام ليْلي.
I'm off work.	*ána baštíɣliš.* *ána gā3id.*	أنا بشْتِغْلِش. أنا قاعِد.
I have weekends off.	*ána fāḍi ʔāxir ilʔisbū3.*	أنا فاضي آخِر الإسْبوع.

office	*máktab (mkātib)*	مكْتب (مُكاتِب)
office worker	*muwázẓaf máktab*	مُوَظّف مكْتب
company representative	*mandūb šírka*	منْدوب شِرْكة
to stay late at the office	*(i)tʔáxxar fi -lmáktab, yitʔáxxar fi -lmáktab*	اِتْأخّر في المكْتب، يِتْأخّر في المكْتب
to go on a business trip	*sāfar [24] ma3 iššúɣul*	سافر مع الشُّغُل
to have a meeting	*3índu ʔijtimā3*	عِنْدو اِجْتِماع
client	*zbūn (zabāyin)* *3amīl (3úmala)*	زْبون (زباين) عميل (عُملا)
to earn (money); get paid	*gábaḍ, yúgbuḍ*	قبَض، يُقْبُض
wage, pay	*dúf3a*	دُفْعة
salary	*rātib* *gábḍa*	راتِب قبْضة
My salary is just okay.	*rātbi kwáyyis.*	راتْبي كْوَيِّس.
payday	*yōm ilgábḍa*	يوْم القبْضة
I get paid on the first of the month.	*ána bágbuḍ áwwal iššáhir.*	أنا بقْبُض أوّل الشّهِر.
bonus, incentive	*ḥāfiz (ḥawāfiz)* *bōnas*	حافِز (حَوافِز) بوْنص
pay raise	*3alāwa* *zyāda*	علاوَة زْيادة
to get a raise	*áxad [55] 3alāwa*	أخد علاوَة
to give __ a raise	*á3ṭa [55] __ 3alāwa*	أعْطى __ علاوَة
promotion	*tárgiya*	ترْقِيِة
to get promoted	*(i)trágga, yitrágga*	اِتْرقّى، بِترقّى

I got a promotion this month.	*ána -traggēt iššáhir hād.*	أنا اتْرقّيْت الشّهِر هاد.
unemployed, jobless	*bištíyliš* *gā3id* *3áṭil*	بِيشْتِغْلش قاعِد عاطِل
unemployment	*baṭāla*	بطالة
to resign	*istagāl, yistagīl*	إِسْتقال، يِسْتقيل
to quit one's job	*sāb [55] iššúyul*	ساب الشُّغُل
to lay off, make redundant	*istáyna 3an, yistáyni 3an*	إِسْتغْنى عن، يِسْتغْني عن
to fire	*fáṣal, yífṣil* *ṭárrad, yṭárrid*	فصل، يِفْصِل طرّد، يْطرُّد
to get fired	*infáṣal [min šúylu], yinfíṣil [min šúylu]*	إِنْفصل [مِن شُغْلو]، يِنْفِصِل [مِن شُغْلو]
to retire	*(i)tqā3ad, yitqā3ad*	إتْقاعد، يِتْقاعد
pension	*ma3āš* *rātib taqā3ud*	معاش راتِب تقاعُد
(age of) retirement	*sinn ittaqā3ud*	سِنّ التّقاعُد
I hope to retire when I'm sixty.	*batmánna ʔatqā3ad lámma ʔaṣīr sittīn.*	بتمنّى أتْقاعد لمّا أصير سِتّين.
trade, craft	*ṣán3a*	صنْعة
What do you do?	*šū btištíyil?*	شو بْتِشْتِغِل؟
I'm a ___.	*ána ___.* *baštíyil ___.*	أنا ___. بِشْتِغِل ___.
accountant	*muḥāsib*	مُحاسِب
actor	*mumássil*	مُمثّل
architect	*muhándis mi3māri*	مُهنْدِس مِعْماري

artist	*fannān*	فنّان
athlete	*riyāḍi*	رياضي
baker	*xabbāz*	خبّاز
bank teller; banker	*muwáẓẓaf bank*	مُوَظّف بنْك
bank manager	*mudīr bank*	مُدير بنْك
barber	*ḥallāg*	حلّاق
bus driver	*sawwāg bāṣ*	سوّاق باص
butcher	*laḥḥām*	لحّام
carpenter	*najjār*	نجّار
cashier	*muḥāsib*	مُحاسِب
chef	*ṭabbāx* *šēf*	طبّاخ شيْف
cleaner	*3āmil naḍāfa*	عامِل نضافة
cook	*ṭabbāx*	طبّاخ
customer service representative	*mandūb xídmit il3úmala*	منْدوب خِدْمِةْ العُملا
dentist	*daktōr snān*	دكْتوْر سْنان
doctor	*daktōr (dakātra)*	دكْتوْر (دكاتْرة)
editor	*muḥárrir*	مُحرّر
electrician	*kahrabāʔi*	كهْربائي
engineer	*muhándis*	مُهنْدِس
farmer	*fallāḥ*	فلّاح
fire fighter	*iṭfāʔi* *rájul iṭfāʔ*	إطْفائي رجُل إطْفاء
fisherman	*ṣayyād (sámak)*	صيّاد (سمك)
flight attendant	*muḍīf ṭayarān*	مُضيف طَيَران
garbage collector	*zabbāl*	زبّال

| gardener | *janāyni* | جناْيني |
| hairdresser (for women) | *kawāfēra* | كَوافيْرة |

imam	*imām*	إمام
judge	*gāḍi*	قاضي
laborer	*3āmil (3umāl)*	عامِل (عُمال)
lawyer	*muḥāmi*	مُحامي
maid	*xaddāma*	خدّامة
mechanic	*mēkānīki*	ميْكانيكي
musician	*mūsīqār*	موسيقار
nurse	*mumárriḍ*	مُمرِّض
painter (artist)	*rassām*	رسّام
painter, house painter	*dahhīn*	دهّين
pharmacist	*ṣáydali (ṣayādla)*	صَيْدلي (صَيادْلة)
pilot	*ṭayyār*	طيّار
plumber	*sabbāk*	سبّاك
police officer	*šúrṭi*	شُرْطي
politician	*siyāsi*	سِياسي
priest	*qissīs*	قِسّيس
professor	*ustāz jām3a*	أُسْتاذ جامْعة
real estate agent	*simsār (samāsra)*	سِمْسار (سماسْرة)
repairman	*mṣálliḥ*	مُصلِّح
sailor	*baḥḥār*	بحّار
salesperson	*mandūb mabī3āt*	منْدوب مبيعات
secretary	*sikirtēr*	سِكِرْتيْر

servant, housekeeper, maid	*xaddāma*	خدّامة
shop assistant	*bayyā3*	بيّاع
shopkeeper	*bayyā3 xúḍra* *xuḍárji*	بيّاع خُضْرة خُضْرْجي
soldier	*3áskari (3asākir)*	عسْكري (عساكِر)
taxi driver	*sawwāg tāksi*	سوّاق تاكْسي
teacher	*ustāz (asádza)*	أُسْتاذ (أساتْذة)
technician	*fánni*	فنّي
travel agent	*wakīl safriyyāt (wúkala safriyyāt)*	وكيل سفْريّات (وُكلا سفْريّات)
veterinarian	*(daktōr) báyṭari*	(دكْتوْر) بَيْطري
waiter, waitress	*garsōn*	غرْسوْن
writer	*kātib (kuttāb)*	كاتِب (كُتّاب)

10 School and Education

education	ta3līm	تعْليم
educated, literate	mit3állim	مِتْعلِّم
to learn	(i)t3állam, yit3állam	اِتْعلَّم، يِتْعلَّم
illiterate	úmmi	أُمّي
illiteracy	ummíyya	أُمّية
	jáhil	جهِل
What is the illiteracy rate in Palestine?	gaddēš mu3áddal ilʔummíyya fi falasṭīn?	قدّيْش مُعدّل الأُمّية في فلسْطين؟
school	mádrasa (madāris)	مدْرسة (مدارِس)
student	ṭālib (ṭullāb)	طالِب (طُلّاب)
preschool	ḥaḍāna	حضانة
kindergarten	ráwḍa	رَوْضة
elementary school, primary school	mádrasa ʔibtidāʔíyyi ibtidāʔi	مدْرسة اِبْتِدائية اِبْتدائي
when I was in elementary school, ...	lámma kúnit fi -lʔibtidāʔi, ...	لمّا كُنِت في الاِبْتِدائي، ...
first grade (year)	ṣaff áwwal	صفّ أوّل
Her son is in first grade.	íbinha b-ṣaff áwwal.	اِبِنْها بْصفّ أوّل.
middle school	mádrasa ʔi3dādíyya i3dādi	مدْرسة إعْدادية إعْدادي
high school, secondary school	mádrasa sānawíyya sānawi	مدْرسة ثانَوية ثانوي
university, college	jām3a kullíyya	جامْعة كُلية

academy	akadīmíyya má3had (ma3āhid)	أكاديمية مَعْهد (معاهِد)
language academy	márkaz ta3līm luȳāt	مرْكز تعْليم لُغات
I teach Arabic at a language academy in Palestine.	ána bagárri 3árabi fi -márkaz ta3līm luȳāt fi -falasṭīn.	أنا بقرّي عربي في مرْكز تعْليم لُغات في فلسْطين.
class(room); class; year	ṣaff (ṣfūf)	صفّ (صْفوف)
fifth grade	ṣaff xāmis	صفّ خامِس
in the sixth grade	b-ṣṣaff issādis	بِالصّفّ السّادِس
period, hour, lesson	ḥíṣṣa (ḥíṣaṣ)	حِصّة (حِصص)
I have six classes a day.	bāxud sitt ḥíṣaṣ fi -lyōm.	باخُد سِتّ حِصص في اليوْم.
Class starts at 8 o'clock and finishes at 9 o'clock.	ilḥíṣṣa btíbda -ssā3a tamānya w bitxálliṣ issā3a tís3a.	الحِصّة بْتِبْدا السّاعة تمانْيَة وبِتْخلِّص السّاعة تِسْعة.
lecture, class	muḥāḍara	مُحاضرة
to attend a lecture	ḥíḍir [55] muḥāḍara	حِضِر مُحاضرة
studies	grāya drāsa	قْرايَة دْراسة
lesson	dars (drūs)	درْس (دْروس)
curriculum	mánhaj (manāhij)	منْهج (مناهِج)
question	suʔāl (ásʔila)	سُؤال (أسْئِلة)
to ask a question in class	sáʔal suʔāl fi -lḥíṣṣa	سأل سُؤال في الحِصّة
answer	jawāb	جَواب
to answer	jāwab, yjāwib	جاوَب، يْجاوِب
to raise one's hand	ráfa3 [23] īdu	رفع إيدو
right, correct	ṣaḥḥ	صحّ
wrong, incorrect; mistake	ȳálaṭ	غلط

He got three questions wrong.	*jāwab ɣálaṭ 3ála tálat ásʔila.*	جاوَب غلط على تلات أسْئِلة.
lecture hall	*qā3it ilmuḥāḍarāt*	قاعِةْ المُحاضرات
desk	*ṭāwla*	طاوْلة
text book	*ktāb (kútub)*	كْتاب (كُتْب)
notebook	*dáftar (dafātir)*	دفْتر (دفاتِر)
to take notes	*sájjal mulāḥaẓāt*	سجّل مُلاحظات
to copy	*nágal, yíngil*	نقل، يِنْقِل
backpack	*šánta (šúnat)*	شنْطة (شُنط)
blackboard	*lōḥ*	لوْح
chalk	*ṭabāšīr*	طباشير
whiteboard	*lōḥ ábyaḍ*	لوْح أبْيَض
map	*xarīṭa (xarāyiṭ)*	خريطة (خرايِط)
library	*máktaba*	مكْتَبة
gymnasium	*nādi ḥadīd* *jim*	نادِي حديد جيْم
playground, school yard	*mál3ab (malā3ib)*	ملْعب (ملاعِب)
cafeteria	*kāftērya* *istirāḥa*	كافْتيرْيا اِسْتِراحة
laboratory	*muxtábar*	مُخْتبر
auditorium, theater	*másraḥ (masāriḥ)*	مسْرح (مسارح)
school bus	*bāṣ mádrasa*	باص مدْرسة
summer vacation	*ijāzit iṣṣēf* *3úṭlit iṣṣēf*	إجازِةْ الصّيْف عُطْلِةِ الصّيْف

winter vacation	*ijāzit iššáta* *3úṭlit nuṣṣ issána*	إجازِةْ الشَّتا عُطلِةْ نُصّ السَّنة
break(time), recess; lunch break	*fōrṣa* *istirāḥa*	فوْرْسة اسْتِراحة
We have a fifteen-minute break between classes.	*bnāxud rúbi3 sā3a fōrṣa* *bēn ilḥíṣaṣ.*	بْناخُد رُبِع ساعة فوْرْسة بيْن الحِصص.
test, exam	*imtiḥān*	إِمْتِحان
to take a test	*áxad [55] imtiḥān*	أخد إِمْتِحان
mid-term (exam)	*imtiḥān nuṣṣ issána*	اِمْتِحان نُصّ السَّنة
final exam	*imtiḥān āxir issána*	اِمْتِحان آخِر السَّنة
entrance exam	*imtiḥān duxūl*	اِمْتِحان دُخول
an oral exam	*imtiḥān šáfawi*	اِمْتِحان شفَوي
a written exam	*imtiḥān kitābi*	اِمْتِحان كِتابي
to pass a test	*níjiḥ bi-lʔimtiḥān, yínjaḥ* *bi-lʔimtiḥān*	نِجِح بِالاِمتِحان، يِنْجح بِالاِمتِحان
to fail a test	*ságaṭ bi-lʔimtiḥān, yúsguṭ* *bi-lʔimtiḥān*	سقط بِالاِمْتِحان، يُسْقُط بِالاِمْتِحان
exam results	*natāyij ilʔimtiḥānāt*	نتايِج الاِمْتِحان
grade, mark	*3alāma*	علامة
to get a good grade	*áxad [55] 3alāma 3ālya*	أخد علامة عالْيَة
a passing grade	*3alāmit innajāḥ*	علامِةْ النَّجاح
a failing grade	*3alāmit irrusūb* *3alāmit lisgúṭ*	علامِةْ الرُّسوب علامِةْ السْقوط
report card	*šihāda*	شِهادة

to study	*gára, yígra* *dáras, yídrus*	قرا، يِقْرا درس، يُدْرُس
He needs to study for the test.	*lāzim yígra la-lʔimtiħān*	لازِم يِقْرا لِلامْتِحان.
homework	*wājib*	واجِب
to do homework	*ħall ilwājib, yħill ilwājib*	حلِّ الواجِب، يْحِلِّ الواجِب
to check, revise, review	*rāja3, yrāji3*	راجع، يُراجِع
essay, paper, composition	*mawqū3 ta3bīr*	مَوْضوع تَعْبير
The students have to write an essay about a historical event.	*lāzim iṭṭullāb yíktibu mawqū3 ta3bīr 3an ħádas tārīxi.*	لازِم الطُّلّاب يِكْتِبوا مَوْضوع تَعْبير عن حدث تاريخي.
teacher	*ustāz (asádza)*	أُسْتاذ (أَساتْذة)
Good morning, teacher!	*ṣabāħ ilxēr, ustāz!*	صباح الخيْر أُسْتاذ!
professor	*ustāz jām3a*	أُسْتاذ جامْعة
principal	*mudīr*	مُدير
to teach	*gárra, ygárri* *dárras, ydárris*	قرّا، يْقرّي درّس، يْدرّس
to teach a course	*á3ṭa [55] dáwra*	أَعْطى دَوْرة
Do you teach at the university?	*bitgárri fi -jjām3a?*	بِتْقرّي في الجامْعة؟
Ahmad is teaching me Arabic.	*áħmad bigarrīni 3árabi.*	أحْمد بيقرّيني عربي.
to teach a lesson	*šáraħ dars, yíšraħ dars*	شرح درْس، يِشْرح درْس
to correct a test	*ṣállaħ imtiħān, yṣálliħ imtiħān*	صلّح اِمْتِحان، يْصلّح اِمْتِحان
to enroll, register	*sájjal, ysájjil*	سجّل، يْسجِّل
enrollment	*tasjīl*	تسْجيل
I intend to enroll in an Arabic class next month.	*nāwi ʔasájjil fi -l3árabi -ššahr ijjāy.*	ناوي أسجِّل في العربي الشّهْر الجّاي.

school year	*sána dirāsíyya*	سنة دِراسية
semester	*fáṣil*	فصِل
tuition	*rusūm ijjām3a*	رُسوم الجّامْعة
scholarship	*mínħa*	مِنْحة
student loan	*qarḍ*	قرْض
university	*jām3a*	جامْعة
to get into college, start university	*ṣār fi -jjām3a, yṣīr fi -jjām3a*	صار في الجّامْعة، يْصير في الجّامْعة
to go to college, study at university	*gára fi -jjām3a*	قرا في الجّامْعة
department, faculty	*qísim (aqsām) kullíyya*	قِسِم (أقْسام) كُلِّية
I got into the faculty of medicine, but later I changed to law.	*sajjálit fi kullíyyit iṭṭíbb, ba3dēn ħawwálit ħuqūq.*	سجَّلِت في كُلِّيّة الطِبّ، بعْدين حوَّلِت حُقوق.
major	*taxáṣṣuṣ*	تخصُّص
minor	*taxáṣṣuṣ fár3i*	تخصُّص فرْعي
to major in	*dáras __ fi -jjām3a itxáṣṣaṣ, yitxáṣṣaṣ*	درس ___ في الجّامْعة اِتْخصّص، بِتْخصّص
What are you majoring in?	*šū btígra fi -jjām3a? šū mitxáṣṣiṣ?*	شو بْتِقْرا في الجّامْعة؟ شو مِتْخصِّص؟
I'm majoring in English literature.	*bágra ādāb inglīzi. mitxáṣṣiṣ ādāb inglīzi.*	بقْرا آداب إنْجْليزي. مِتْخصِّص آداب إنْجْليزي.
university campus	*ħáram jām3a (aħrām jām3a)*	حرم جامْعة (احْرام جامْعة)
dormitories	*sákan jām3a*	سكن جامْعة
Do you live on campus?	*ínta 3āyiš fi sákan ijjām3a?*	إنْتَ عايِش في سكن الجّامْعة؟
to graduate from	*(i)txárraj min, yitxárraj min*	اِتْخرّج مِن، بِتْخرّج مِن

When did you graduate from university?	*wagtēš itxárrajit min ijjām3a?*	وَقْتيْش اِتْخرّجِت مِن الجّامعة؟
I graduated from university in 2005.	*(i)txárrajit min ijjām3a fi -l?alfēn w xámsa.*	اِتْخرّجِت مِن الجّامْعة في الأَلْفيْن وخمْسة.
freshman (1st year university student)	*sána ?ūla* *ṭālib jdīd*	سنة أُولى طالِب جْديد
sophomore (2nd year)	*sána tānya*	سنة تانْية
junior (3rd year)	*sána tālta*	سنة تالْتة
senior (4th year)	*sána rāb3a* *xirrīj*	سنة رابْعة خِرّيج
All the freshmen have to attend an orientation ceremony.	*kull ṭullāb sána ?ūla lāzim yíḥḍaru -lliqā? itta3rīfi.*	كُلّ طُلّاب سنة أُولى لازِم يِحْضروا اللِّقاء التّعْريفي.
degree, certificate, diploma	*šihāda*	شِهادة
He got a certificate for completing the course.	*áxad šiháda bá3id ma xállaṣ iddáwra.*	أخد شِهادة بعِد ما خلّص الدَوْرة.
to get a bachelor's degree	*áxad [55] šihādit ilbakālōryus*	أخد شِهادةِ البكالوْرْيوس
college student	*ṭālib jām3a*	طالِب جامْعة
to do a Master's degree	*áxad [55] māstar* *áxad [55] mājistēr*	أخد ماسْتر أخد ماجِسْتيْر
Doctorate	*duktōrā*	دُكْتوْراه
thesis, dissertation	*risālit mājistēr* *risālit duktōrā*	رِسالةِ ماجِسْتيْر رِسالةِ دُكْتوْراه
subject	*mādda (mawādd)*	مادّة (مَوادّ)
What was your favorite subject in school?	*šū ?áktar mādda kunt tḥíbbha fi -lmádrasa?*	شو أكْتر مادّة كُنْت تْحِبّها في المدْرسة؟

I really enjoyed studying history, but I hated science class.	kunt aḥíbb ittārīx, bass kúnit ákrah ḥíṣṣit il3ulūm.	كُنْت أحِبّ التّاريخ، بسّ كُنِت أكْرهْ حِصّةْ العُلومْ.
to be good at	kān [55] šāṭir fi	كان شاطِر في
He's really good at math.	húwwa šāṭir ktīr fi -rriyāḍiyyāt.	هُوَّ شاطِر كْتير في الرِّياضِيّات.
biology	aḥyāʔ	أحْياء
chemistry	kīmya	كيمْيا
dentistry	ṭibb ilʔasnān	طِبّ الأسْنان
economics	iqtiṣād	اِقْتِصاد
geography	juɣrāfya	جُغْرافْيا
geology	jiyōlōjya	جيوْلوْجْيا
geometry	hándasa riyāḍíyya	هنْدسة رِياضية
history	tārīx	تاريخ
law	ḥuqūq	حُقوق
linguistics	luɣāt	لُغات
literature	ādāb ádab	آداب أدب
mathematics	riyāḍiyyāt	رِياضِيّات
medicine	ṭibb	طِبّ
philosophy	fálsafa	فلْسفة
physical education (P.E.)	tárbiya riyāḍíyya	ترْبِيَة رِياضية
physics	fīzya	فيزْيا
political science	3ulūm siyāsíyya	عُلوم سِياسية
psychology	3ilm nafs	عِلْم نفْس
science	3ulūm	عُلوم
social studies	dirāsāt ijtimā3íyya	دِراسات اِجْتِماعية

11 Health and Medicine

health	ṣíḥḥa	صِحَّة
healthy, in good health	ṣíḥḥtu kwáyysa	صِحْتو كُوَيّسة
sickness, illness, disease	máraḍ (amrāḍ)	مرض (أمْراض)
sick, ill; patient	marīḍ (márḍa)	مريض (مرْضى)
in poor health	ta3bān	تعْبان
handicapped	mu3āq	مُعاق
wheelchair	kúrsi mutaḥárrik	كُرْسي مُتحرّك
doctor	daktōr (dakātra)	دكْتور (دكاتْرة)
I don't feel well. I think I need to go see a doctor.	ḥāsis ḥāli ta3bān. bíddi ʔarūḥ 3a iddaktōr.	حاسِس حالي تعْبان. بِدّي أروح عَ الدّكْتور.
specialist	axiṣāʔi	أخِصّائي
cardiologist	axiṣāʔi galb	أخِصّائي قلْب
eye doctor, ophthalmologist	daktōr 3uyūn	دكْتور عُيون
to make an appointment with	áxad [55] máw3id 3ind	أخد مَوْعِد عِنْد
hospital	mustášfa	مُستشْفى
doctor's office, clinic	3iyāda	عِيادة
nurse	mumárriḍ	مُمرّض
to get a (medical) check-up	3ámal [55] fáḥiṣ ṭíbbi	عمل فحِص طِبّي
to diagnose	šáxxaṣ, yšáxxiṣ	شخّص، يْشخّص
diagnosis	tašxīṣ	تشْخيص
to examine	fáḥaṣ, yífḥaṣ	فحص، يِفْحص
examination	fáḥiṣ (fuḥūṣāt)	فحِص (فُحوصات)

The doctor examined him and diagnosed him with the flu.	iddaktōr fáḥaṣu w gāl má3u ʔinfluwánza.	الدّكْتوْر فحصو وقال معو إنْفلُوَنْزا.
problem	múškila (mašākil)	مُشْكِلة (مشاكِل)
What's wrong?	šū -lmúškila?	شو المُشْكِلة؟
I'm sick.	ána 3ayyān.	أنا عيّان.
pain	wája3 (awjā3)	وَجع (أوْجاع)
to have a backache	ḍáhru ʔája3u, ḍáhru yūja3u	ضهْرو أجعو، ضهْرو يوجعو
to have a headache	rāsu ʔája3u	راسو أجعو
I have a really bad headache.	rāsi bijá3ni ktīr.	راسي بيجعْني كْتير.
My shoulder has been hurting for ages.	kítfi bijá3ni min zamān.	كِتْفي بيجعْني مِن زمان.
He has a stomachache.	báṭnu bijá3u.	بطْنو بيجعو.
It hurts here.	fī wája3 hān.	في وَجع هان.
migraine	ṣudā3 níṣfi	صُداع نِصْفي
dizziness	dōxa	دوْخة
dizzy	dāyix	دايْخ
to faint	úɣma 3lē, yúɣma 3alē	أغْمى عليْه، يُغْمى عليْه
to have a cold	áxad [55] bard	أخد برْد
to be congested, have nasal congestion	mráššiḥ	مْرشّح
to have the flu	má3u ʔinfluwánza mfálwiz	معو اِنْفلوَنْزا مْفلْوِز

معو má3u (or معاه ma3ā), literally 'with one,' is a prepositional phrase that is used like a verb. (See the book Palestinian Arabic Verbs p. 108)

| to have a fever | ḥarārtu 3ālya súxun | حرارْتو عالْية سُخْن |
| to have a sore throat, have tonsilitis | lúwazu miltihbāt | لُوَزو مِلْتِهْبات |

to cough	gaḥḥ, yguḥḥ kaḥḥ, ykuḥḥ	قَحَّ، يْقُحّ كَحَّ، يْكُحّ
to have a cough	3índu gáḥḥa	عِنْدو قَحَّة
to vomit, throw up	nátag, yúntug istáfraɣ, yistáfriɣ	نَتَق، يُنْتُق إِسْتَفْرَغ، يِسْتَفْرِغ
rash	ḥasāsíyya fi -jjílid	حساسية في الجِّلِد
to have a rash	3índu ḥasāsíyya	عِنْدو حساسية
diarrhea	ishāl	إسْهال
having diarrhea	3índu ʔishāl míshil	عِنْدو إسْهال مِسْهِل
constipated	3índu ʔimsāk	عِنْدو إمْساك
to have indigestion	3índu 3úsur háḍim	عِنْدو عُسُر هضِم
diabetes	súkkar máraḍ issúkkar	سُكَّر مرض السُّكَّر
to be diabetic	má3u súkkar	معو سُكَّر
to have asthma	3índu rábu 3índu ʔázma	عِنْدو ربْوْ عِنْدو أزْمَة
to have high blood pressure	3índu ḍáɣiṭ	عِنْدو ضغِط
AIDS, HIV	īdz	إيدْز

Although medically there is a clear difference between HIV and AIDS, in everyday speech, this distinction is commonly ignored.

cancer	saraṭān	سرطان
to get injured	injáraḥ, yinjíriḥ	إنْجرح، يِنْجِرِح
injured	majrūḥ	مَجْروح
to get a bruise	ákal [8]ḍárba	أكَل ضُرْبة
bruised	wārim	وارِم

wound, cut	járiḥ (jrūḥ)	جرح (جْروح)
to get stitches	(i)tɣárraz, yitɣárraz	اِتْغرَّز، يِتْغرَّز
stitch	ɣúrza (ɣúraz)	غُرْزة (غُرز)
burn	ḥárig (ḥrūg)	حرِق (حُروق)
burned	maḥrūg	محْروق
bandage, Band-Aid	lízig jrūḥ	لِزِق جْروح
to break	inkásar, yinkísir	اِنْكسر، يِنْكِسِر
He broke his arm.	inkásarat ʔīdu	اِنْكسرت إيدو
a broken bone	3áḍma maksūra	عضْمة مكْسورة
cast (UK: plaster); splint	jibṣ	جِبْص
x-ray	ṣūrit ʔaší33a	صورِةْ أُشِعَّة
medicine	dáwa (ádwiya)	دَوا (أدْوِيَة)
prescription	rūšítta	روشِتّا
to prescribe	wáṣaf, yūṣif	وَصف، يوصِف
aspirin	asbirīn	أسْبيرين
pill	ḥábbit dáwa	حبَّةْ دَوا
antibiotics	muḍādd ḥáyawi	مُضادّ حَيَوي
injection, shot	íbra (íbar)	إبْرة (إبر)
to get a shot	áxad [55] íbra	أخد إبْرة
to draw blood	sáḥab damm, yísḥab damm	سحب دمّ، يِسْحب دمّ
to run a blood test	3ámal [55] fáḥiṣ damm	عمل فحِص دمّ
to cure, heal	ṭāb, yṭīb	طاب، يْطيب
recovery, healing	taḥássun	تحسُّن
to treat	3ālaj, y3ālij	عالج، يْعالج
treatment	3ilāj	عِلاج
infection	3ádwa	عدْوَى

contagious	*mú3di*	مُعْدي
Are you contagious?	*máraḑak mú3di?*	مرضك مُعْدي؟
surgeon	*daktōr jirāḩa* *jarrāḩ*	دكتْور جِراحة جرّاح
surgery	*3amalíyya*	عملية
to perform surgery on, operate on	*3ámal [55] 3amalíyya la-*	عمل عملية لـ
to undergo surgery, have an operation	*3ámal [55] 3amalíyya*	عمل عملية
to have an abortion	*názzalat [55] [f.]* *3ámlat [f.] ijhāḑ*	نزّلت عْملت إجْهاض
plastic surgeon	*daktōr tajmīl*	دكْتْور تجْميل
plastic surgery	*3amalíyyit tajmīl*	عمليّة تجْميل
pregnancy	*ḩámil*	حمِل
to get pregnant by	*ḩíblat min, tíḩbal min [f.]* *ḩámlat min, tíḩmil min [f.]*	حِبْلت مِن، تِحْبل مِن حمْلت مِن، تِحْمِل مِن
pregnant	*ḩāmil [f., invar.]*	حامِل
to give birth	*wíldat, tūlad [f.]*	وِلْدت، تولد
When are you due?	*wagtēš ḩatūladi?*	وَقْتيْش حتولدي؟
She's due in early July.	*ḩatūlad fi ʔáwwal sáb3a.*	حتولد في أوّل سبْعة.
How far along is she?	*b-ʔáyy šáhir ṣārat?*	بْأيّ شهِر صارت؟
She's six-months pregnant.	*híyya fi -ššahr issādis.*	هِيَّ في الشّهْر السّادِس.
to use birth control (pills)	*áxdat [f.] ḩbūb máni3 ḩámil*	أخْدت خْبوب منع حمِل
condom	*kōndōm* *wāqi zákari*	كوْنْدوْم واقي زكْري

dentist	daktōr snān	دكْتوْر سْنان
to have a cavity	3índu tasáwwus	عِنْدو تسوُّس
to have a toothache	snānu bija3ū	سْنانو بيجعوه
to have a chipped tooth	sínnu maksūr	سِنّو مكْسور
to get a filling	ḥáša sínnu, yíḥši sínnu 3ámal [55] ḥášwa fi sínnu	حشى سِنّو، يِحْشِي سِنّو عمل حشْوَة في سِنّو
to get a tooth pulled	xála3 sinn, yíxla3 sinn	خلع سِنّ، يِخْلع سِنّ
to get a cleaning	náḍḍaf [7] snānu	نضّف سْنانو
I'm going to the dentist's to get a check-up and a cleaning.	rāyiḥ 3ind daktōr lisnān á3mal fáḥiṣ w anáḍḍif snāni.	رايِح عِنْد دكْتور السْنان أعْمل فحِص وأنضِّف سْناني.
to get one's teeth whitened	báyyaḍ snānu, ybáyyiḍ snānu 3ámal [55] la-snānu tabyīḍ	بيّض سْنانو، يْبيِّض سْنانو عمل لسْنانو تبْييض

technology	*tuknōlōjya*	تُكْنُولُوْجْيا
computer	*kumbyūtar*	كُمْبْيوتر
to turn on the computer	*šáyyal [21] ilkumbyūtar*	شغّل الكُمْبْيوتر
to turn off the computer	*ṭáfa [55] -lkumbyūtar*	طفى الكُمْبْيوتر
laptop	*lāb tōb*	لاب توب
screen, monitor	*šāša*	شاشة
keyboard	*kībōrd*	كيبوْرْد
mouse	*māws*	ماوْس
to click on	*3aṣṣ 3ála, y3uṣṣ 3ála* *ḍáɣaṭ 3ála, yíḍɣaṭ 3ála*	عصّ على، يْعُصّ على ضْغط على، يِضْغط على
file	*maláff* *fāyl*	ملفّ فايْل
folder	*mujállad* *fōldar*	مُجلّد فوْلْدر
I can't remember what folder the file is in.	*miš zākir ilmaláff b-ʔayy mujállad.*	مِش زاكِر الملفّ بْأيّ مُجلّد.
to open a file	*fátaḥ [55] maláff*	فتح ملفّ
to save	*ḥífiẓ, yíḥfaẓ* *sáyyav, ysáyyiv*	حِفِظ، يِحْفظ سيّف، يْسيّف
computer program	*barnāmij kumbyūtar*	برْنامِج كُمْبْيوتر
to close (the program)	*sákkar [5] (ilbarnāmij)*	سكّر (البرْنامِج)
to delete	*ḥázaf, yíḥzif*	حذف، يِحْذِف
internet	*nit* *íntirnit*	نِت إِنْترْنِت

on the internet, online	3a -nnit	عَ النِّت
to get on the internet, go online	fátaɦ [55] innít	فتح النِّت
wifi	wāyirlis wāy fāy	وايَرْلِس واي فاي
Is wifi available here?	fī wāyirlis hān?	في وايَرْلِس هان؟
web site	máwqi3 (mawāqi3)	مَوْقِع (مَواقِع)
web page	ṣáfɦa	صفْحة
to download	ɦámmal, yɦámmil názzal, ynázzil	حمَّل، يْحمِّل نزَّل، يْنزِّل
to upload	ráfa3, yírfa3	رفع، يِرْفع
email	īmēl	إيميْل
to send an email	bá3at [17] īmēl bá3at [17] risāli 3ála -lʔīmēl	بعت إيميْل بعت رِسالة عَ الإيميْل
username	ism ilmustáxdim yūzar nēm	اِسْم المُسْتخْدِم يوزر نيْم
password	kílmit issírr pāswōrd	كِلْمِة السِّر باسْووْرْد
Enter your username and password.	íktib ism ilmustáxdim tába3ak w kílmit issírr.	اِكْتِب اِسْم المُسْتخْدِم تبعك وكِلْمِة السِّرّ.
Facebook	fēsbōk	فيْسْبوْك
to click "like"	ɦaṭṭ [55] lāyk	حطّ لايْك

Twitter	twítar	تْوِتر
printer	ṭáb3a	طابْعة

to print	ṭába3, yíṭba3	طبع، يِطْبع
scanner	skānar	سْكانر
to scan	sáḥab [11] ṣūra 3ámal [55] skān	سحب صورة عمل سْكان
fax, fax machine	fāks	فاكْس
to fax	bá3at [17] fāks	بعت فاكْس
(landline) telephone, phone	talafōn	تلفوْن
cell phone	jawwāl mōbāyl	جوّال موْبايْل
app	taṭbīq	تطْبيق
to send a text message	bá3at [17] risāla	بعت رِسالة
ringtone	náɣama ránna	نغمة رنّة
vibration	rajjāj	رجّاج
silent mode	ṣāmit sāylant	صامِت سايْلنْت
(cell) phone number	ráqam jawwāl	رقم جوّال
What's your number?	gaddēš ráqamak?	قدّيْش رقمك؟
to call, phone (someone)	(i)ttáṣal [55] fi	اِتِّصل في
(phone) call	ittiṣāl	اِتِّصال
line	xaṭṭ	خطّ
to ring	rann, yrinn	رنّ، يْرِنّ
The phone's ringing!	ijjawwāl birínn!	الجّوّال بيرِنّ!
to get a phone call	ajā -ttiṣāl, yijī -ttiṣāl	أجاه اِتِّصال، بِجيه اِتِّصال
to answer the phone	radd 3a -jjawwāl	ردَّ عَ الجّوّال

Hello?	ālō?	آلوْ؟
to talk on the phone	ḥáka [55] 3a -jjawwāl	حكى عَ الجّوّال
to hang up (the phone)	sákkar [5] ilxáṭṭ	سكّر الخطّ
to hang up on	sákkar [5] ilxáṭṭ fi wíjih __	سكّر الخطّ في وِجِهْ ــــ
to call a wrong number	(i)ttáṣal [55] 3a ráqam ɣálaṭ	إتّصل عَ رقم غلط
receiver	sammā3it talafōn	سمّاعِةْ تلفوْن

Getting Around

transportation	*muwāṣalāt* [pl.]	مُواصلات
to take the bus	*ṭíli3 [55] fi -lbāṣ*	طِلع في الباص
to get on, get in, take (a bus, taxi, etc.)	*ríkib, yírkab*	رِكِب، يِرْكب
to get off, get out of	*nízil [55] min*	نزِل مِن
transportation, shipping	*nágil*	نقِل
freight; truck	*šáḥin*	شحِن
pick-up truck	*sayyāra nuṣṣ nágil*	سيّارة نُصّ نقِل
ship	*safīna*	سفينة
boat	*ḥásaka*	حسكة
bus	*bāṣ*	باص
I usually go to work by bus.	*bi-l3āda barūḥ 3a -ššúɣul fi -lbāṣ.*	بِالعادة بروح عَ الشُّغُل في الباص.
to miss the bus	*rāḥ 3alē -lbāṣ, yrūḥ 3alē -lbāṣ*	راح عليْه الباص، يْروح عليْه الباص
bus stop	*máwgif bāṣat (mawāgif bāṣāt)*	مَوْقِف باصّات (مَواقِف باصّات)
bus driver	*sawwāg bāṣ*	سوّاق باص
metro, subway (UK: underground)	*mítro*	مِترْوْ
I take the metro every day.	*ána báṭla3 fi -lmítro kull yōm.*	أنا بطْلع في المِترْوْ كُلّ يوْم.
subway station	*maḥáṭṭit mítro*	محطّة مِترْوْ
taxi	*tāksi* *sayyārit újra*	تاكْسي سيّارةِ أُجْرة

We took a taxi downtown.	ṭlí3na 3a -lbálad fi tāksi.	طْلِعْنا عَ البلد في تاكْسي.
taxi driver	sawwāg tāksi	سوّاق تاكْسي
to hail a taxi	ašār la-tāksī, yʾāšir la-tāksī	أشّر لتاكْسي، يْأشّر لتاكْسي
taxi meter	3addād tāksi	عدّاد تاكْسي
to negotiate the fare	fāṣal 3a -ssí3ir, yfāṣil 3a -ssí3ir	فاصِل عَ السِّعِر، يْفاصِل عَ السِّعِر
left	šmāl	شْمال
Turn left!	xūd šmāl!	خُد شْمال!
right	yamīn	يَمِين
Turn right!	xūd yamīn!	خُد يَمِين!
straight	guddāmak fi wíjhak	قُدّامك في وِجْهك
Go straight!	ḍállak dúɣri	ضّلّك دُغْري
bicycle	baskalēt	بسْكليْت
to ride a bicycle	ríkib baskalēt	رِكِب بسْكليْت
cyclist	sawwāg baskalēt	سوّاق بسْكليْت
bicycle lane, bike path	ṭarīg baskalētāt	طريق بسْكليْتات
pedal	da33āsa dawwāsa	دعّاسة دوّاسة
chain	janzīr (janazīr)	جنْزير (جنازير)
bike seat	kúrsi baskalēt	كُرسي بسْكليْت
motorcycle	fízba mōtsíkil	فِزْبة موْتْسِكِل
helmet	xūza (xúwaz)	خوذة (خُوَذ)

car	sayyāra	سيّارة
to drive, steer	sāg, ysūg	ساق، يْسوق
driver	sawwāg	سوّاق
passenger	rākib	راكِب
driver's license	rúxṣit swāga (rúxaṣ swāga)	رُخْصِةْ سْواقة (رُخص سْواقة)
traffic jam	záḥma	زحْمة
stuck in traffic	m3állig fi -zzáḥma	مْعلَّق في الزَّحْمة
The traffic is horrible right now!	iṭṭarīg záḥma ktīr halgēt.	الطَّريق زحْمة كْتير هلْقيْت.
rush hour	wagt izzáḥma	وَقْت الزَّحْمة
Let's not go downtown right now. It's rush hour.	balāš nínzal 3a -lbálad halgēt, iddínya záḥma.	بلاش نِنْزل عَ البلد هلْقيْت، الدِّنْيا زحْمة.
to pass, overtake	idjāwaz, yidjāwaz	اِتْجاوَز، بِتْجاوَز
to stop	wígif, yūgaf	وِقِف، يوقف
to yield to	wássa3 la-, ywássi3 la-	وَسَّع لـ، يْوسِّع لـ
to have the right of way	ílu lʔāwlawíyya	إلو الأوْلَوية
pedestrians	mušā [pl.]	مُشاة
sidewalk (UK: pavement)	raṣīf (árṣifa)	رصيف (أرْصِفة)
cross walk, pedestrian crossing (UK: zebra crossing)	xaṭṭ mušā (xṭūṭ mušā)	خطّ مُشاة (خْطوط مُشاة)
to cross the street	gáṭa3 iššāri3, yígṭa3 iššāri3	قطع الشَّارِع، بِقْطع الشَّارِع
traffic light	išārit murūr	إشارِةْ مُرور
green light	išāra xáḍra	إشارة خضْرا
red light	išāra ḥámra	إشارة حمْرا
yellow light	išāra ṣáfra	إشارة صفْرا
to run a red light	gáṭa3 [7] ilʔišāra -lḥámra	قطع الإشارة الحمْرا
to park	ṣaff, yṣuff	صفَّ، يْصُفَّ

parking lot	máwgif (mawāgif)	مَوْقِف (مواقِف)
parking garage	karāj	كراج
to park on the street	ṣaff fi -ššāri3	صفّ في الشّارِع
lane	xaṭṭ (xṭūṭ) masār	خطّ (خْطوط) مسار
to change lanes	ɣáyyar [55] ilxáṭṭ	غيِّر الخطّ
a four-lane road	ṭarīg árba3 xṭūṭ	طريق أُرْبع خْطوط
intersection	taqāṭu3	تقاطُع
round-about	duwwār mīdān (mayadīn)	دُوّار ميدان (مَيادين)
highway, expressway (UK: **motorway**)	xaṭṭ sarī3	خط سريع
bridge, overpass	jísir (jsūr)	جِسِر (جْسور)
speed limit	ḥadd issúr3a	حدّ السُّرْعة
license plate (UK: **number plate**)	láwḥit innímira	لَوْحِةْ النِّمْرة
car insurance	ta?mīn sayyāra	تأُمين سيّارة
to pick up	rákkab, yrákkib	ركّب، يْركّب
to drop off	názzal, ynázzil	نزّل، يْنزّل
You can just drop me off on the corner.	nazzílni 3a -lláffa	نزّلْني عَ اللَّفّة.
to give a lift to, take	wáṣṣal, ywáṣṣil áxad __ má3u	وَصّل، يْوَصّل أخد ___ معو
Can you give me a ride home?	btígdar twaṣṣílni 3a -ddār?	بْتِقْدر تْوَصِّلْني عَ الدّار؟
hood	kabbūd	كبّود

windshield	gzāz guddamāni gzāz amāmi	قْزاز قُدّماني قْزاز أمامي
trunk	šántit sayyāra	شنْطِةْ سيّارة
the front seat	ilkúrsi -lguddamāni	الكُرْسي القُدّماني
the back seat	ilkúrsi -lwarrāni	الكُرْسي الوَرّاني
car door	bāb issayyāra	باب السّيّارة
car door handle	máskit ilbāb	مسْكِةِ الباب
window	šubbāk (šababīk)	شُبّاك (شبابيك)
to roll the window up	3álla -ššubbāk, y3álli -ššubbāk ráfa3 [23] iššubbāk	علّى الشُبّاك، يْعلّي الشُبّاك رفع الشُبّاك
to roll the window down	názzal iššubbāk	نزّل الشُبّاك
The door is ajar.	ilbāb maftū̄.	الباب مفْتوح.
steering wheel	stīrin	سْتيرِن
turn signal	ɣammāz	غمّاز
He never uses his turn signal.	bya3ṭīš ɣammāz bi-lmárra.	بْيَعْطيش غمّاز بِالمرّة.
rear view mirror	mrāya warrāníyya	مْرايَة وَرّانية
side view mirror	mrāya -lli 3a -jjánab	مْراية اللي عَ الجّنِب
glove compartment	ṣandūg tāblōn	صنْدوق طبْلوْن
dashboard	tāblōn issayyāra	طبْلوْن السّيّارة
emergency brake, hand brake	hānd brēk	هانْد بْريْك
tire (UK: tyre)	3ájal	عجل
to check the tire pressure	gās [46] ḍáɣiṭ il3ájal	قاس ضغِط العجل
to get a flat tire	náffas il3ájal, ynáffis il3ájal	نفّس العجل، يْنفّس العجل
spare tire	3ájal spēr	عجل سْبيْر
to change a flat tire	ɣáyyar [55] il3ájal	غيّر العجل
automatic	ōtōmātik	أوْتوْماتِك

manual, stick-shift	*3ādi*	عادي
He can't drive a stick.	*bi3rífš ysūg gīr 3ādi.*	بيعْرِفْش يْسوق غير عادي.
pedal	*dá3sa* *dawwāsa*	دعْسِة دوّاسة
clutch	*klatš*	كُلتْش
brake	*brēk* *stōb*	بْريْك سْتوْب
to brake	*dá3as brēk, yíd3as brēk*	دعس بْريْك، يِدْعس بْريْك
gas pedal, accelerator	*dá3sit ilbanzīn*	دعْسِةْ البنْزين
to accelerate, speed up	*síri3, yísri3* *dá3as banzīn*	سِرِع، يِسْرِع دعس بنْزين
to slow down	*báttaʔ, ybáttiʔ* *wátta [21] -ssúr3a*	بطّأ، يْبطّئ وطّى السُّرْعة
gear; stick shift	*gīr*	غير
in gear	*mlábbis ɣayār* *m3áššig*	مْلبّس غَيار مْعشُّق
1st gear	*ɣayār áwwal*	غيار أوّل
reverse (gear)	*lāvērs*	لافيْرْس
to back up	*ríji3 wára, yírja3 wára*	رِجِع وَرا، يِرْجع وَرا
to change gears	*ɣáyyar [55]* *báddal [19]*	غيّر بدّل
I put the car in reverse and started backing up.	*ḥattēt ilgīr lāvērs w rijā3t la-wára.*	حطّيْت الغير لافيْرْس ورْجِعِت وَرا.
speedometer	*3addād (issúr3a)*	عدّاد (السُّرْعة)
to do the speed limit	*iltázam bi-ssúr3a, yiltízim bi-ssúr3a*	إِلتزِم بِالسُّرْعة، يِلْتزِم بِالسُّرْعة
to speed, go over the speed limit	*txátta ssír3a, yitxátta ssír3a*	إِتْخطّى السُّرْعة، يِتْخطّى السُّرْعة

The police pulled me over for speeding.	iššúrṭa waggafátni b-sábab issúr3a.	الشُّرْطة وقّفتْني بْسبب السُّرْعة.
gas (UK: **petrol**)	banzīn	بنْزين
We've run out of gas.	ilbanzīn xállaṣ.	البنْزين خلّص.
The tank is full.	ittánk malyān.	التّنْك ملْيان.
gas gauge	3addād banzīn	عدّاد بنْزين
gas station	maḥáṭṭit banzīn	مْحطّة بنْزين
gas pump	maḍáxxit banzīn	مضخّة بنْزين
to get gas	3ábba banzīn, y3ábbi banzīn	عبّى بنْزين، يْعبّي بنْزين
to change the oil	ɣáyyar [55] izzāt	غيّر الزّيْت
to put on one's seatbelt, wear one's seat belt	ḥaṭṭ [55] ḥzām ilʔamān	حطّ حْزام الأمان
to start a car	šáɣɣal [21] issayyāra	شغّل السّيّارة
The car won't start.	issayyāra miš rāḍya tištíɣil.	السّيّارة مِش راضْية تِشْتِغِل.
to turn off the engine	ṭáfa [55] -lmātōr	طفى الماتوْر
fender; bumper	ṣaddām ráfraf (rafārif)	صدّام رفْرف (رفارِف)
(car) roof	ságif (sgūf)	سقِف (سْقوف)
to get in a fender-bender	3ámal [55] ḥādis basīṭ	عمل حادِث بسيط
dent	xábṭa	خبْطة
There's a dent in the side of the car.	fī xábṭa fi -ssayyāra min ijjánab.	في خبْطة في السّيّارة مِن الجّنِب.
headlight	ḍaww guddamāni ḍaww amāmi	ضوّ قُدّماني ضوّ أمامي
Turn on your headlights when it starts to get dark.	íḍwi -ḍḍaww lámma tíbda t3áttim.	اِضوي الضّوّ لمّا تِبْدا تْعتِّم.
to get in an accident, have an accident	3ámal [55] ḥādis	عمل حادِث

to crash	*xábaṭ, yúxbuṭ*	خبط، يُخْبُط
He crashed (his car) into a tree.	*xábaṭ sayyārtu fi šájara.*	خبط سيّارْتو في شجرة.
The car was totaled in the accident.	*(i)tkássarit issayyāra fi -lḥādis.*	اِتْكسّرت السّيّارة في الحادِث.

English	Transliteration	Arabic
city	madīna (múdun)	مدينة (مُدُن)
town	bálad (blād)	بلد (بْلاد)
village	qárya	قَرْيَة
downtown	ilbálad	البلد
square, plaza	mīdān (mayadīn)	ميدان (مَيادين) مُرَبَّع
park	ḥadīqa (ḥadāʔiq)	حديقة (حدائِق)
fountain	nāfūra (nawāfīr)	نافورة (نَوافير)
street	šāri3 (šawāri3)	شارِع (شَوارِع)
alley, narrow street	ḥāra	حارة
corner	láffa zāwya	لفَّة زاوْيَة
bakery	fúrun (frān)	فُرُن (فُران)
bank	bank (bnūk)	بنْك (بْنوك)
butcher shop	málḥama maḥáll láḥma	مَلْحمة محلّ لحْمة
city hall	baladíyya	بلدية
fire station	difā3 mádani	دِفاع مدني
grocery store	dukkāna	دُكَّانة
museum	mátḥaf (matāḥif)	مَتْحف (متاحِف)
police station	márkaz šúrṭa	مرْكز شُرْطة
post office	máktab barīd (makātib barīd)	مكْتب بريد (مكاتِب بريد)

supermarket; grocery store	*sūbar mārkit*	سوْبر مارْكِت
restaurant	*máṭ3am (maṭā3im)*	مطْعم (مطاعِم)
café, coffee shop	*kāfi* *kāfi šōp*	كافي كافي شُب
(traditional) coffee shop	*gáhwa*	قهْوَة
to go to a café	*rāḥ [55] 3a -lkāfi*	راح عَ الكافي

Buildings and Construction

to build	*bána, yíbni*	بِنى، يِبْني
construction	*binā?* *tašyīd*	بِناء تشْييد
construction worker	*bánna*	بنّا
building, structure	*3imāra* *bināya*	عِمارة بِناية
apartment building	*3imāra sakaníyya*	عِمارة سكنية
office building	*3imārit makātib*	عِمارةْ مكاتِب
tower; high-rise building	*burj (abrāj)*	بُرْج (أبْراج)
skyscraper	*nāṭaḥit saḥāb*	ناطحِةْ سحاب
to demolish	*hadd, yhidd*	هدّ، يْهِدّ
elevator (UK: lift)	*asānsēr* *máṣ3ad*	أصانْصيْر مصْعد
stairs, staircase	*dáraj*	درج
escalator	*dáraj kahrabā?i*	درج كهْرُبائي
to go upstairs	*ṭíli3 [55] 3a -ddáraj*	طِلِع عَ الدَّرج
to go downstairs	*nízil [55] 3a -ddáraj*	نِزِل عَ الدَّرج
basement	*búdrum*	بُدْرُم
story, floor	*ṭābig (ṭawābig)*	طابِق (طَوابِق)
ground floor	*ṭābig árḍi* *il?árḍi*	طابِق أرْضي الأرْضي
top floor	*ṭābig axīr* *āxir ṭābig*	طابِق أخير آخِر طابِق
concrete	*bāṭōn*	باطوْن

brick	*blōk*	بْلُك
	ḥájar	حجر
wood	*xášab*	خشب
glass	*gzāz*	قْزاز
metal	*má3dan*	معْدن
iron; steel	*ḥadīd*	حديد

16 Bank

bank	bank (bnūk)	بنْك (بْنوك)
Bank of Palestine	bank falasṭīn	بنْك فلسْطين
to borrow money from the bank	áxad [55] qarḍ min ilbank	أخد قرْض مِن البنْك
to lend money (to)	dāyan, yḍāyin	دايَن، يْدايِن
loan	qarḍ (qrūḍ)	قرْض (قْروض)
to finance	máwwal, ymáwwil	موّل، يموّل
mortgage, home loan	ráhin 3aqāri (rhūn 3aqāríyya)	رهِن عقاري (رْهون عقارية)
payment, installment	gisṭ (agsāṭ)	قِسْط (أقْساط)
to make a payment on a loan	dáfa3 [55] gisṭ ilqárḍ	دفع قِسْط القرْض
to pay in installments	dáfa3 [55] tagsīṭ	دفع تقْسيط
to settle, pay off (a debt)	sadd, ysidd	سدّ، يْسِدّ
debt	dēn (dyūn)	ديْن (دْيون)
interest	fāyda (fawāyid)	فايْدة (فَوايِد)
This accounts pays 5% interest.	hāda liḥsāb bījīb xámsa fi -lmíyya fāyda.	هادا الحِساب بيجيب خمْسة في المية فايْدة.
to earn interest	áxad [55] fawāyid	أخد فوايِد
account	ḥsāb	حْساب
savings account	ḥsāb tawfīr	حْساب تَوْفير
savings	taḥwīša	تحْويشة
to save, put aside	ḥáwwaš, yḥáwwiš	حوّش، يْحوّش
He has over 100,000 shekels in savings.	húwwa mḥáwwiš áktar min mīt alf šēkil.	هُوَّ مْحوِّش أكْتر مِن مية ألْف شيْكِل.
I try to save a little money every month.	ána baḥāwil aḥáwwiš šwáyyit maṣari kull šáhir.	أنا بحاوِل أحوِّش شْوَيِّة مصاري كُلّ شهِر.

to deposit	*áwda3, yūdi3*	أوْدع، يودِع
to withdraw	*sáḥab, yísḥab*	سحب، يِسْحب
ATM	*ṣarrāf* *ṣarrāf āli* *[ATM]*	صرّاف صرّاف آلي ATM
to write a check	*kátab [38] šek*	كتب شيْك
to sign	*máḍa, yímḍi* *wáqqa3, ywágqqi3*	مضى، يِمْضي وَقَّع، يْوَقِّع
signature	*tawqī3* *máḍya* *ímḍa*	تَوْقيع مضْيَة إمْضا

post office	máktab barīd (makātb barīd)	مكْتب بريد (مكاتِب بريد)
mail	barīd	بريد
airmail	barīd jáwwi	بريد جوّي
letter	risāla (rasāyil)	رِسالة (رسايِل)
envelope	ẓarf (ẓrūf)	ظرْف (ظْروف)
postcard	biṭāqit barīd	بِطاقِةْ بريد
address	3inwān (3anawīn)	عِنْوان (عناوين)
stamp	ṭābi3 (ṭawābi3)	طابِع (طوابِع)
to affix a stamp	lázzag ṭābi3, ylázzig ṭābi3	لزّق طابِع، يْلزّق طابِع
to stamp (with a postmark)	xátam, yíxtim	ختم، يِخْتِم
to send, mail	bá3at, yíb3at	بعت، يِبْعت
package, parcel	ṭard (ṭrūd)	طرْد (طْرود)
mailbox	ṣandūg barīd (ṣanādīg barīd)	صنْدوق بريد (صناديق بريد)
counter, window	šubbāk (šababīk) kāntar	شُبّاك (شبابيك) كانْتر
mail carrier	sā3i barīd	ساعي بريد
to deliver the mail	wáṣṣal [13] ilbarīd	وَصّل البريد

library, bookstore, stationery shop	*máktaba*	مكْتْبة
book	*ktāb (kútub)*	كْتاب (كُتُب)
page	*şáfḥa*	صفْحة
page number	*ráqam şáfḥa*	رقم صفْحة
bookmark	*fāşil ktāb* *bōk mārk*	فاصِل كْتاب بوْك مارْك
reference book	*márji3*	مرْجِع
novel	*riwāya*	رِوايَة
story	*gíşşa (gíşaş)*	قِصّة (قِصص)
fairy tale	*gíşşa xayālíyya*	قِصّة خَيالية
prose	*náṯir*	نثِر
writer, author	*kātib (kuttāb)*	كاتِب (كُتّاب)
poetry	*ší3ir (aš3ār)*	شِعِر (أَشْعار)
poem	*gaşīda (gaşāyid)*	قصيدة (قصايِد)
poet	*šā3ir (šú3ara)*	شاعِر (شُعرا)
newspaper	*jarīda (jarāyid)*	جريدة (جرايِد)
headline	*3inwān (3anāwīn)*	عِنْوان (عناوين)
article	*maqāl*	مقال
column	*3amūd şáḥafi (3awamīd şaḥafíyya)*	عمود صحفي (عَواميد صحفية)
to publish	*nášar, yúnšur*	نشر، يِنْشُر
to print	*ṭába3, yíṭba3*	طبع، يِطْبع
stationery	*qurṭāsíyya*	قُرْطاسية

pen	gálam (glām)	قلم (قْلام)
ballpoint pen	gálam jāff	قلم جافّ
pencil	gálam rṣāṣ	قلم رْصاص
eraser	maḥḥāya	محّايَة
to erase	máḥa, yímḥi máḥḥa, ymáḥḥi	محّى، يِمْحي محّى، يمْحّي
(pair of) scissors	mgaṣṣ	مْقصّ
ink	ḥíbir (aḥbār)	حِبِر (أحْبار)
typewriter	āla kātba	آلة كاتْبة
paper	wárag (wrāg)	وَرق (وْراق)
a sheet of paper	wáraga	وَرقة
ruler	másṭra (masāṭir)	مسْطرة (مساطِر)
(adhesive) tape	lízig	لِزِق
paperclip	málgaṭ wárag (malāgiṭ wárag)	ملْقط وَرق (ملاقِط وَرق)
pin, pushpin; staple	dabbūs (dababīs)	دبّوس (دبابيس)
stapler	dabbāsa	دبّاسة
to staple	dábbas, ydábbis	دبّس، يْدبّس
to sharpen a pencil	bárra gálam, ybárri gálam	برّى قلم، يْبرّي قلم
to photocopy	ṣáwwar, yṣáwwir	صوّر، يْصوّر
a photocopy	núsxa (núsax)	نُسْخة (نُسخ)
photocopy machine	mākīnit taṣwīr	ماكينِةْ تصْوير

19 Shopping

shopping	*šírya*	شِرْيَة
to go shopping	*rāḥ [55] yíštiri* *rāḥ [55] yitsáwwag*	راح يِشْتِري راح يِتْسوَّق
We went shopping downtown yesterday.	*nzílna ništíri ɣrāḍ min ilbálad.*	نْزِلْنا نِشْتِري غْراض مِن البلد.
to buy	*ištára, yištíri*	إِشْترى، يِشْتِري
to sell	*bā3, ybī3*	باع، يْبيع
to pay for __	*dáfa3 [55] ḥagg__*	دفع حقّ__
I've already paid for the vegetables.	*ána dafá3it ḥagg ilxúḍra.*	أنا دفعِت حقّ الخُضْرة.
How much did you pay for that?	*gaddēš dafá3it 3a hād?*	قدّيْش دفعِت عَ هاد؟
to pay in cash	*dáfa3 [55] kāš* *dáfa3 [55] nágdi*	دفع كاش دفع نقْدي
to pay by credit card	*dáfa3 [55] bi-lbiṭāqa*	دفع بِالبِطاقة
change (money back)	*ilbāgi*	الباقي
You gave me too much change.	*a3ṭētni zyāda 3a -lbāgi.*	أعْطيْتْني زْيادة عَ الباقي.
receipt	*fātūra (fawatīr)*	فاتورة (فَواتير)
price	*ḥagg* *sí3ir (as3ār)*	حقّ سِعِر (أسْعار)
to cost	*kállaf, ykállif*	كلّف، يُكلّف
cheap	*rxīṣ (rxāṣ)*	رْخيص (رْخاص)
expensive	*ɣāli*	غالي
(for) free	*b-balāš* *majānan*	بْبلاش مجاناً

fee	rusūm	رُسوم
bill	ḥsāb	حْساب
How much do I owe?	gaddēš liḥsāb?	قدّيْش الحِْساب؟
advertisement, ad	i3lān	إعْلان
discount, sale	xáṣim (xṣūmāt)	خصِم (خُصومات)
40% off	xáṣim arba3īn fi -lmíyya	خصِم أرْبعين في المية
coupon	qasīma širāʔíyya	قسيمة شِرائية
bargain	ṣáfqa ittifāg	صفْقة اِتِّفاق
Wow! That's a real bargain!	yā salām! hādi ṣáfqa ḥílwa!	يا سلام! هادي صفْقة حِلوَة.
to haggle over, bargain	fāṣal, yfāṣil sāwam, ysāwim	فاصِل، يْفاصِل ساوَم، يْساوِم
I'm not very good at haggling.	ána miš šāṭir ktīr bi-limfāṣala.	أنا مِش شاطِر كْتير بالمْفاصلة.
fixed price	tas3īra síʔir nihāʔi	تسْعيرة سِعِر نِهائي
shopping center	márkaz tijāri (marākiz tijāríyya)	مرْكز تِجاري (مراكِز تِجارية)
(shopping) mall	mōl	موْل
market, shopping area	sūg (swāg)	سوق (سْواق)
Let's go shopping this weekend.	xallīna nrūḥ ništíri āxir ilʔisbū3	خلّينا نْروح نِشْترِي آخِر الإسْبوع.
store, shop	maḥáll	محلّ
There are a lot of nice shops on this street.	hāda -ššāri3 fī maḥallāt ḥílwa ktīr.	هادا الشّارِع فيه محلّات حِلْوة كْتير.
supermarket	sūbar mārkit	سوْبر مارْكِت

cashier	*muḥāsib* *kāšīr*	مُحاسِب كاشير
shop keeper	*ṣāḥib maḥáll*	صاحِب محلّ
shop assistant	*muwázzaf b-maḥáll*	مُوَظَّف بْمحلّ
customer	*zbūn (zabāyin)*	زْبون (زباين)
to serve a customer	*bā3 zbūn* *sā3ad [55] zbūn*	باع زْبون ساعد زْبون
(plastic) bag	*kīs (kyās)*	كيس (كْياس)
shopping bag, paper bag	*kīs wárag*	كيس وَرق
Would you like a bag (for that)?	*bíddak kīs?*	بِدّك كيس؟
to wrap	*ɣállaf, yɣállif*	غلَّف، يْغلِّف
to return (a purchased item)	*rájja3, yrájji3*	رجَّع، يْرجِّع
to exchange	*báddal, ybáddil*	بدَّل، يْبدِّل
Can I exchange this for another color?	*múmkin abádlu 3a lōn tāni?*	مُمْكِن أبدْلو عَ لوْن تاني؟
to get a refund	*áxad [55] maṣārī*	أخد مصاريه

restaurant	*máṭ3am (maṭā3im)*	مطْعم (مطاعِم)
fast food restaurant	*máṭ3am wajbāt sarī3a*	مطْعم وَجْبات سريعة
waiter	*garsōn*	غرْسوْن
waitress	*garsōna*	غرْسوْنة
menu	*mínyu* *qāʔima*	مِنْيو قائِمة
to order	*ṭálab, yúṭlub*	طلب، يُطْلُب
bill	*ḥsāb* *fātūra (fawatīr)*	حْساب فاتورة (فْواتير)
to pay the bill	*dáfa3 [55] liḥsāb*	دفع الِحْساب
Waiter! Can I have the bill, please!	*law samáḥit, hātli liḥsāb.*	لَوْ سمحِت هاتْلي الِحْساب.
cook, chef	*ṭabbāx* *šef*	طبّاخ شيْف
tip	*bayɣīš* *ikrāmíyya*	بغْشيش إكْرامية
I never know how much to leave for a tip.	*3úmri mā 3rífit gaddēš lāzim á3ṭi bayɣīš.*	عُمْري ما عُرِفِت قدّيْش لازِم أعْطي بغْشيش.
service	*xídma*	خِدْمة
a table for two	*ṭāwla la-šaxṣēn*	طاوْلة لشخْصيْن

to relax, rest	*irtāḥ, yitāḥ*	اِرْتاح، يِرْتاح
relaxation	*rāḥa* *istirxā?*	راحة اِسْتِرْخاء
to go for a walk	*(i)tmášša, yitmášša*	اِتْمشّى، يِتْمشّى
Let's go for a walk in the park.	*yálla nrūḥ nitmášša fi -lḥadīqa.*	يَلّا نْروح نِتْمشّى في الحديقة.
to fly a kite	*ṭáyyar ṭábag, yṭáyyir ṭábag*	طيّر طبق، يْطيرّ طبق
day off	*ijāza* *3úṭla*	إجازة عُطْلة
Today's my day off.	*ilyōm ijāzti.* *ilyōm 3úṭliti.*	اليوْم إجازْتي. اليوْم عُطْلِتي.
fun, enjoyable	*bisálli*	بيسلّي

بيسلّي *bisálli* is actually a verb, so if the subject is a feminine noun, it would be بِتْسلّي *bitsálli*.

friend	*ṣāḥib (ṣḥāb)* *ṣadīq (aṣdiqā?)*	صاحِب (صْحاب) صديق (أصْدِقاء)
to meet up with friends	*(i)tlāga ma3 ṣḥābu, yitlāga ma3 ṣḥābu*	اِتْلاقى مع صْحابو، يِتْلاقى مع صْحابو
to hang out (with friends)	*ṭíli3, yíṭla3* *ṭašš, yṭušš*	طِلِع، يِطْلِع طشّ، يْطُشّ
We hung out at the shopping mall yesterday evening.	*ṭlí3na 3a -lmōl imbāriḥ fi -llēl.*	طْلِعْنا عَ الموْل إمْبارِح في اللّيْل.
to read	*gára, yígra*	قرا، يِقْرا

newspaper	*jarīda (jarāyid)*	جريدة (جرايِد)
I like to sit in a coffe shop and read the newspaper before I go to work.	*baḥíbb á3gud fi -lkāfi ágra -jjarīda gábil ma arūḥ 3a -ššúɣul.*	بحِبّ أقْعُد في الكافي أقْرا الجريدة قبِل ما أروح عَ الشُّغُل.
magazine	*majálla*	مجلّة
book	*ktāb (kútub)*	كْتاب (كُتُب)
novel	*riwāya*	رِوايَة
comic book, graphic novel	*gíṣṣa muṣáwwara riwāya muṣáwwara*	قِصّة مُصوّرة رِوايَة مُصوّرة
television	*tilfizyōn*	تِلْفِزْيوْن
to watch TV	*(i)tfárraj [55] 3a -ttilfizyōn*	اِتْفرّج عَ التِلْفِزْيوْن
TV show, TV program	*barnāmij (barāmij)*	برْنامِج (برامِج)
What's your favorite TV program?	*šū áktar barnāmij bitḥíbbu fi -ttilfizyōn?*	شو أكْتر برْنامِج بِتْحِبّو في التِّلْفِزْيوْن؟
What do you like to watch on TV?	*3a šū bitḥíbb titfárraj fi -ttilfizyōn?*	عَ شو بِتْحِبّ تِتْفرّج في التِّلْفِزْيوْن؟
I like watching Palestinian dramas (soaps).	*baḥíbb atfárraj 3a lidrāmā -lfalasṭīníyya.*	بحِبّ أتْفرّج عَ الدِّراما الفلسْطينية.
drama	*drāmā*	دْراما
comedy program	*barnāmij kōmīdi*	برْنامِج كوْميدي
sports program	*barnāmij riyāḍi*	برْنامِج رِياضي
sporting event	*fa3ālíyya riyāḍíyya ḥádaṯ riyāḍi (aḥdāṯ riyāḍíyya)*	فعالية رِياضية حدث رِياضي (أحْداث رِياضية)
soccer match	*mubārāt kōra mubārāt kúrit qádam*	مبُاراةْ كوْرة مُباراةْ كُرِةْ قدم
movie	*fílim (aflām)*	فِلِم (أفْلام)
documentary	*fílim waṯāʔiqi*	فِلِم وَثائِقي

children's program	*barnāmij aṭfāl*	برْنامِج أطْفال
cartoon	*rusūm (mutaḥárrika)* *kartūn*	رُسوم (مُتحرِّكة) كرْتون
game show	*barnāmij musābagāt*	برْنامِج مُسابقات
reality TV show	*barnāmij min ilwāqi3* *barnāmij wāqi3i*	برْنامِج مِن الواقِع برْنامِج واقِعي
series	*musálsal*	مُسلْسل
sitcom	*musálsal kōmīdi*	مُسلْسل كوْميدي
episode	*ḥálaga*	حلقة
season	*máwsim (mawāsim)*	مَوْسِم (مَواسِم)
I haven't seen the second season of this show yet.	*líssa maḥḍírtiš ilmáwsim ittāni min hāda - lmusálsal.*	لسّا محْضِرْتِش المَوْسِم التّاني مِن هادا المُسلْسل.
the news	*ilʔaxbār*	الأخْبار
weather report	*nášra jawwíyya*	نشْرة جوّية
talk show	*barnāmij ḥiwāri*	برْنامِج حِواري
Have you ever been on TV?	*3úmrak ṭlí3it 3a -ttilfizyōn?*	عُمْرك طْلِعِت عَ التِّلْفِزْيوْن؟
channel	*qanā (qanawāt)*	قناة (قنَوات)
What's on TV (now)?	*šū fī 3a -ttilfizyōn halgēt?*	شو في عَ التِّلْفِزْيوْن هلْقيْت؟
There's an interesting program on channel 3.	*fī barnāmij ḥílu 3a -lqanā -ttālta.*	في برْنامِج حِلوع عَ القناة التّالْتة.
to turn the TV on	*ḍáwa [7] -ttilfizyōn*	ضَوى التِّلْفِزْيوْن
to turn the TV off	*ṭáfa [55] -ttilfizyōn*	طفى التِّلْفِزْيوْن
volume	*ṣōt*	صوْت
to turn the volume up	*3álla [13] -ṣṣōt*	علّى الصَّوْت
I can't hear what they're saying. Could you turn the TV up a bit?	*miš sāmi3 šū bíḥku, múmkin t3álli -ṣṣōt šwáyya?*	مِش سامِع شو بيحْكو، مُمْكِن تْعلّي الصَّوْت شْوَيّة؟
to turn the volume down	*wáṭṭa -ṣṣōt, ywáṭṭi -ṣṣōt*	وطّى الصَّوْت، يْوَطّي الصَّوْت

I'm trying to study. Could you turn the TV down a bit?	gā3id bágra, múmkin twáṭṭi -ṣṣōt šwáyya?	قاعِد بقْرا، مُمْكِن تْوَطّي الصّوْت شْوَيّة؟
antenna	antēnna	أنْتينّة
satellite dish	diš ṣáḥin	دِش صَحِن
radio	rādyō	رادْيوْ
to listen to the radio	sími3 [38] -rrādyō	سِمِع الرّادْيوْ
radio station	maḥáṭṭit rādyō idā3a	محطّة رادْيوْ إداعة
stereo (home music system)	stēryō	سْتيرْيوْ
speakers; headphones, earphones	sammā3āt	سمّاعات
disc (CD, vinyl record)	isṭuwāna	اِسْطُوانة
CD	sī dī	سي دي
CD player	mušáyyil istuwānāt	مُشغِّل اِسْطُوانات
cassette (tape)	šrīṭ kāsētt	شْريط كاسيتّ
song	uyníyya (ayāni)	أغْنية (أغاني)
track	trāk	تْراك
to play (a CD, song, etc.)	šáyyal, yšáyyil	شغّل، يْشغِّل
to forward, skip to the next track	gáddam, ygáddim	قدّم، يْقدِّم
to rewind, go back to (the previous track)	rájja3 [19]	رجّع
to stop, pause	wággaf [55]	وقّف
MP3 (file)	(maláff) [MP3]	ملفّ MP3)

to download an MP3	*ḥámmal [12] maláff [MP3]*	حمّل ملفّMP3
MP3 player	*(mušáyyil) [MP3]*	MP3 (مُشغِّل)
to visit	*zār, yzūr*	زار، يْزور
a visit	*zyāra*	زْيارة
to go on a visit	*rāḥ [55] zyāra*	راح زْيارة
to have guests over	*3índu ḍyūf*	عِندو ضْيوف
to entertain guests	*sálla liḍyūf, ysálli liḍyūf*	سلّى الِضْيوف، يْسلّي الِضْيوف
to sew; knit	*xáyyaṭ, yxáyyiṭ*	خيّط، يْخيّط
sewing machine	*mākīnit xyāṭa*	ماكينِةْ خْياطة
sewing needle	*íbrit xyāṭa (íbar xyāṭa)*	إبْرِةْ خْياطة (إبر خْياطة)
thread	*xēṭ (xīṭān, xyūṭ)*	خيْط (خيطان، خْيوط)
a ball of wool	*ṭúbbit ṣūf*	طبّةْ صوف
thimble	*kaštabān*	كشْتبان
to knit	*násaj, yínsij*	نسج، يِنْسِج
to crochet	*3ámal [55] krōšē*	عمل كْروْشيه
to embroider	*ṭárraz, yṭárriz*	طرّز، يْطرّز
to patch, darn	*rága3, yírga3* *rágga3, yrággi3*	رقع، يِرْقع رقّع، يْرقّع
art	*fann (fnūn)*	فنّ (فْنون)
artist	*fannān*	فنّان
to draw, sketch, paint	*rásam, yúrsum*	رسم، يُرْسُم
a painting	*láwḥa*	لوْحة
a drawing	*rásma*	رسْمة

photography	*taṣwīr*	تصْوير
photo(graph)	*ṣūra (ṣúwar)*	صورة (صُوَر)
to take a photo of	*ṣáwwar [18]*	صوّر
Excuse me. Would you take a photo of us?	*law sámaḥit, múmkin tṣawwírna?*	لَوْ سمحِت، مُمْكِن تْصوِّرْنا؟
to take a selfie	*áxad [55] sílfi* *ṣáwwar [18] sílfi*	أخد سِلْفي صوّر سِلْفي
photographer	*muṣáwwir*	مُصوّر
camera	*kāmira*	كاميرا
to hunt	*ṣād, yṣīd*	صاد، يْصيد
hunting	*ṣēd*	صيْد
hunter	*ṣayyād*	صيّاد
hunting dog	*kalb ṣēd*	كلْب صيْد
hunting rifle	*bārūdit ṣēd*	بارودِةْ صيْد
to fish, go fishing	*ṣād sámak*	صاد سمك
fishing	*ṣēd sámak*	صيْد سمك
fishing pole	*sinnāra*	سِنّارة
fishing tackle	*3íddit iṣṣēd*	عِدّةْ الصيْد
bait	*ṭú3um*	طُعُم
cinema, movies, movie theater	*sīnēma*	سينيْما
Let's go to the cinema this weekend.	*xallīna nrūḥ 3a -ssīnēma āxir ilʔisbū3.*	خلّينا نْروح عَ السّينيْما آخِر الإسْبوع.
movie ticket	*tázkara (tazākir)*	تذْكرة (تذاكِر)
How much is a (movie) ticket?	*gaddēš ḥagg ittázkara?*	قدّيْش حقّ التذْكرة؟
movie, film	*fílim (aflām)*	فِلِم (أفْلام)

auditorium, screening room	qā3it sīnēma	قاعِةْ سيْنيْما
What's playing?	šū -lfílim?	شو الفِلِمْ؟
A new movie is coming out on Friday. Want to go?	fī fílim jdīd ḥayínzil yōm ijjúm3a, bíddak trūḥ?	في فِلِم جْديد حينِزِل يوْم الجُمْعة، بدّك تْروح؟
They're showing a classic movie this evening.	ḥayí3riḍu fílim gadīm ilyōm bi-llēl.	حيعْرِضوا فِلِم قديم اليوْم في اللّيْل.
seat	kúrsi (karāsi) máq3ad (maqā3id)	كُرْسي (كراسي) مقْعد (مقاعِد)
What are our seat numbers?	gaddēš arqām karāsīna?	قدّيْش أرْقام كراسينا؟
screen	šāša	شاشة
to sit close to the screen	gá3ad [55] guddām iššāša	قعد قُدّام الشّاشة
to sit in the middle	gá3ad [55] fi -nnuṣṣ	قعد في النُّصّ
I don't like to sit too close to the screen.	baḥíbbiš ág3ud garīb 3a -ššāša.	بحِبِّش أقْعُد قريب عَ الشّاشة.
popcorn	(dūra) fišār dūra faššāra	(دُرة) فِشار دُرة فشّارة
action movie	fílim ákšin	فِلِم أكْشِن
romantic comedy	fílim rōmānsi kōmīdi	فِلِم روْمانْسي كوْميدي
drama	fílim drāmā	فِلِم دْراما
horror movie	fílim rú3ub	فِلِم رُعُب
thriller	fílim iťāra	فِلِم إثارة
period piece	fílim tārīxi	فِلِم تاريخي
science fiction (sci-fi)	fílim xayāl 3ílmi	فِلِم خَيال عِلْمي
fantasy	fílim fantāzya	فِلِم خَيال
What kind of movies do you like?	šū nū3 lʔaflām ílli bitḥíbbha?	شو نوع الأفْلام اللي بِتْحِبّها؟

I love action movies, but I can't stand romantic movies.	*baħíbb aflām ilʔákšin, bass baħíbbiš ilʔaflām irrōmānsíyya bi-lmárra.*	بحِبّ أفْلام الأكْشِن، بسّ بحِبِّش الأفْلام الرّوْمانْسية بالمرّة.
(movie) star	*nájim (nujūm)*	نجِم (نُجوم)
theater	*másraħ (masāriħ)*	مسْرح (مسارِح)
on stage	*3a -lmásraħ*	عَ المسْرح
aisle	*mamárr*	ممرّ
actor	*mumássil*	مُمثِّل
to act	*mással, ymássil*	مثَّل، يْمثِّل
to play the role of __	*lí3ib [55] dōr __* *mással dōr __*	لِعِب دوْر____ مثَّل دوْر____
intermission	*istirāħa* *fāṣil*	إسْتِراحة فاصِل
spectator	*mutafárrij* *mušāhid*	مُتفرِّج مُشاهِد
audience, crowd	*jumhūr (jamahīr)*	جُمْهور (جماهير)
to applaud	*zággaf, yzággif*	زقَّف، يْزقِّف
Some people say سقَّف، يْسقِّف *sággaf, ysággif* 'to applaud.'		
applause	*tazgīf*	تزْقيف
circus	*sīrk*	سيرْك
acrobat	*bahlawān*	بهْلَوان
clown	*muhárrij*	مُهرِّج
cigarette	*sigāra (sagāyir)*	سِجارة (سجايِر)
to smoke	*dáxxan sigāra, ydáxxin sigāra* *šírib [8] sigāra*	دخِّن سِجارة، يْدخِّن سِجارة شِرِب سِجارة
smoking	*tadxīn*	تدْخين

No smoking!	*mamnū3 ittadxīn*	ممْنوع التّدْخين
smoker	*mudáxxin*	مُدخِّن
non-smoker	*miš mudáxxin*	مِش مُدخِّن
Do you smoke?	*ínta bitdáxxin?*	اِنْت بِتْدخِّن؟
Would you like a cigarette?	*tāxud sigāra?* *tíšrab sigāra?*	تاخُد سِجارة؟ تِشْرب سِجارة؟
No, thank you. I don't smoke.	*lā, šúkran. badáxxniš.*	لا شُكْراً. بدخُنِش.
to quit smoking	*báṭṭal ydáxxin,* *ybáṭṭil ydáxxin* *báṭṭal idduxān*	بطّل يدخِّن، يْبطّل يْدخِّن بطّل الدُّخان
cigar	*sīgār*	سيجار
pipe	*ɣalyōn*	غلْيوْن
tobacco	*wárag duxxān* *tíbiɣ* *timbāk*	وَرق دُخّان تِبِغ تِمْباك
matches	*kabrīt*	كبْريت
lighter	*gaddāḥa* *wallā3a*	قدّاحة ولّاعة
to light (a cigarette)	*wálla3 sigāra, ywálli3 sigāra*	ولّع سِجارة، يْولّع سِجارة
ashtray	*matákka* *ṭaffāya*	متكّة طفّايَة

<table><tr><td colspan="3">Some people say مكتّة makátta 'ashtray.'</td></tr></table>

cigarette butt	*gúm3it sigāra*	قُمْعِة سِجارة
a pack of cigarettes	*3ílbit duxxān (3ílab duxxān)*	عِلْبِة دُخّان (عِلب دُخّان)
shisha, hookah, water-pipe	*šīša* *argīla*	شيشة أرْجيلة

to smoke a hookah	*šáyyaš, yšáyyiš* *árgal, yʔárgil*	شيّش، يْشيِّش أرْجل، يْأرْجِل
mouth-piece (of shisha)	*mábsam (mabāsim)*	مبْسم (مباسِم)
glass container (of shisha)	*gzāzit šīša*	قْزازِةْ شيشة
hose (of shisha)	*barbīš šīša*	برْبيش شيشة
coal	*fáḥim*	فحِم

music	*aɣāni* [pl.; lit. songs] *mūsīqa*	أغاني موسيقى
to listen to music	*sími3 [38] aɣāni*	سِمِع أغاني
song	*uɣníyya (aɣāni)*	أُغْنية (أغاني)
singer	*muɣánni*	مُغَنّي
to sing	*ɣánna, yɣánni*	غَنّى، يْغَنّي
singing	*ɣúna*	غُنا
I love singing, but I'm not very good at it.	*baħíbb aɣánni bass ána miš ktīr šāṭir fi -lɣúna.*	بحِبّ أغنّي بسّ أنا مِش كْتير شاطِر في الغُنا.
Who's your favorite singer?	*mīn muɣannīk ilmufáḍḍal?*	مين مُغَنّيك المُفَضّل؟
band, group	*fírga*	فِرْقة
What kind of music do you like?	*šū bitħíbb tísma3?* *šū nū3 ilʔaɣāni -lli bitħíbbha?*	شو بِتْحِبّ تِسْمع؟ شو نوع الأغاني اللي بِتْحِبّها؟
folk music, popular music	*aɣāni ša3bíyya*	أغاني شعْبية
pop music (specifically more Western-sounding music)	*aɣāni pōp* *mūsīqa -lpōp*	أغاني بوْب موسيقى البوْب
rap (music)	*(aɣāni) rāp*	(أغاني) راب
classical music	*mūsīqa klāsīkíyya* *mūsīqa gadīma*	موسيقى كلاسيكية موسيقى قديمة
rock music	*aɣāni rōk* *mūsīqa -rrōk*	أغاني روْك موسيقى الرّوْك
jazz	*aɣāni jāz* *mūsīqa -ldjāz*	أغاني جاز موسيقى الجاز

English	Transliteration	Arabic
Arabic classical music	*aɣāni 3arabíyya gadīma*	أغاني عربية قديمة
musician	*mūsīqār*	موسيقار
musical instrument	*āla mūsīqíyya*	آلة موسيقية
to play (an instrument)	*3ázaf (3ála), yí3zif (3ála)*	عزف (على)، يِعْزِف (على)
I can play the guitar.	*bá3rif á3zif gītār.*	بعرِف أعْزِف غيتار.
guitar	*gītār*	غيتار
piano	*byānō*	بْيانو
violin	*kamān* *kamānja*	كمان كمانْجة
drum	*ṭábil (ṭbūl)* *dram*	طبِل (طْبول) دْرم
flute, mizmaar (wooden flute)	*mizmār (mazāmīr)*	مِزْمار (مزامير)
oud, lute	*3ūd*	عود
ney (reed flute)	*nāy*	ناي
guitar string	*wátar ilgītār (awtār ilgītār)*	وَتر الغيتار (أوْتار الغيتار)
piano keys	*zrār libyānō* [pl.]	زْرار البْيانو
to tune (a guitar, piano)	*zábbaṭ, yzábbiṭ*	زبَّط، يْزبِّط
in tune	*zābiṭ* *náɣamtu mazbūṭa*	زابِط نغْمتو مزْبوطة
out of tune	*miš zābiṭ* *našāz*	مِش زابِط نشاز
orchestra	*fírga mūsīqíyya*	فِرْقة موسيقية
to dance	*rágaṣ, yúrguṣ*	رقص، يُرْقُص

a dance	*rágṣa*	رقْصة
dancer	*raggāṣ*	رقّاص
ballet dancer	*raggāṣ balē*	رقّاص بليْه
belly dancing	*rágiṣ šárgi*	رقِص شرْقي

Games and Sports

toy, game; doll, puppet	*lí3ba (lí3ab)*	لِعْبة (لِعب)
teddy bear	*dabdūb (dabadīb)*	دبْدوب (دباديب)
to play a game	*lí3ib [55] lí3ba*	لِعِب لِعْبة
to play billiards	*lí3ib [55] bilyārdō*	لِعِب بِلْيارْدوْ
to play cards	*lí3ib [55] šádda*	لِعِب شدّة
turn	*dōr (dwār)*	دوْر (دْوار)
Whose turn is it?	*3a mīn iddōr?*	عَ مين الدّوْر؟
It's your turn.	*dōrak.*	دوْرك.
chess	*iššiṭaránj*	الشُّطرنْج
move	*ḥáraka*	حركة
Check! (in chess)	*kiš!*	كِش!
Checkmate!	*kiš málik!*	كِش ملِك!
(chess) piece	*gíṭ3a (gíṭa3)*	قِطْعة (قِطع)
king	*málik*	ملِك
queen	*wazīr*	وَزير
bishop	*fīl*	فيل
knight	*ḥṣān*	حْصان
rook	*gál3a*	قلْعة
pawn	*júndi*	جُنْدي
backgammon	*ṭāwlit zāhir*	طاوْلِةْ زهِر
dice	*záhra* *ḥájar nard*	زهْرة حجر نرْد

sport	*riyāḍa*	رِياضة
Do you like sports?	*bitḥíbb irriyāḍa?*	بِتْحِبّ الرِّياضة؟
I like watching sports, but I don't play any.	*baḥíbb áḥḍar riyāḍa bass mā bál3abha.*	بحِبّ أَحْضَر رِياضة بسّ ما بلْعبْها.
ball; soccer (UK: **football**)	*kōra*	كوْرة
goal	*gōn*	غوْن
to score a goal	*jāb [55] gōn*	جاب غوْن
soccer game (UK: **football match**)	*lí3bit kōra*	لِعْبِةْ كوْرة
soccer field (UK: **football pitch**)	*mál3ab kōra (malā3ib kōra)*	ملْعب كوْرة (ملاعِب كوْرة)
(American) football	*kúrit qádam amrīkíyya*	كُرةْ قدم أُمْريكية
baseball	*bēsbōl* *kúrit ilmáḍrab* [lit. bat ball]	بيْسْبول كُرةْ المضْرب

مضْرب translates 'bat' in the context above, but it can more broadly refer to any equipment for hitting in a sport: bat, racket, club, etc.

basketball	*(kúrit) sálla*	(كُرةْ) سلّة
basketball hoop	*šábakit issálla*	شبِكِةْ السّلّة
boxing	*mulākama*	مُلاكمة
golf	*gōlf*	غوْلْف
golf club	*nādi gōlf*	نادي غوْلْف
golf course	*mál3ab gōlf*	ملْعب غوْلْف
hockey	*hōki*	هوكي
to ski, go skiing	*(i)dzállaj, yidzállaj*	اِتْزلّج، يِتْزلّج
tennis	*tins* *tínis*	تِنْس تِنِس
tennis court	*mál3ab ittíns (malā3ib ittíns)*	ملْعب التِّنْس (ملاعِب التِّنْس)

(tennis/volleyball) net	nit	نِت
tennis net	šábakit ittíns	شبكِةْ التِّنس
tennis racket	rākit máḍrab ittíns (maḍārib ittíns)	راكِت مِضْرب التِّنس (مضارِب التِّنس)
volleyball	(kúra) ṭāʔira	(كُرة) طائِرة
volleyball net	šábakit iṭṭāʔira	شبكِةْ الطّائِرة
to kick (a ball)	šāṭ, yšūṭ	شات، يْشوت
to hit	ḍárab, yúḍrub	ضرب، يُضْرُب
to throw	ráma, yírmi	رمى، يِرْمي
to catch	másak, yímsik	مسك، يِمْسِك
to win (a game)	ríbiḥ, yírbaḥ	رِبِح، يِرْبح
to lose (a game)	xísir, yíxsar	خِسِر، يِخْسر
to beat (a team)	fāz 3ála, yfūz 3ála	فاز على، يْفوز على
to lose to (a team)	xísir [55] guddām	خِسِر قُدّام
Who won?	mīn fāz?	مين فاز؟
player	lā3ib	لاعِب
team	farīg (fírag)	فريق (فِرق)
to play against (a team, a player)	lí3ib [55]ḍidd	لِعِب ضِدّ
champion	báṭal (abṭāl)	بطل (أبْطال)
score	natīja (natāyij)	نتيجة (نتايِج)
What's the score?	ákam innatīja?	أكمِ النّتيجة؟
The score is two to four.	innatīja tnēn árba3a.	النّتيجة تْنيْن أرْبعة.
(They're tied) three to three.	talāta -lkull.	تلاتة الكُلّ.
The match ended in a draw/tie.	ilmabārā xállaṣat ta3ādul.	المباراة خْلّصت تعادُل.

fitness	*layāqa* *fítnis*	لَياقة فِتنِس
to exercise, work out	*lí3ib* *(i)tmárran, yitmárran* *(i)ddárrab, yiddárrab*	لِعِب اِتْمَرّن، يِتْمَرّن اِتْدرّب، يِتْدرّب
How often do you exercise?	*kull gaddēš bitmárran?*	كُل قدّيْش بْتِتْمرّن؟
I try to exercise at least twice a week.	*baħāwil atmárran agáll íši marrtēn bi-lʔisbū3.*	بحاوِل أتْمرّن أقلّ إشي مرّتيْن بِالإسْبوع.
I had a really good workout at the gym this morning.	*l3íbit tamrīn ħílu fi -nnādi -lyōm iṣṣúbiħ.*	لعِبِت تمْرين حِلو في النّادي اليوْم الصُّبِح
gym, health club	*nādi ħadīd* *jim*	نادي [حديد] جِم
to go to the gym	*rāħ [55] 3a -lħadīd*	راح عَ الحديد
I go to the gym every morning.	*ána barūħ 3a -lħadīd kull yōm iṣṣúbiħ.*	أنا بروح عَ الحديد كُلّ يوْم الصُّبِح.
to join a gym, become a member of a gym	*ištárak fi -nnādi, yištírik fi -nnādi*	اِشْترك في النّادي، يِشْترِك في النّادي
member	*múštarik* *3úḍu (a3ḍāʔ)*	مُشْترِك عُضو (أعْضاء)
membership	*ištirāk* *3uḍwíyyi*	اِشْترِاك عُضْوية
How much is a monthly membership at this gym?	*bákam lištirāk fi -nnādi?*	بكم الاِشْترِاك في النّادي؟
Is there a contract?	*fī 3áqid?*	في عقِد؟
personal trainer	*mudárrib šáxṣi* *mudárrib xuṣūṣi*	مُدرّب شخصي مُدرّب خُصوصي

I'd like to hire a personal trainer.	bíddi mudárrib šáxṣi.	بِدّي مُدرِّب شخْصي.
training session	ḥíṣṣit tamrīn jálsit tamrīn	حِصّةْ تمْرين جلْسِةْ تمْرين
How much does it cost per training session?	bákam ḥíṣṣit ittamrīn?	بكم حِصّةْ التّمْرين؟
My goal is to gain muscle.	hádafi ʔazīd 3áḍal.	هدفي أزيد عضل.
to gain weight	zād wázin, yzīd wázin	زاد وَزِن، يْزيد وَزِن
I feel like I've gained a bit of weight.	ḥāsis ḥāli zídit šwáyya.	حاسِس حالي زِدِت شْوَيّة.
to lose weight	ḍí3if, yíḍ3af xass, yxiss	ضِعِف، يِضْعف خسّ، يْخِسّ
I want to lose weight.	bíddiʔáḍ3af. bíddi ʔaxíss.	بِدّي أضْعف. بِدّي أخِسّ.
I need to lose five kilos.	bíddi áḍ3af xámsa kēlō.	بِدّي أضْعف خمْسة كيْلوْ.
to go on a diet	3ámal [55] rujīm 3ámal [55] dāyt	عمل رُجيم عمل دايْت
I'm on a diet.	ána 3āmil rujīm.	أنا عامِل رُجيم.
locker room, changing room	ɣúrfit ilɣayār	غُرْفةْ الغَيار
locker	xazāna	خزانة
to change one's clothes	ɣáyyar [55] awā3ī	غيِّر أواعيه
gym clothes, workout clothes	awā3ī -nnādi	أواعي النّادي
a barbell	bār	بار
a dumbbell	dámbil	دمْبِل
free weights	awzān ḥúrra	أوْزان حُرّة
to lift weights	šāl [7] wázan	شال وَزن
weight machine	jihāz ḥadīd (ájhizit ḥadīd) mākīnit ḥadīd	جِهاز حديد (أجْهِزةْ حديد) ماكينةِ حديد

to adjust the weight	zábbaṭ ilwázin, yzábbiṭ ilwázin	زبِّط الوَزِن، يْزَبِّط الوَزِن
Excuse me, how do you use this machine?	ba3d íznak, kēf btištíγil hādi -lmākīna?	بعْد إذْنك، كيْف بْتِشْتِغِل هادي الماكينة؟
to do cardio exercise	lí3ib [55] kārdyō	لِعِب كارْدْيوْ
to burn calories	ħárag issu3rāt ilħarāríyya, yíħrig issu3rāt ilħarāríyya	حرق السُّعْرات الحرارية، يِحْرِق السُّعْرات الحرارية
running machine, treadmill	maššāya	مشّايَة
elliptical trainer	jihāz ilíptikal	جِهاز إيليبْتيكال
stationary bicycle	baskalēt sābit	بسْكليْت ثابِت
to run	jára, yíjri	جرى، يِجْري
I usually spend 20 minutes on the running machine.	bi-l3āda bájri 3išrīn dgīga 3a -lmaššāya.	بِالعادة بجْري عِشْرين دْقيقة عَ المشّايَة.
to jog, go jogging	hárwal, yhárwil	هرْوَل، يْهرْوِل
exercise; workout	tamrīn (tamarīn)	تمْرين (تمارين)
to do sit-ups, work one's abs	lí3ib [55] mí3da	لِعِب مِعْدة
to do pull-ups	lí3ib [55] 3úgla	لِعِب عُقْلة
to do push-ups	lí3ib [55] ḍáγiṭ	لِعِب ضغِط
How many sit-ups can you do?	kam 3áddit mí3da btígdar tí3mal?	كم عدِّةْ مِعْدة بْتِقْدر تِعْمل؟
a set	jáwla	جوْلة
a rep	3ádda	عدّة
to do aerobics	lí3ib [55] tamārīn hawāʔíyya	لِعِب تمارين هوائية
to do yoga	lí3ib [55] yōgā	لِعِب يوْغا
to push	ḍáγaṭ, yídγaṭ	ضغط، يِضْغط
to pull	sáħab, yísħab	سحب، يِسْحب

to lift	*ráfa3, yírfa3* *šāl, yšīl*	رفع، يِرْفع شال، يْشيل
to lower	*názzal, ynázzil*	نزّل، يْنزِّل
Lift the barbell over your head, then slowly lower it back down.	*írfa3 ilbār fōg rāsak w názzlu bišwēš.*	اِرْفع البار فوْق راسك ونزّلُو بِشْويْش.
to breathe in	*áxad [55] náfas*	أخد نفس
to breathe out	*ṭálla3 náfas, yṭálla3 náfas*	طلّع نفس، يْطلّع نفس
Don't forget to breathe!	*mā tínsa titnáffas!*	ما تِنْسى تِتْنفّس.
a jump rope; jumping rope	*naṭṭ ḥábil*	نطّ حبِل
to jump rope	*lí3ib [55] naṭṭ ḥábil*	لِعِب نطّ حبِل
scale	*mīzān*	ميزان
to weigh oneself	*(i)twázzan, yitwázzan*	اِتْوَزّن، يِتْوَزّن

24 Travel and Vacations

travel, traveling	*sáfar*	سفر
to travel, go on a journey	*sāfar, ysāfir*	سافِر، يْسافِر
vacation	*ijāza* *3úṭla*	إجازة عُطْلة
to take a vacation	*áxad [55] ijāza*	أخد إجازة
a trip	*ríḥla*	رِحْلة
tourism	*siyāḥa*	سِياحة
tourist	*sāyiḥ (suyyāḥ)*	سايِح (سُيّاح)
to go on a tour	*ṭāliḥ jáwla*	طالِع جَوْلة
tour guide	*múršid siyāḥi*	مُرْشِد سِياحي
tourist police	*šúrṭa siyāḥíyya*	شُرْطة سِياحية

at the seaside	*3a -lbáḥar*	عَ البحر
seaside resort	*fúndug 3a ilbáḥar*	فُنْدُق عَ البحر
at the beach	*3a -lbáḥar* *3a -ššaṭ*	عَ البحر عَ الشّطّ
on the coast	*3a -ssāḥil*	عَ السّاحِل
beach	*šaṭṭ (šawāṭiʔ)*	شطّ (شَواطِئ)
I just got back from the beach.	*táwwi rjí3it min ilbáḥar.*	توّي رْجِعِت مِن البحر.
sand	*rámil (rimāl)*	رمِل (رِمال)
to build a sand castle	*bána [15] qál3a rámil*	بنى قلْعة رمِل
sun umbrella, beach umbrella	*šamsíyya*	شمْسية
to sunbathe	*áxad [55] ḥammām šámis* *itšámmas, yitšámmas*	أخد حمّام شمِس اِتْشمّس، يِتْشمّس

to sunburn	ḥárgatu -ššámis [lit. the sun burned one], tíḥrigu -ššámis inḥárag min iššámis, yinḥírig min iššámis	حرْقتو الشّمِس، تِحرِقو الشّمِس إنْحرق مِن الشّمِس، يِنْحِرِق مِن الشّمِس
I'm so sunburned! It hurts!	inḥarágit min iššámis, btíja3.	إنْحرقِت مِن الشّمِس، بْتِجع.
to put on sunblock	ḥaṭṭ [55] wāqi šámis	حطّ واقي شمِس
to tan	3ámal [55] tān áxad [55] lōn	عمل تان أخد لوْن
tanned	3āmil tān māxid lōn	عامِل تان ماخِد لوْن
to go into the water	raḥ [55] yísbaḥ	راح يِسْبح
waves	mōj	موْج
to swim	sábaḥ, yísbaḥ	سبح، يِسْبح
swimming	sbāḥa	سْباحة
swimming pool	másbaḥ bírka	مسْبح بِرْكة
Do you know how to swim?	btí3rif tísbaḥ?	بْتِعْرِف تِسْبح؟
I can swim pretty well.	bá3rif ásbaḥ mnīḥ.	بعْرِف أسْبح مْنيح.
I don't know how to swim.	ba3rífiš ásbaḥ.	بعْرِفِش أسْبح.
to dive, go scuba diving	ɣáṭas, yúɣṭus ɣāṣ, yɣūṣ	غطس، يُغْطُس غاص، يْغوص
to snorkel	ḥábas náfas, yíḥbis náfas kátam náfas, yíktim náfas	حبس نفس، يِحْبِس نفس كتم نفس، يِكْتِم نفس
to go camping	ṭíli3 [55] taxyīm	طِلع تخْيِم
camp	muxáyyam	مُخيّم
tent	xēma (xíyam)	خيْمة (خِيَم)

to go hiking, trek	*ṭíli3 [55] sēr*	طِلع سيْر
suitcase	*šánta (šúnat)*	شنْطة (شُنط)
to pack one's suitcase	*jáhhaz šánṭitu, yjáhhiz šánṭitu* *ḥáḍḍar šánṭitu, yḥáḍḍir šánṭitu*	جهّز شنْطِتو، يْجهّز شنْطِتو حضّر شنْطِتو، يْحضّر شنْطِتو
to unpack one's suitcase	*fáḍḍa šánṭitu, yfáḍḍi šánṭitu*	فضّى شنْطِتو، يْفضّي شنْطِتو
passport	*jawāz sáfar*	جَواز سفر
to get a passport	*3ámal [55] jawāz sáfar*	عمل جَواز سفر
passport photo	*ṣūrit jawāz issáfar*	صورةِ جَواز السّفر
visa	*vīza*	فيزا
to issue a visa	*áxad [55] vīza*	أخد فيزا
tourist visa	*vīza siyāḥíyya*	فيزا سِياحية
residence permit	*iqāma*	إقامة
work permit	*taṣrīḥ šúɣul*	تصْريح شُغُل
valid	*sāri*	ساري
to expire	*intáha, yintíhi*	اِنْتهى، يِنْتِهي
abroad	*bárra*	برّا
to travel abroad	*sāfar bárra*	سافر برّا
Have you ever been abroad?	*3úmrak sāfarit gábil hēk?*	عُمْرك سافرتِ قبِل هيْك؟
border	*ḥdūd [pl.]*	حْدود
customs	*jamārik [pl.]*	جمارِك
customs officer	*muwáẓẓaf jamārik*	مُوظّف جمارِك
to declare	*ṣárraḥ, yṣárriḥ* *á3lan, yí3lin*	صرّح، يْصرّح أعْلن، يِعْلِن
to smuggle	*hárrab, yhárrib*	هرّب، يْهرّب

exchange office	*máktab ṣrāfa (makātib ṣrāfa)*	مكْتب صْرافة (مكاتِب صْرافة)
to change money	*ṣárraf, yṣárrif*	صرّف، يْصرِّف
I'd like to change $100 to shekels pounds, please.	*bíddi ʔaṣárrif mīt dōlār la-šēkil law samáḥit.*	بدّي أصرّف ميةْ دوْلار لشيْكِل لَو سمحِت.
exchange rate	*síʒir ʒúmla*	سِعِر عُمْلة
ticket	*tázkara (tazākir)* *tíkit*	تذْكرة (تذاكِر) تِكِت
to buy a ticket	*ištára [19] tázkara* *ištára [19] tíkit*	إشْترى تذْكرة إشْترى تِكِت
airplane	*ṭayyāra*	طيّارة
flight	*ṭayarān* *ríḥla*	طيَران رِحْلة
to fly	*sāfar bi-ṭṭayyāra*	سافر بِالطّيّارة
(airplane) to take off	*áqlaʒ, yíqlaʒ*	أقْلع، يِقْلع
to land	*hábaṭ, yúhbuṭ*	هبط، يُهْبُط
to book a seat	*ḥájaz kúrsi*	حجز كُرْسي
I'd like to book a seat on the next available flight.	*bíddi áḥjaz kúrsi ʒála ʔágrab ríḥla.*	بِدّي أحْجز كُرْسي على أقْرب رِحْلة.
first class	*iddáraja -lʔūla*	الدّرجة الأولى
I've never flown first class before.	*ʒúmri ma sāfárit fi -ddáraja -lʔūla.*	عُمْري ما سافرِت في الدّرجة الأُولى.
business class	*dárajit rijāl ilʔa3māl* *ilbíznis*	درجِةْ رِجال الأعْمال البِزْنِس
economy class, coach	*iddáraja -lʔiqtiṣādíyya* *iddáraja -ssiyāḥíyya*	الدّرجة الاِقْتِصادية الدّرجة السِّياحية

airfare	si3r ittázkara	سِعْر التَّذْكرة
The airfare was reasonable.	kwáyyis sí3r ittázkara.	كْوَيِّس سِعْر التّذْكرة.
airport	maṭār	مطار
aisle seat	kúrsi jamb ilmamárr	كُرْسي جنْب الممرّ
window seat	kúrsi jamb iššubbāk	كُرْسي جنْب الشُّبّاك
I prefer an aisle seat.	baḥíbb ág3ud jamb ilmamárr.	بحِبّ أقْعُد جنب الممرّ.
gate	bawwāba	بوّابة
to board	ṭíli3 [55] 3a -ṭṭayyāra	طِلع عَ الطيّارة
to be delayed	(i)tʔájjal, yitʔájjal((i)tʔáxxar, yitʔáxxar	اِتْأَجّل، يِتْأَجّلِ تْأَخّر، يِتْأَخّر
Your flight has been delayed by two hours.	riḥíltak itʔajjálit sā3tēn.	رِحْلِتك اِتْأَجّلت ساعْتيْن.
to be canceled	iltáɣa, yíltiɣi	اِلْتغى، يِلْتِغي
Our flight leaves in 30 minutes from gate 5.	ṭayyárítna ḥatítḥárrak kamān nuṣṣ sā3a min bawwāba ráqam xámsa.	طيّارِتْنا حتِتْحرّك كمان نُصّ ساعة مِن بوّابة رقم خمْسة.
pilot	ṭayyār	طيّار
flight attendant	muḍīf	مُضيف
to transfer, change planes	ṭíli3 [55] trānzīt	طِلع تْرانْزيت
I had a 3-hour layover in Dubai.	nzilt trānzīt tálat sā3āt fi dubáyy.	نْزِلْت تْرانْزيت تلات ساعات في دُبيّ.
train	giṭār	قِطار
to take the train	ríkib [13] ilgiṭār	رِكِب القِطار
first class	iddáraja -lʔūla	الدَّرجة الأولى
second class	iddáraja -ttānya	الدَّرجة التانْيَة
third class	iddáraja -ttālta	الدَّرجة التّالْتة
train station	maḥáṭṭit ilgiṭār	محطّة القِطار

one-way ticket	tázkarit zahāb	تذْكِرِةْ ذهاب
round-trip ticket	tázkarit zahāb w 3áwda	تذْكِرِةْ ذهاب وعَوْدة
waiting room	ɣúrfit intiẓār	غُرْفِةِ اِنْتِظار
platform	manáṣṣa	منصّة
track, rails	quḍbān	قُضْبان
railway, railroad	síkkit ḥadīd	سِكّةْ حديد
to arrive	wíṣil, yūṣal	وِصِل، يوصل
to depart	rāḥ [55] ṭíli3 [55]	راح طِلِع
compartment	ɣúrfa (ɣúraf)	غُرْفة (غُرَف)
(train) car	magṭūra 3árabit ilgiṭār	مقْطورة عربِةْ القِطار
express	giṭār sarī3	قطار سريع
non-express train	giṭār 3ādi	قطار عادي
bus	bāṣ	باص
to take the bus	ṭíli3 [55] fi -lbāṣ	طِلِع في الباصّ
I took a bus from Rafah to Gaza.	ṭlí3it fi -lbāṣ min ráfaḥ la-ɣázza.	طْلِعِت في الباصّ مِن رفح لغزّة.
air-conditioned	mukáyyif	مُكيِّف
comfortable	murīḥ	مُريح
uncomfortable, tiring	mút3ib	مُتْعِب
bus station	maḥáṭṭit bāṣāt	محطّةْ باصات
to ride while evading the fare; to hitchhike	ṭíli3 [55] b-blāš	طِلِع بْبلاش
hotel	fúndug (fanādig)	فُنْدُق (فنادِق)

reservation	ḥájiz	حجز
I have a reservation.	fī ḥájiz b-ʔísmi.	في حجِز بْاِسْمي.
to reserve, book	ḥájaz, yíḥjiz	حجز، يِحْجِز
room	ɣúrfa (ɣúraf)	غُرْفة (غُرف)
I want to book a room.	bíddi ʔáḥjiz ɣúrfa.	بِدّي أحْجِز غُرْفة.
a single room	ɣúrfa la-šáxṣ wāḥad	غُرْفة لشخْص واحد
a double room	ɣúrfa la-šaxṣēn	غُرْفة لشخْصيْن
a twin room	ɣúrfa bi-srīrēn	غُرْفة بِسْريريْن
How much is it per night?	bákam illēla?	بكم اللّيْلة؟
I'd like to stay for three nights.	bíddi ʔág3ud tálat layāli. bíddi ʔanām tálat layāli.	بِدّي أقْعُد تلات لَيالي. بِدّي أنام تلات لَيالي.
to check in (at a hotel or the airport)	sájjal [10] duxūlu	سجّل دُخولو
to check out	sájjal [10] xurūgu	سجّل خُروجو
What time is checkout?	wagtēš ma3ād ilxurūg?	وَقْتيْش معاد الخُروج؟
lobby	istigbāl ṣāla qā3a	اِسْتِقْبال صالة قاعة
porter	šayyāl 3attāl	شيّال عتّال

25 Government and Politics

government	ḥukūma	حُكومة
to govern, rule over	ḥákam, yúḥkum	حكم، يُحْكُم
cabinet	májlis wúzara kabēnit	مجْلِس وُزرا كابيْنِت
ministry, department	wizāra	وِزارة
minister, secretary	wazīr (wúzara)	وَزير (وُزرا)
prime minister	raʔīs wúzara	رئيس وُزرا
parliament	barlamān májlis innuwwāb	برْلمان مجْلِس النُّوّاب
member of parliament, MP	ʒúḍu barlamān	عُضو برْلمان
president	raʔīs (rúʔasa)	رئيس (رُؤُساء)
vice president	nāʔib raʔīs	نائِب رئيس
republic	jumhūríyya	جُمْهورية
authority	súlṭa	سُلْطة
Palestinian National Authority	issúlṭa -lwaṭaníyya -lfalasṭīníyya	السُّلْطة الوَطنية الفلسْطينية
kingdom	mámlaka (mamālik)	ممْلكة (ممالِك)
monarchy, royalty	malakíyya	ملكية
king	málik (mulūk)	ملِك (مُلوك)
queen	málika	ملِكة
prince	amīr (úmara)	أمير (أُمرا)
princess	amīra	أميرة
emperor	imbirāṭōr (abāṭira)	إمْبِراطوْر (أباطِرة)
empress	imbirāṭōra	إمْبِراطوْرة

empire	imbirāṭūríyya	إِمْبِراطورية
people, nation	šá3ib	شعِب
citizen	muwāṭin	مُواطِن
to vote	ṣáwwat, yṣáwwit	صَوَّت، يْصَوِّت
voter	nāxib	ناخِب
majority	aɣlabíyya	أغْلبية
minority	aqallíyya	أقَلّية
(political) party	ḥízib (áḥzāb)	حِزِب (أحْزاب)
to nominate	ráššaḥ, yráššiḥ	رشَّح، يْرشِّح
nomination	taráššuḥ	ترشُّح
elections	intixābāt [pl.]	انْتِخابات
to elect	intáxab, yíntixib	انْتخب، يِنْتخِب
He was elected president.	intaxabū raʔīs.	انْتخبوه رئيس.
presidential term	fátra riʔāsíyya	فتْرة رِئاسية
democracy	dīmuqrāṭíyya	ديمُقْراطية
democratic	dīmuqrāṭi	ديمُقْراطي
constitution	dustūr (dasatīr)	دُسْتور (دساتير)
reform	iṣlāḥ	إصْلاح
dictator	diktātōr	دِكْتاتوْر
dictatorship	diktātōríyya	دِكْتاتوْرية
capital, capital city	3āṣima (3awāṣim)	عاصِمة (عَواصِم)
Jerusalem is the capital of Palestine.	ilqúds 3āṣimit falasṭīn.	القُدْس عاصِمِةْ فلسْطين.
province	muḥāfaẓa	مُحافظة
state	wilāya	وِلايّة

politics	siyāsa	سِياسة
political; politician	siyāsi	سِياسي
summit	muʔtámar ilqímma	مُؤْتمر القِمّة
demonstration, protest	muẓāhara	مُظاهرة
march	masīra	مسيرة
to demonstrate, protest	idẓāhar, yidẓāhar	إِتْظاهر، يِتْظاهر
demonstrator, protester	mutaẓāhir	مُتظاهِر
revolution	sáwra	ثَوْرة
society	mújtama3	مُجْتمع
social	ijtimā3i	إِجْتِماعي
free	ḥurr (aḥrār)	حُرّ (أُحْرار)
freedom	ḥurríyya	حُرّية

26 Crime and Justice

crime	jarīma (jarāyim)	جريمة (جرايِم)
criminal	mújrim	مُجْرِم
to commit a crime	irtákab jarīma, yirtíkib jarīma	اِرْتكب جريمة، يِرْتِكِب جريمة
to break the law	xālaf ilqānūn, yxālif ilqānūn	خالف القانون، يْخالِف القانون
theft	sírga	سِرْقة
to steal, rob	sárag, yísrig	سرق، يِسْرِق
thief	ḥarāmi sarrāg	حرامي سرّاق
to break into a house	dáxal 3a dār, yúdxul 3a dār	دخل عَ دار، يُدْخل عَ دار
rape	iɣtiṣāb	اِغْتِصاب
to rape	iɣtáṣab, yiɣtíṣib	اِغْتَصب، يِغْتِصِب
murder	gátil	قتِل
to murder, kull	gátal, yúgtul	قتل، يُقْتُل
murderer	gātil (gátala)	قاتِل (قتلة)
assault	i3tidāʔ hujūm	اِعْتِداء هجوم
to assault, attack	hájam 3ála, yíhjim 3ála i3táda 3ála, yi3tídi 3ála	هجم على، يِهْجِم على اِعْتدى على، يِعْتِدي على
vandalism	taxrīb	تخْريب
to vandalize	xárrab, yxárrib	خرّب، يْخرّب
to arrest	másak, yímsik gábaḍ 3ála, yúgbuḍ 3ála i3tágal, yi3tígil	مسك، يِمْسِك قبض على، يُقْبُض على اِعْتقل، يِعْتِقِل

to be arrested	inmásak, yinmísik ingábaḍ 3alē, yingíbiḍ 3alē	إِنْمَسك، يِنْمِسِك إِنْقبض عليه، يِنْقِبِض عليه
to interrogate	istájwab, yistájwib	إِسْتَجْوَب، يِسْتَجْوِب
court	máḥkama (maḥākim)	مَحْكمة (محاكِم)
justice	3adāla	عدالة
judge	gāḍi (guḍā)	قاضي (قُضاة)
lawyer	muḥāmi	مُحامي
prosecutor	innāʔib il3āmm ilmúdda3i -l3āmm	النّائِب العامّ المُدّعي العامّ
law	qānūn (qawanīn)	قانون (قَوانين)
legal	qānūni	قانوني
illegal	miš qānūni	مِش قانوني
I think that's illegal.	aẓúnn ínnu hāda miš qānūni.	أظُنّ إِنّو هادا مِش قانوني.
judgment, sentence	ḥúkum (aḥkām)	حُكُم (أَحْكام)
to convict	adān, ydīn	أدان، يْدين
punishment	3uqūba	عُقوبة
The judge sentenced him to five years in prison.	ilgāḍi ḥakam 3alē xams snīn síjin.	القاضي حكم عليْه خمْس سْنين سِجِن.
prison	síjin (sjūn) ḥábis (ḥbūs)	سِجِن (سْجون) حبِس (حْبوس)
to be sentenced	inḥákam 3alē, yinḥíkim 3alē	إِنْحكم عليْه، يِنْحِكِم عليْه
He was sentenced to life in prison.	inḥákam 3alē bi-ssíjin ilmuʔábbad.	إِنْحكم عليْه بِالسِّجْن المُؤبّد.
in prison, imprisoned	maḥbūs masjūn	مخْبوس مسْجون
prisoner	sajīn (sú#jana)	سجين (سُجنا)

to escape from prison	*šárad min ilḥábis , yúšrud min ilḥábis* *šárad min issíjin, yúšrud min issíjin*	شرد مِن الحبِس، يُشْرُد مِن الحبِس شرد مِن السِّجِن، يُشْرُد مِن السِّجِن
death sentence, capital punishment	*i3dām*	إعْدام
I don't believe in the death penalty.	*ána miš migtíni3 b-3uqūbit ilʔi3dām.*	أنا مِش مِقْتِنِع بْعُقوبِةْ الإعْدام.
accused of	*muttáham b(i)-*	مُتّهم بِـ
charge, accusation	*túhma (túham)*	تُهْمة (تُهم)
defense	*difā3*	دِفاع
to be hanged	*inšánag, yinšínig*	اِنْشنق، يِنْشِنِق

27 Money

money	*maṣāri*	مَصاري
currency	*3úmla*	عُمْلة
dollar	*dōlar*	دوْلار
euro	*yūrō*	يوْرو
pound sterling	*jnēh istarlīni*	جْنيْه اِسْترْليني
shekel	*šēkil*	شيْكِل

Palestinians do not have a sovereign currency. The Palestinian economy primarily relies on the Israeli shekel for day-to-day transactions. The Jordanian dinar, Egyptian pound, and US dollar are used to lesser extents.

agora, agorot (100 agorot = 1 shekel)	*agōra*	أغوْرة
coin	*maṣāri ḥadīd*	مصاري حديد
bill	*maṣāri wárag*	مصاري وَرق
a 100-shekel bill	*mīt šēkil wárag*	ميةْ شيكل وَرق
change (coins)	*ṣrāfa*	صُرافة
to break a bill, make change	*fakk, yfikk*	فكّ، يْفِكّ
Could you break this bill, please?	*múmkin tfíkkili hādi, law samáḥit?*	مُمْكِن تْفِكِّلّي هادي لَوْ سمحِت؟

tax	*ḍarība (ḍarāyib)*	ضريبة (ضرايِب)
to tax	*fáraḍ ḍarība 3ála, yífriḍ ḍarība 3ála*	فرض ضريبة على، يِفْرِض ضريبة على
to pay taxes	*dáfa3 [55] iḍḍarāyib*	دفع الضّرايِب
tax evasion	*(i)ttahárrub min iḍḍarība*	التهرُّب مِن الضّريبة
VAT, sales tax	*ḍarībit ilqīma -lmuḍāfa*	ضريبةِ القيمة المُضافة

income	*dáxil*	دخِل

expenses	maṣārīf [pl.]	مصاريف
funds	maṣāri	مصاري
financial, fiscal, monetary	māli	مالي
rich	ɣáni (áɣniya)	غني (أَغْنِيا)
wealth	sárwa	ثرْوَة
poor	fagīr (fúgara)	فقير (فُقرا)
poverty	fágir	فقِر
upper class	iṭṭábaqa -lɣaníyya	الطّبقة الغنية
middle class	iṭṭábaqa -lmutawássiṭa	الطبقة المتُوَسِّطة
working class	ṭábaqit il3ummāl	طبقِةْ العُمّال

Business and Commerce

business	šúɣul a3māl [pl.] bíznis	شُغُل أَعْمال بِزْنِس

commerce, trade;
  business, commercial
  venture
	tijāra	تِجارة

commercial	tijāri	تِجاري
merchant	tājir (tujjār)	تاجِر (تُجّار)
store, shop	mádjar (matājir)	مَتْجِر (متاجِر)
businessman	rájul 3ámal	رجُل أَعْمال
businesswoman	sáyyidit a3māl	سيِّدِةْ أَعْمال
to start one's own business	fátaḥ [55] šúɣlu -lxāṣṣ	فتح شُغْلو الخاصّ
entrepreneur	ryādi	ريادي
company	šírka	شِرْكة
to go on a business trip	sāfar [24] fi ríḥlit šúɣul	سافر في رِحْلِةْ شُغْل
committee	lájna (lijān)	لجْنة (لِجان)
board, council	májlis (majālis)	مجْلِس (مجالِس)
chair, chairman	raʔīs (rúʔasa)	رئيس (رُؤْسا)
administration	idāra	إدارة
to meet	gābal, ygābil	قابل، يْقابِل
meeting	ijtimā3	اِجْتِماع
appointment	máw3id	مَوْعِد (مَواعيد)
to cancel	láɣa, yílɣi	لغى، يِلْغي

to postpone	ájjal, yʔájjil	أجَّل، يْأجِّل
conference	muʔtámar	مُؤْتمر
seminar	nádwa	نَدْوَة
proposal	muqtáraɧ 3árḍ (3urūḍ)	مُقْترح عرْض (عُروض)
office	máktab (makātib)	مكْتب (مكاتِب)
head office, head quarters	maqárr raʔīsi márkaz raʔīsi (marākiz raʔīsíyya)	مقرّ رئيسي مرْكز رئيسي (مراكِز رئيسية)
factory	máṣna3 (maṣāni3)	مصْنع (مصانع)
to manufacture	ṣánna3, yṣánni3	صنَّع، يْصنِّع
industry	majāl ṣinā3a	مجال صِناعة

29 Agriculture

agriculture	*zirā3a*	زِراعة
farm	*mázra3a (mazāri3)*	مَزْرعة (مَزارِع)
farmer	*muzāri3* *fallāħ*	مُزارِع فلّاح
barn, pen, corral, coop, stable	*zrība (zarāyib)*	زْريبة (زرايِب)
cattle	*bágar*	بقر
cow	*bágara*	بقرة
to milk	*ħálab, yíħlib*	حلب، بِحْلِب
donkey	*ħmār (ħamīr)*	حْمار (حمير)
mule	*báɣil (byāl)*	بغِل (بْغال)
pig	*xanzīr (xanazīr)*	خِنْزير (خنازير)
goat	*3ánza*	عِنْزة
(male sheep) **ram**	*xarūf (xirfān)*	خروف (خِرْفان)
(female sheep) **ewe**	*ɣánama (ɣánam)*	غنمة (غنم)

The collective form غنم *ɣánam* is used to refer to sheep (male and female) in the plural.

The farmer is out feeding his sheep.	*ilmuzāri3 ṭíli3 yír3a ilɣánam.*	المُزارِع طِلِع يِرْعى الغنم.
shepherd	*rā3i ɣánam (ru3āt ɣánam)*	راعي غنم (رُعاةْ غنم)
chicken, hen	*jāja (jāj)*	جاجة (جاج)
rooster (UK: **cock**)	*dīk (dyūk)*	ديك (دْيوك)
chick	*ṣūṣ (ṣūṣān)*	صوص (صوصان)
to lay an egg	*bāḍat [f.] bēḍa, tbīḍ bēḍa*	باضت بيْضة، تْبيض بيْضة

ducks	*baṭṭ*	بطّ
geese	*wizz*	وِزّ
turkey	*ħábaša (ħábaš)* *dīk rūmi (dyūk rūmíyya)*	حبشة (حبش) ديك رومي (دْيوك رومية)
camel	*jámal (jmāl)*	جمل (جْمال)
horse	*ħṣān (ħúṣun)*	حْصان (حُصُن)
to graze	*rá3a, yír3a*	رعى، يِرْعى
hay	*tíbin*	تِبِن
field	*arḍ* *ħáqil*	أرْض حقِل
to plow	*ħárat, yúħrut*	حرت، يُحْرُت
tractor	*traktōr* *jarrār*	تْرِكْتوْر جرّار
orchard	*ħadīqa (ħadāʔiq)* *bustān (basātīn)*	حديقة (حدائِق) بُسْتان (بساتين)
to plant	*zára3, yízra3*	زرع، يِزْرع
to irrigate	*ṣága, yíṣgi*	سقى، يِسْقي
harvest	*ħaṣād*	حصاد
to harvest	*ħáṣad, yúħṣud*	حصد، يُحْصُد
wheat	*ğámiħ*	قمِح
corn	*dura*	دُرة
grain, cereals	*ħbūb [pl.]*	حْبوب

war	*ḥarb (ḥrūb)*	حرْب (حْروب)
peace	*salām*	سلام
to declare war on	*á3lan ilḥárb 3ála, yí3lin ilḥárb 3ála*	أعْلن الحرْب على، يِعْلِن الحرْب على
to be at war with	*kān [55] fī ḥarb ḍidd*	كان في حرْب ضِدّ
military	*3áskari*	عسْكري
army	*jēš*	جيْش
air force	*guwwāt jawwíyya*	قُوّات جوّية
navy	*guwwāt baḥríyya*	قُوّات بحْرية
soldier	*júndi (jnūd)*	جُنْدي (جْنود)
sailor	*baḥḥār*	بحّار
to recruit, enlist	*jánnad, yjánnid*	جنّد، يْجنّد
battle	*má3raka (ma3ārik)*	معْركة (معارِك)
attack	*hujūm*	هُجوم
to attack	*hájam, yíhjim*	هجم، يهْجِم
to defend	*dāfa3, ydāfi3*	دافع، يْدافع
defense	*difā3*	دِفاع
bomb	*gúmbila*	قُنْبلة (قَنابِل)
grenade	*gúmbila yadawíyya*	قُنْبلة يَدَوية
to explode	*infájar, yinfíjir*	اِنْفجر، يِنْفِجر
explosion	*infijār*	اِنْفِجار
mine	*lúɣum (alɣām)*	لُغْم (ألغام)
missile	*ṣārūx (ṣawārīx)*	صاروخ (صَواريخ)
tank	*dabbāba*	دبّابة

to occupy	iḥtáll, yiḥtáll	اِحْتَلّ، يِحْتِلّ
occupation	iḥtilāl	اِحْتِلال
to liberate	ḥárrar, yḥárrir	حرّر، يْحرّر
liberation	taḥrīr	تحْرير

The Mind

mind; intelligence	3ágil (3gūl)	عقِل (عْقول)
consciousness	wá3i	وَعي
to think about	fákkar b(i)-, yfákkir b(i)-	فكّر بِـ، يْفكّر بِـ
What are you thinking about?	b-šū bitfákkir?	بْشو بِتْفكّر؟
to remember	(i)dzákkar, yidzákkar	اِتْزكّر، بِتْزكّر
Do you remember me?	zākírni?	زاكِرْني؟
to remind __ about	zákkar b(i)-, yzákkir b(i)-	زكّر بِـ، يْزكّر بِـ
Remind me to set my alarm.	zakkírni ʔaḥúṭṭ ilmunábbih.	زكّرْني أحطّ المنبّه.
to plan on	xáṭṭaṭ la-, yxáṭṭiṭ la-	خطّط لـ، يْخطّط لـ
plan	xúṭṭa (xúṭaṭ)	خُطّة (خُطط)
to forget	nísi, yínsa	نِسي، يِنْسى
memory	zākira	زاكِرة
to believe	ṣáddag, yṣáddig	صدّق، يْصدّق
I don't believe that!	miš mṣáddig ha-lʔíši.	مِش مْصدّق هالإشي.
to understand	fíhim, yífham	فِهِم، يِفْهم
to decide	qárrar, yqárrir	قرّر، يْقرّر
decision	qarār	قرار
to know	3írif, yí3rif	عِرِف، يِعْرِف
knowledge	má3rifa (m3ārif)	معْرِفة (معارِف)
to imagine	(i)txáyyal, yitxáyyal	اِتْخيّل، بِتْخيّل
imagination	xayāl	خَيال
to guess	ḥázzar, yḥázzir	حزّر، يْحزّر
How did you guess?	kēf ḥazzárit?	كيْف حزّرِت؟
guess	taḥzīr	تحْزير

to predict, expect	(i)twáqqa3, yitwáqqa3	اِتْوَقَّع، يِتْوَقَّع
prediction	tawáqqu3	تَوَقُّع
crazy, insane	majnūn (majanīn)	مجْنون (مجانين)
intelligent, clever	záki (ázkiya)	ذكي (أَذْكِيا)
intelligence	zakāʔ	ذكاء
stupid	yábi (áybiya) múxxu txīn	غبي (أغْبِيا) مُخّو تْخين
stupidity, idiocy	yabāwa	غباوَة

32   Feelings

feeling, emotion	iḥsās (aḥāsīs) 3āṭifa (3awāṭif)	إحْساس (أحاسيس) عاطِفة (عَواطِف)
to feel	ḥass b(i)-, yḥiss b(i)-	حسّ بِـ، يْحِسّ بِـ
to feel good	ḥass iḥsās ḥílu	حسّ إحْساس حِلو
to feel bad	ḥass b-ʔiḥsās bíši3	حسّ بْإحْساس بِشِع
How do you feel?	šū ḥāsis?	شو حاسِس؟
to laugh	ḍíḥak, yíḍḥak	ضِحك، يِضْحك
laughter	ḍíḥka	ضِحْكة
to cry	3áyyaṭ, y3áyyiṭ ṣáyyaḥ, yṣáyyiḥ	عيّط، يْعيّط صيّح، يْصيّح
to smile	ibtásam, yibtísim	إبْتسم، يِبْتِسِم
to frown	káššar, ykáššir 3ágad ḥawājbu	كشّر، يْكشّر عقد حَواجْبو
happy	mabsūṭ farḥān	مبْسوط فرْحان
I'm really happy about the news.	mabsūṭ ktīr 3a ha-lʔaxbār.	مبْسوط كْتير عَ هالأخْبار.
sad; upset	za3lān	زعْلان
angry with	m3áṣṣib min	مْعصّب مِن
to annoy	nárfaz, ynárfiz dāyag, ydāyig	نرْفز، يْنرْفِز ضايَق، يْضايِق

Notice the pronunciation of ضايَق is with *d* and is also commonly spelled دايَق. People often preserve spelling from MSA even when the pronunciation is different in Palestinian Arabic. Othertimes, the spelling is altered to reflect the true pronunciation. There are, of course, no official rules in the dialect; it's largely up to individual preference.

annoyed by, fed up with	middāyag min	مِتْضايَق مِن

I'm really annoyed at myself for that.	*ána 3an jadd middāyag min ḥāli min wára ha-ššáɣla.*	أنا عن جدّ مِتْضايَق مِن حالي مِن وَرا هالشّغْلة
annoying	*múz3ij*	مُزْعِج
to surprise	*fājaʔ, yfāji?*	فاجِئ، يُفاجِئ
That really surprises me.	*hādi -ššáɣla bitfājíʔni 3an jadd.*	هادي الشّغْلة بِتْفاجِئْني عن جدّ.
surprising	*mufāji?*	مُفاجِئ
to be surprised	*(i)tfājaʔ, yitfāja?*	إتْفاجِئ، يِتْفاجِئ
surprised	*mitfāji?*	مِتْفاجِئ
excited about	*mitḥámmis la-*	مِتْحمّس لـ
exciting	*mušáwwiq* *ḥamāsi* *muḥámmis*	مُشوّق حماسي مُحمّس
tired	*ta3bān*	تعْبان
tiring	*mút3ib*	مُتْعِب
to fear, be afraid of	*xāf min, yxāf min*	خاف مِن، يْخاف مِن
fear	*xōf*	خوْف
proud of	*faxūr fi*	فخور في
embarrassed by	*múḥrij min* *xajlān min* *místiḥi min*	مُحْرج مِن خجْلان مِن مِسْتِحي مِن
thankful, grateful	*šākir* *mumtánn*	شاكِر مُمْتنّ

33 Personality

personality	*šaxṣíyya*	شخْصية
modest	*mutawāḍi3*	مُتَواضِع
shy	*xajūl*	خجول
friendly, kind	*laṭīf* *binḥább*	لطيف بينْحبّ

بينْحبّ *binḥább* is actually a verb that literally translates 'to be loved,' so if the subject is a feminine noun, it would be بْتِنْحبّ *btinḥább*.

sociable	*ijtimā3i*	إِجْتِماعي
cruel, harsh	*jílif* *gāsi*	جِلِف قاسي
kind	*ṭáyyib* *ḥanūn*	طيُّب حنون
generous	*karīm*	كريم
greedy	*ṭammā3*	طمّاع
hard-working, diligent	*mújtahid* *šayɣīl*	مُجْتهِد شغّيل
lazy	*kasūl*	كسول
serious	*jáddi*	جدّي
funny, jovial, likeable	*dámmu xafīf*	دمّو خفيف
nice, pleasant, sweet	*laṭīf* *ẓarīf*	لطيف ظريف
jovial, merry, lively	*míriḥ* *bašūš*	مِرِح بشوش
strange	*ɣarīb*	غريب

| jealous, envious | *ɣayyūr*
ḥasūd | غيّور
حسود |

to like, love	*ḥabb [3]*	حبّ
I like traveling and learning foreign languages.	*baḥíbb asāfir w at3állam luɣāt ajnabíyyi.*	بحبّ أسافِر وأتْعلّم لُغات أجْنبية.
to enjoy	*istámta3, yistámti3*	اِسْتمْتع، يِسْتمْتع
to hate	*kírih, yíkrah*	كِرِهْ، يِكْرهْ
I hate getting up early.	*bákrah áṣḥa bádri.*	بكْرهْ أصْحى بدْري.
interested in	*mihtámm b(i)-*	مِهْتمّ بِـ
I'm not interested in politics.	*ána miš mihtámm bi-ssiyāsa.*	أنا مِش مِهْتمّ بالسِّياسة.
hobby	*hiwāya*	هِوايَة
What are your hobbies?	*šū hiwāyātak?*	شو هِواياتك؟
to praise	*mádaḥ, yímdaḥ*	مدح، يِمْدح
praise	*mádiḥ*	مدح
to criticize	*intáqad, yintíqid*	اِنْتقد، يِنْتِقِد
criticism	*intiqād* *náqid*	اِنْتِقاد نقِد
to complain about	*šáka, yíški*	شكى، يِشْكي
complaint	*šákwa (šakāwi)*	شكْوى (شكاوي)
to admire, like	*3ájabu, yí3jibu*	عجبو، يِعْجبو

عجب *3ájab* literally means 'to please,' so to express 'I like something,' we need to phrase it as 'something pleases me.'

I like this color.	*ána bí3jibni hāda -llōn.*	أنا بيعجِبْني هادا اللّوْن.
to prefer __ to	*fáḍḍal, yfáḍḍil*	فضّل، يْفضّل
I prefer the train to the bus.	*bfáḍḍil ilgiṭār áktar min ilbāṣ.*	بفضّل القِطار أكْتر مِن الباص.

agreement	*ittifāg*	اِتِّفاق
to agree with; get along with	*(i)ttáffag ma3, yittíffig ma3*	اتِّفق مع، يِتِّفِق مع
They don't get along (with each other) very well.	*bittífgūš ma3 bá3iḍ.*	بيتِّفْقوش مع بعض.
to disagree with	*ixtálaf ma3, yixtílif ma3*	اِخْتلف مع، يِخْتِلِف مع
to argue about	*jādal 3ála, yjādil 3ála*	جادل على، يْجادِل على

جادل *jādal* is a measure III verb (see the book Palestinian Arabic Verbs). By adding the prefix اِتْ, as in the sentence below, we have the reciprocal measure VI verb اِتْجادل *idjādal* 'to argue <u>with each other</u>.'

They're always arguing (with each other) about politics.	*dāyman bidjādalu bi-ssiyāsa.*	دايْماً بيتْجادلوا بِالسِّياسة.
to have a discussion	*3índu munāqaša*	عِنْدو مُناقشة
certain, sure	*mit?ákkid*	مِتْأكِّد
okay	*ṭáyyib* *tamām* *ōkē* *ṭab*	طيِّب تمام أوْكيْ طب
opinion	*rá?i (ārā?)*	رأي (آراء)
What do you think about __?	*šū rā?yak b(i)-__?*	شو رأْيَك بِـــ؟
I think (that) …	*aẓúnn…* *ba3tígid…*	أظُنّ بعْتِقِد
in my opinion	*b-rā?yi*	بْرأْيي

36 Desires and Intentions

desire	*ráɣba*	رغْبة
intention	*níyya (nawāya)*	نية (نَوايا)
to want	*bíddu*	بِدّو

بِدّو *bíddu* is a pseudo-verb. It is not technically a verb, and is not conjugated as a verb, but it acts as a verb. (See the book Palestinian Arabic Verbs.)

I want to...	*bíddi*	بِدّي
I don't want to eat anything.	*biddīš ākul íši.*	بِدّيش أكُل إشي.
I want a car.	*bíddi sayyāra.*	بِدّي سيّارة.
to wish, hope	*(i)tmánna, yitmánna*	إتْمنّى، بِتْمنّى
I hope (that)...	*batmánna...*	بتْمنّى
I hope to see you again.	*batmánna ʔašūfak márra tānya.*	بتْمنّى أشوفك مرّة تانْية.
I hope nothing happens to him.	*batmánna mā yṣīrlu íši.*	بتْمنّى ما يْصيرْلو إشي.
I wish...	*yā rēt...*	يا ريْت
I wish I were in Palestine.	*yā rēt kúnit fi falasṭīn.*	يا ريْتْني كُنِت في فلسْطين.
I wish I had a car.	*yā rēt law 3índi sayyāra.*	يا ريْت لَوْ عِنْدي سيّارة.
looking forward to	*mitšáwwig*	مِتْشوّق
I'm looking forward to seeing you.	*mitšáwwig ašūfak.*	مِتْشوّق أشوفك.

religion	dīn (adyān)	دين (أَدْيان)
religious (concerning religion)	dīni	ديني
faith, belief	īmān	إيمان
secular	3ilmāni	عِلْماني
to believe in	āman b(i)-, yʔāmin b(i)-	آمن بِ، يْآمِن بِ
Do you believe in God?	ínta bitʔāmin b-ʔallāh? ínta múʔmin bi-llāh?	إنْتَ بِتْآمِن بْالله؟ إنْتَ مُؤْمِن بِالله؟
religious (person)	mutadáyyin	مُتديِّن
He's a very religious man.	húwwa zámala mutadáyyin ktīr.	هُوَّ زلمة مُتديِّن كْتير.
ceremony	ṭáqis (ṭuqūs)	طقِس (طُقوس)
to pray	dá3a, yíd3i	دعا، يِدْعي
prayer	du3āʔ	دُعاء
She prayed to God that her son would be alright.	dá3at allāh ínnu íbinha ykūn mnīḥ.	دعت الله اِنّو اِبنْها يْكون مْنيح.
soul	rōḥ (arwāḥ)	روْح (أَرْواح)
Heaven, Paradise	ijjánna	الجّنّة
a god	ilāh (āliha)	إله (آلِهة)
a goddess	ilāha	إلهة
God, Allah	allāh/álla	الله
prophet	nábi (ánbiya)	نبي (أَنْبِيا)
messenger	rasūl (rúsul)	رسول (رُسُل)
angel	malāk (malāʔika)	ملاك (ملائِكة)
jinn, genie	jínni (jinn)	جِنّي (جِنّ)
Hell	ijjaḥīm	الجّحيم

devil, demon	šīṭān (šayaṭīn)	شيطان (شَياطين)
the Devil, Satan	iššīṭān	الشَّيطان
sin	zamb (znūb)	ذَنْب (ذُنوب)
to sin	áznab, yíznib	أذْنب، يِذْنِب
evil (noun)	šarr (šrūr)	شرّ (شرور)
evil (adjective)	šarrīr (ašrār)	شرّير (أشْرار)
superstition	xurāfa	خُرافة
superstitious (person)	múʔmin bi-lxurāfa	مُؤْمِن بِالخُرافة
good luck	ḥazz ḥílu	حظّ حِلو
bad luck	ḥazz bíši3	حظّ بِشِع
pagan	wátani	وَتني
paganism	ilwataníyya	الوَتنية
Islam	islām	إسْلام
Muslim	múslim	مُسْلِم
Islamic	islāmi	إسْلامي
The Prophet Muhammad	innábi muḥámmad	النَّبي مُحمّد
Christianity	ilmasīḥíyya	المسيحية
Christian	masīḥi	مسيحي
Christ	ilmasīḥ	المسيح
Jesus	3īsa yasū3	عيسى يَسوع

Judaism	ilyahūdíyya	اليَهودية
Jew, Jewish	yahūdi	يَهودي
Buddhism	ilbūdíyya	البودية

Buddhist	*būdi*	بودي
Buddha	*būda*	بودا
Hinduism	*ilhindūsíyya*	الهِنْدوسية
Hindu	*hindūsi*	هِنْدوسي
atheism	*ilḥād*	إلْحاد
atheist	*múlḥid*	مُلْحِد
mosque	*jāmi3 (jawāmi3)*	جامِع (جَوامِع)
masjid (small mosque)	*másjid (masājid)*	مسْجِد (مساجِد)
Friday prayer	*ṣalāt ijjúm3a*	صلاةْ الجُمْعة
imam	*imām (aʔímma)*	إمام (أئِمّة)
Friday sermon	*xúṭbit ijjúm3a*	خُطْبِةْ الجُمْعة
to preach	*wá3aẓ, yū3aẓ*	وَعظ، يوعظ
call to prayer	*adān*	أدان
to call to prayer	*áddan, yʔáddin*	أدّن، يْأْدِّن
ablution (ceremonial washing before praying)	*wḍūʔ*	وُضوء
to perform ritual abllutions	*(i)twáḍḍa, yitwáḍḍa*	إتْوَضّى، يِتْوَضّى
to perform prayer	*ṣálla, yṣálli*	صلّى، يْصلّي
prayer	*ṣalā (ṣalawāt)*	صلاة (صلَوات)
dawn prayer	*ṣalāt ilfájir* *ṣalāt iṣṣúbiḥ*	صلاةْ الفجِر صلاةْ الصُبِح
Duha prayer (voluntary morning prayer)	*ṣalāt iḍḍúḥa*	صلاةْ الضُحى
noon prayer	*ṣalāt iḍḍúhur*	صلاةْ الضُهُر
afternoon prayer	*ṣalāt il3áṣir*	صلاةْ العصِر
sunset prayer	*ṣalāt ilmáɣrib*	صلاةْ المغْرِب
evening prayer	*ṣalāt il3íša*	صلاةْ العِشا

Eid prayers	ṣalāt il3īd	صلاةُ العيد
Quran	qurʔān	قُرآن
to recite the Quran	tála -lqurʔān, yítlu -lqurʔān	تلى القُرآن، يِتْلو القُرآن
sura (chapter of Quran)	sūra (súwar)	سورة (سُوَر)
verse	āya	آيَة
Hadith	ḥadīs (aḥādīs)	حديث (أحاديث)
Sunnah	issúnna	السُّنّة
church	kanīsa (kanāyis)	كنيسة (كنايِس)
church service	xídmit ilkanīsa	خِدْمِةْ الكنيسة
minister, pastor	kāhin (káhana)	كاهِن (كهنة)
priest (Catholic, Orthodox)	qasīs (qsūs) rāhib (ruhbān)	قسيس (قُسوس (راهِب (رُهْبان)
nun	rāhiba	راهِبة
pope	bāba	بابا
to preach about	báššar b(i)-, ybáššir b(i)-	بشَّر بِ، يْبشِّر بِ
sermon	máw3iẓa (mawā3iẓ)	مَوْعِظة (مَواعِظ)
pulpit	mánbar (manābir)	مِنْبر (منابِر)
altar	mádbaḥ (madābiḥ)	مذْبح (مدابِح)
choir	jáwga	جَوْقة
Bible	liktāb ilmuqáddas	الكْتاب المُقدّس
The New Testament	ilʔinjīl	الإنْجيل
evangelical	injīli	إنْجيلي
to baptize	3ámmad, y3ámmid	عمَّد، يْعمِّد
baptism	ṭa3mīd	تعْميد

language	lúɣa	لُغة
foreign language	lúɣa ʔajnabíyya	لُغة أَجْنبية
(foreign) accent	lákna	لكْنة
native language	lúɣa ʔumm	لُغة أُمّ
Chinese	ṣīni	صيني
Dutch	hōlāndi	هوْلانْدي
English	inglīzi	إنْجْليزي
Farsi	fārisi	فارِسي
French	faránsi	فرنْسي
German	almāni	ألْماني
Greek	yūnāni	يوناني
Hebrew	3íbri	عِبْري
Hindi	híndi	هِنْدي
Italian	īṭāli	إيطالي
Japanese	yābāni	ياباني
Korean	kūri	كوري
Portuguese	burtuɣāli	بُرْتُغالي
Russian	rūsi	روسي
Spanish	asbāni	أسْباني
Turkish	túrki	تُرْكي
Arabic	3árabi	عربي
Classical Arabic; Modern Standard Arabic	(3árabi) fúṣḥa [lit. pure (Arabic)]	(عربي) فُصْحى

Arabs generally don't differentiate between Classical Arabic (of the Quran) and MSA.

dialect; accent	*láhja*	لَهْجة
colloquial language; colloquial Arabic	*3ammíyya*	عامِّية
Egyptian Arabic	*máṣri*	مِصْري
Moroccan Arabic	*máɣribi*	مَغْرِبي
Levantine Arabic	*šāmi*	شامي
Gulf Arabic	*xalīji*	خليجي

to learn	*(i)t3állam, yit3állam*	اِتْعلم، بِتْعلَّم
practice, exercise	*tadrīb* *tamrīn (tamārīn)*	تَدْريب تَمْرين (تمارين)
to practice	*(i)ddárab 3ála, yiddárrab 3ála* *(i)tmárran 3ála, yitmárran 3ála*	اِتْدرَّب على، بِتْدرَّب على اِتْمرّن على، بِتْمرّن على
level	*mústawa (mustawayāt)*	مُسْتَوى (مُسْتَوَيات)
beginner's	*mubtádi?*	مُبْتَدِئ
intermediate	*mutawássiṭ*	مُتَوَسِّط
advanced	*mutaqáddim*	مُتَقدّم

writing	*kitāba*	كِتابة
to write	*kátab, yíktib*	كتب، بِكْتِب
reading	*grāya*	قْرايَة
to read	*gára, yígra*	قرا، بِقْرا
alphabet	*liḥrūf il?abjadíyya*	الِحْروف الأبْجدية
letter	*ḥarf (ḥrūf)*	حرْف (حْروف)
Chinese characters	*liḥrūf iṣṣīníyya*	الِحْروف الصّينية
to spell	*hájja, yhájji*	هجّى، يْهجّي
spelling	*táhjiya* *imlā?*	تهْجِية إمْلاء

handwriting, penmanship	*xaṭṭ (īd)*	خطّ (إيد)
I have such bad penmanship.	*ána xáṭṭi miš ḥílu.*	أنا خطّي مِش حِلو.
is legible	*bingára*	بينْقِرا
is illegible	*bingarāš*	بينْقِراش
His handwriting is completely illegible.	*xáṭṭu mā bingarāš bi-lmárra.*	خطّو بينْقِراش بالمرّة.
calligraphy	*taxṭīṭ* *fann irrásim bi-lxáṭṭ*	تخْطيط فنّ الرّسِم بِالخطّ
speaking, speech	*ḥáki*	حكي
I need to practice speaking more.	*ána lāzim atdárrab 3a -lḥáki ʔáktar.*	أنا لازِم أتْدرّب عَ الحكي أكْتر.
You can't understand anything he says.	*btigdáriš tífham wála kílma mínnu.*	بْتِقْدِرِش تِفْهم وَلا كِلْمة مِنّو.
to speak	*ḥáka [55]* *itkállam, yitkállam*	حكى اِتْكلّم، يِتْكلّم
Can you speak Arabic?	*btí3rif tíḥki 3árabi?*	بْتِعْرِف تِحْكي عربي؟
I know a few words.	*bá3rif kam kílma.*	بعْرِف كم كِلْمة.
I know some basic Arabic.	*bá3rif asāsiyyāt fi -l3árabi.*	بعْرِف أساسِيّات في العربي.
I can speak a little Arabic.	*bá3rif áḥki šwáyyit 3árabi.*	بعْرِف أحْكي شوَيّة عربي.
I can get by in Arabic.	*bamášša ḥāli fi -l3árabi.*	بمشّي حالي في العربي.
I speak Arabic pretty well.	*báḥki 3árabi mnīḥ.*	بحْكي عربي مْنيح.
broken Arabic	*3árabi mkássar*	عربي مْكسّر
fluently	*b-ṭalāqa* *bi-shūla*	بْطلاقة بِسْهولة
I am fluent in Arabic.	*ána báḥki 3árabi b-ṭalāqa.*	أنا بحْكي عربي بْطلاقة.
pronunciation	*núṭug* *láfiẓ*	نُطُق لفِظ

to pronounce	*náṭag, yúnṭug* *láfaẓ, yúlfuẓ*	نطق، يُنْطُق لفظ ، يُلْفُظ
How do you pronounce this word?	*kēf btúnṭug hādi -lkílma?*	كِيْف بْتُنْطُق هادي الكِلْمة؟
Your Arabic pronunciation is quite good.	*nutg il3árabi 3índak ktīr mnīḥ.*	نُطْق العربي عِنْدك كْتير مْنيح.
listening	*istimā3* *samā3*	اِسْتِماع سماع
I need to work on my listening skills in Arabic.	*lāzim aštíɣil 3ála tamārīn ilʔistimā3 bi-l3árabi.*	لازِم أَشْتِغِل على تمارين الاِسْتِماع بِالعربي.
to listen to	*sími3, yísma3*	سِمِع، يِسْمع
vocabulary	*kalimāt [pl.]* *mufradāt [pl.]*	كلِمات مُفْردات
word	*kílma (kalimāt)*	كِلْمة (كلِمات)
dictionary	*qāmūs (qawāmīs)*	قاموس (قَواميس)
to look up a word in the dictionary	*dáwwar [9] 3a kílma fi -lqāmūs*	دوَّر عَ كِلْمة في القاموس
flashcard	*biṭāqa ta3līmíyya*	بِطاقة تعْليمية
to repeat	*3ād, y3īd*	عاد، يْعيد
repetition	*i3āda*	إعادة
grammar	*náḥu* *qawā3id*	نحو قَواعِد
grammatical	*náḥawi*	نَحَوي
grammatical rule	*qā3ida naḥawíyya (qawā3id naḥawíyya)*	قاعِدة نَحْوِية (قَواعِد نَحَوية)
to inflect, conjugate, decline	*ṣárraf, yṣárrif*	صرَّف، يْصرِّف

inflection, conjugation, declension	taṣrīf	تصْريف
suffix	āxir ilkílma	آخِر الكِلْمة
prefix	áwwal ilkílma	أوّل الكِلْمة
case	ḥāla	حالة
tense	záman (azmān)	زمن (أزْمان)
gender	jins (ajnās)	جِنْس (أجْناس)
singular	múfrad	مُفْرد
dual	muťánna	مُثنّى
plural	jámi3	جمِع
masculine	muđákkar	مُذكّر
feminine	muʔánnať	مُؤنّث
neuter	muḥāyid	مُحايِد
the present tense	záman ilmuḍāri3	زمن المُضارِع
the past tense	záman ilmāḍi	زمن الماضي
the future tense	záman ilmustáqbal	زمن المُسْتقْبل
article	adāt ta3rīf	أداةْ تعْريف
preposition	ḥarf jarr	حرْف جرّ
noun	ísim (asmā?)	إِسِم (أسْماء)
verb	fí3il (af3āl)	فِعِل (أفْعال)
adjective	ṣífa	صِفة
adverb	ẓarf (ẓurūf)	ظرْف (ظُروف)
subject	fā3il	فاعِل
object	maf3ūl bíhi	مفْعول بِهِ
definite	mu3árraf má3rifa	مُعرّف معْرِفة
indefinite	nákira	نكِرة

word order	tartīb ilkalimāt	ترْتيب الكلِمات
sentence	júmla (júmal)	جُمْلة (جُمل)
paragraph	fáqara	فقرة
vowel	ḥarf 3ílla ḥarf mutaḥárrik	حرْف عِلّة حرْف مُتحرِّك
consonant	ḥarf sākin	حرْف ساكِن
syllable	máqṭa3	مقْطع
punctuation	tarqīm	ترْقيم
punctuation mark	3alāmit tarqīm	علامِةْ ترْقيم
period	núgṭa (núgaṭ)	نُقْطة (نُقط)
comma	fāṣla (fawāṣil)	فاصْلة (فَواصِل)
exclamation mark	3alāmit ta3ájjub	علامِةْ تعجُّب
question mark	3alāmit istifhām	علامِةْ اِسْتِفْهام
quotation marks	3alāmtēn tanṣīṣ [dual]	علامْتينْ تنْصيص
colon	nugṭitēn fōg bá3aḍ [dual]	نُقْطِتينْ فوْق بعض
parenthesis, bracket	gōs (gwās)	قوْس (قُواس)
(a pair of) parentheses	gōsēn [dual]	قوْسينْ

country, nation	*bálad (blād)*	بلد (بْلاد)
What countries have you been to?	*šū liblād ílli zurítha?*	شو البْلاد اللي زُرِتْها؟
international	*dáwli*	دَوْلي
worldwide	*3ālami*	عالمي
culture	*łaqāfa*	ثقافة
foreign; foreigner	*ájnabi (ajānib)*	أجْنبي (أجانِب)

Where are you from?	*min wēn ínta?*	مِن وِيْن إنْتَ؟
I'm from Palestine.	*ána min falasţīn.*	أنا مِن فلسْطين.
I'm Palestinian.	*ána falasţīni.*	أنا فلسْطيني.

| Arab | *3árabi (3árab)* | عربي (عرب) |
| The Arab World | *il3ālam il3árabi* | العالم العربي |

Countries are feminine in Palestinian Arabic. The only exceptions are five Arab countries, noted as masculine below, but even these may be treated as feminine by many speakers.

Egypt	*máşir*	مصِر
Egyptian	*máşri*	مصْري
Sudan	*issūdān [m.]*	السّودان
Sudanese	*sūdāni*	سوداني
Libya	*lībya*	ليبْيا
Libyan	*lībi*	ليبي
Tunisia	*tūnis*	تونِس
Tunisian	*tūnisi*	تونِسي

Algeria Algerian	ijjazāʔir jazāʔiri	الجّزائِر جزائِري
Morocco Moroccan	ilmáɣrib [m.] máɣribi	المغْرِب مغْرِبي
Palestine Palestinian	falasṭīn falasṭīni	فلسْطين فلسْطيني
Jordan Jordanian	ilʔúrdun [m.] úrduni	الأُرْدُن أُرْدُني
Lebanon Lebanese	libnān [m.] libnāni	لِبْنان لِبْناني
Syria Syrian	sūriya sūri	سوريا سوري
Iraq Iraqi	il3irāq [m.] 3irāqi	العِراق عِراقي
Kuwait Kuwaiti	likwēt kwēti	الِكْوِيْت كْوِيْتي
Qatar Qatari	qáṭar qáṭari	قطر قطري
Bahrain Bahraini	ilbaḥrēn baḥrēni	البحْرِيْن بحْرِيْني
The Emirates Emirati	ilʔimārāt imārāti	الإمارات إماراتي
Saudi Arabia Saudi	issu3ūdíyya su3ūdi	السُّعودية سُعودي
Oman Omani	3umān 3umāni	عُمان عُماني

| Yemen | ilyáman | الْيَمن |
| Yemeni | yámani | يَمَني |

| Somalia | iṣṣūmāl | الصّومال |
| Somali | ṣūmāli | صومالي |

Nationalities, adjectives, and languages are regularly formed from the names of countries by adding the suffix ي -i, as seen in the section above. This requires first removing any definite articles and ـا -a or يا -ya endings. These forms are only listed for countries in the following section if there is a notable variation or irregular plural.

Ethiopia	aṯyōbya	أثْيوبْيا
Nigeria	nayjīrya	نَيْجيرْيا
South Africa	jnūb afrīqya	جنوب أفْريقْيا

Norway	innarwīj	النَّرْويج
Sweden	isswīd	السْويد
Swedish	swīdi	سْويدي
Finland	finlánda	فِنْلَنْدا
Denmark	iddinimārk	الدِّنيمارْك
Germany	almānya	ألْمانْيا
German	almāni (almān)	ألْماني (ألْمان)
The Netherlands, Holland	hōlānda	هوْلانْدا
Belgium	beljīka	بلْجيكا
Ireland	irlánda	إيرْلَنْدا
Great Britain	brīṭānya	بْريطانْيا
British	brīṭāni	بريطاني
England	ingíltra	إنْجِلْتْرا
English	inglīzi (inglīz)	إنْجْليزي (إنْجْليز)

Scotland	askutlánda	أسْكُتْلَنْدا
Wales	wēlz	ويلْز
France	faránsa	فرنْسا
French	faránsi	فرنْسي
Spain	asbānya	أسْبانْيا
Portugal	ilburtuɣāl	البُرْتُغال
Switzerland	swīsra	سْويسْرا
Italy	īṭālya	إيطالْيا
Austria	innámsa	النّمْسا
Austrian	namsāwi	نمْساوي
The Czech Republic	litšīk	التِشيك
Czech	tšīki	تْشيكي
Slovakia	slōvākya	سْلوْفاكْيا
Poland	bōlánda	بوْلنْدا
Hungary	ilmájar / hungārya	المجر / هُنْقارْيا
Romania	rōmānya	روْمانْيا
Bulgaria	bulɣārya	بُلْغارْيا
Turkey	túrkya	تُرْكْيا
Turkish	túrki (atrāk)	تُرْكي (أتْراك)
Ukraine	ukrānya	أُكْرانْيا
Russia	rūsya	روسْيا
Iran	īrān	إيران
Afghanistan	afɣānistān	أفْغانِسْتان
Afghan	afɣāni	أفْغاني
Pakistan	bākistān	باكِسْتان

India	*ilhínd*	الهِنْد
Indian	*híndi*	هِنْدي
China	*iṣṣīn*	الصّين
South Korea	*kūrya -jjnūbíyya*	كورْيا الجُنوبية
Japan	*ilyābān*	اليابان
Taiwan	*tāywān*	تايْوان
Thailand	*tāylānda*	تايْلانْدا
Vietnam	*vitnām*	فِتْنام
Malaysia	*mālīzya*	ماليزْيا
Indonesia	*indōnīsya*	إنْدوْنيسْيا
The Philippines	*ilfilibbīn*	الفِلِبّين
Australia	*ustrālya*	أُسْترالْيا
New Zealand	*nyūzlanda*	نيوزْلنْدا
Canada	*kánada*	كندا
The United States	*ilwilāyāt ilmuttáḥida*	الوِلايات المتّحِدة
American	*amrīki (amirikān)*	أمْريكي (أمِريكان)
Mexico	*ilmaksīk*	المكْسيك
Colombia	*kōlōmbya*	كوْلوْمْبيا
Venezuela	*vinzwēla*	فِنْزوِيلا
Brazil	*ilbarāzīl*	البرازيل
Argentina	*ilʔarjantīn*	الأرْجنْتين
Chile	*tšīli*	تْشيلي
Chilean	*tšīli*	تْشيلي

40 Palestine

Palestine	*falasṭīn* [f.]	فلسْطين
Gaza Strip	*giṭā3 ɣázza*	قِطاع غزّة

All cities are feminine in Arabic.

Gaza (City)	*ɣázza*	غزّة
Al Nuseirat	*linṣērāt*	النِّصيرات
Dair Al Balah	*dēr ilbálaḩ*	ديْر البلح
Khan Younes	*xān yūnis*	خان يونِس
Rafah	*ráfaḩ*	رفح

The West Bank	*iḑḑáffa -lɣarbíyya*	الضفّة الغرْبية
Jerusalem	*ilqúds*	القُدْس
Jericho	*arīḩa*	أريحا
Nablus	*nāblis*	نابْلِس
Al Nasra	*innāṣra*	النّاصْرة
Qalqilya	*qalqīlya*	قلْقيلْيَة
Ramallah	*rāmálla*	رام الله
Acre, Akko	*3ákka*	عكّا
Haifa	*ḩēfa*	حيْفا
Bisan	*bīsān*	بيسان
Jenin	*jinīn*	جِنين
Tulkarm	*ṭūlkarim*	طولْكرِم
Hebron	*ilxalīl*	الخليل
Ramla	*irrámla*	الرّمْلة
Beer Sabi'	*bīr issábi3*	بير السّبع

Al Aqsa Mosque	*ilmásjid ilʔáqṣa*	المسْجِد الأقْصى
The Dome (of the Rock)	*qúbbit iṣṣáxra*	قُبّة الصّخْرة
Church of the Holy Sepulchre	*kanīsit ilqiyāma*	كنيسِة القِيامة
Salah Al-Din Street	*šāri3 ṣalāḥ iddīn*	شارِع صلاح الدّين
Church of the Nativity	*kanīsit ilmáhd*	كنيسِة المهْد
The Mediterranean Sea	*ilbáḥr ilʔábyaḍ*	البحْر الأبْيَض
The Dead Sea	*ilbáḥr ilmíyyit*	البحْر الميِّت
Mount Hebron	*jábal ilxalīl*	جبل الخليل
Lake Tiberias	*buḥērit ṭabaríyya*	بُحَيْرة طبريّا
Wadi Gaza	*wādi ɣázza*	وادي غزّة

land; ground, soil; earth	*arḍ (arāḍi)*	أَرْض (أَراضي)
island	*jazīra (júzur)*	جزيرة (جُزُر)
peninsula	*šíbih jazīra*	شِبِه جزيرة
mountain	*jábal (jbāl)*	جبل (جْبال)
tunnel	*náfag (anfāg)*	نفق (أَنْفاق)
mountain range	*silsílt jibāl*	سِلْسِلِةْ جِبال
mountainous, hilly	*jábali*	جبلي
hill	*tall (tlāl)*	تَلّ (تْلال)
flat	*musáṭṭaḥ*	مُسطَّح
plateau	*háḍaba (hiḍāb)*	هضبة (هِضاب)
valley	*wādi (widyān)*	وادي (وِدْيان)
ravine, gorge	*maḍīq*	مضيق
cliff	*múnḥádar ṣáxri*	مُنْحدر صخْري

continent	*qārra*	قارّة
North America	*amrīka -ššamālíyya*	أَمْريكا الشَّمالية
South America	*amrīka -jjanūbíyya*	أَمْريكا الجْنوبية
Europe	*ōrōbba*	أُورُوْبّا
Africa	*afrīqya*	أَفْريقْيا
Asia	*āsya*	آسيا
Australia	*usturālya*	أَسْتُرالْيا

water	*máyya*	مِيّة
to freeze	*(i)djámmad, yidjámmad*	اِتْجمَّد، يِتْجمَّد
to melt	*dāb, ydūb*	داب، يْدوب

sea	báħar (biħār)	بحر (بِحار)
bay, gulf	xalīj (xiljān)	خليج (خِلْجان)
canal	qanā (qanawāt)	قناة (قَنوات)
river	náhir (anhār)	نهِر (أنْهار)
stream	májra māʔi (majāri māʔíyya)	مجْرى [مائي] (مجاري [مائية])
lake	buħēra	بُحَيْرة
waterfall, cataract	šallāl	شلّال
swamp	mustánqa3	مُسْتنْقع
ocean	muħīṭ	مُحيط
Pacific Ocean	ilmuħīṭ ilhādi	المُحيط الهادي
Atlantic Ocean	ilmuħīṭ ilʔáṭlasi ilmuħīṭ ilʔaṭlánṭi	المُحيط الأطْلسي المُحيط الأطْلنْطي
Indian Ocean	ilmuħīṭ ilhíndi	المُحيط الهِنْدي
equator	xaṭṭ ilʔistiwāʔ	خطّ الإسْتِواء
the tropics	ilmanāṭig ilʔistiwāʔīyya	المناطِق الإسْتِوائية
the arctic	ilgúṭb iššmāli	القُطْب الشَّمالي
desert	ṣáħra (ṣaħāri)	صحْرا (صحاري)
forest, jungle	ɣāba	غابة
plains, grasslands	suhūl	سُهول
sand dunes	kuŧbān ramlíyya	كُثْبان رمْلية
oasis	wāħa	واحة
volcano	burkān (barākīn)	بُركان (براكين)
lava	ħímam	حِمم
to erupt	infájar, yinfíjir ŧār, yŧūr	اِنْفجر، يِنْفِجِر

		ثار، يْثور
eruption	*infijār*	اِنْفِجار
dormant, extinct	*xāmid*	خامِد
This volcano hasn't erupted in millions of years.	*hāda -lburkān mā -nfájar min malāyīn lisnīn.*	هادا البُرْكان ما انْفجر مِن ملايين السِّنين.
earthquake	*zilzāl*	زِلْزال
an earthquake struck	*zilzāl ḍárab*	زِلْزال ضرب
Did you feel the earthquake this morning?	*ḥassēt bi-zzilzāl iṣṣúbiḥ?*	حسّيْت بِالزِّلْزال الصُّبِح؟
air	*háwa*	هَوا
sky	*sáma (samawāt)*	سما (سموات)
moon	*gámar (agmār)*	قمر (أقْمار)
planet	*káwkab (kawākib)*	كَوْكب (كَواكِب)
sun	*šámis (šmūs)*	شمِس (شْموس)
star	*níjma*	نِجْمة
universe, cosmos	*kōn (akwān)*	كوْن (أكْوان)
space, outer space	*faḍāʔ*	فضاء
comet	*muḍánnab*	مُذنَّب
meteorite, falling star	*šhāb (šúhub)*	شْهاب (شُهُب)
sunlight	*ḍaww iššámis*	ضوّ الشَّمِس
sunrise	*šurūg*	شُروق
The sun rises in the east.	*iššáms btúšrug min iššárg.*	الشّمْس بْتُشْرُق مِن الشّرْق.
sunset	*ɣurūb*	غُروب
The sun sets in the west.	*iššáms btúɣrub min ilɣárb.*	الشّمْس بْتُغْرُب مِن الغرْب.
dusk, twilight	*ɣásaq* *šáfaq*	غسق شفق

compass	*bōṣala*	بوْصلة
map	*xarīṭa*	خريطة
north	*šamāl*	شمال
south	*janūb*	جنوب
west	*ɣarb*	غرْب
east	*šarq*	شرْق
northwest	*šamāl ɣarb*	شمال غرْب
southwest	*janūb ɣarb*	جنوب غرْب
northeast	*šamāl šarq*	شمال شرْق
southeast	*janūb šarq*	جنوب شرْق
Nablus is in the north of Palestine.	*nāblis b-šamāl falasṭīn.*	نابْلِس بْشمال فلسْطين.
Jordan is to the east of Palestine	*ilʔúrdun šarq falasṭīn.*	الأُرْدُن شرْق فلسْطين.
northern	*šamāli*	شمالي
southern	*janūbi*	جنوبي
western	*ɣárbi*	غرْبي
eastern	*šárqi*	شرْقي
the north pole	*ilqúṭb iššamāli*	القُطْب الشَّمالي
the south pole	*ilqúṭb ijjanūbi*	القُطْب الجَّنوبي

weather	*jaww* *ṭaqs*	جَوّ **طَقْس**
What's the weather like today?	*kēf ijjáww ilyōm?*	كيْف الجَوّ اليوْم؟
The weather is __.	*ijjáww __.*	الجَوّ.__
good, nice, fair	*ḥílu*	**حِلو**
bad, miserable	*sáyyiʔ*	**سيِّئ**
What a nice day!	*šū ha-lyōm ilḥílu!*	شو هاليوْم الحِلو!
temperature	*dárajit ḥarāra*	**درجةْ حرارة**
What's the temperature?	*gaddēš dárajit ilḥarāra?*	قدّيْش درجةِ الحرارة؟

Keep in mind that Arabs use Celsius, and not Fahrenheit.

(It's) 25 degrees.	*xámsa w 3išrīn.*	خمْسة وعِشْرين.
It's in the low twenties.	*dárajit ilḥarāra fi ʔáwwal il3išrīn.*	درجةِ الحرارة في أوّل العِشْرين.
in the mid-twenties	*b-nuṣṣ il3išrīn*	**بْنُصّ العِشْرين**
in the high twenties	*b-ʔāxir il3išrīn*	**بْآخِر العِشْرين**
It's around 30 degrees.	*tagrīban talātīn.*	تقْريباً تلاتين.
It's over 30 degrees.	*áktar min talātīn.*	أكْتر مِن تلاتين.
It's below zero. It's below freezing.	*dárajit ilḥarāra taḥt iṣṣífir.*	درجةِ الحرارة تحْت الصِّفِر.
the maximum temperature, the high	*dárajit ilḥarāra -lqúṣwa*	**درجةِ الحرارة القُصْوى**
the minimum temperature, the low	*dárajit ilḥarāra -ddúnya*	**درجةِ الحرارة الدُّنْيا**

الجَوّ *ijjáww* or الدُّنْيا *iddínya* serve as subjects when talking about the weather, where in English the subject would be "it," as in "It's hot," "It's sunny." The predicate can be a true adjective, or a noun used adjectivally. Keep in mind that nouns, unlike true adjectives, are invariable and do not have a feminine form.

It's __.	*ijjáww __.* *iddínya __.*	الجَوّ ___. الدِّنْيا ___.
heat	*šōb* *ḥarr*	شوْب حَرّ
It's very hot.	*ktīr šōb.*	كْتير شوْب.
warm	*dāfi*	دافي
coolness, coldness	*ság3a* *bard*	سقْعة برْد
It's really cold.	*ság3a ktīr* *bard ktīr*	سقْعة كْتير برْد كْتير
It's freezing outside.	*ijjáww tálij bárra.*	الجَوّ تلج برّا.
heat wave	*mōjit šōb* *mōjit ḥarr*	موْجِةْ شوْب موْجِةْ حَرّ
How hot does it get where you're from?	*gaddēš fī šōb b-báladku?*	قدّيْش في شوْب بْبلدْكو؟
Where I'm from, it doesn't usually get over 30 degrees in the summer.	*fi báladna, ilḥarāra mā btítla3 fōg ittlātīn fi -ṣṣēf.*	في بلدْنا، الحرارة ما بْتِطْلع فوْق التّلاتين في الصيْف.
It's hotter than it was yesterday.	*ijjáww ášwab min imbāriḥ.*	الجَوّ أشْوَب مِن إمْبارِح.
I don't like hot weather.	*baḥíbbíš iššōb.*	بحِبِّش الشّوْب.
sky	*sáma [f.] (samawāt)*	سما (سمَوات)
The sky is clear.	*issámaṣāfya.* *ijjáww ṣāfi.*	السّما صافْيَة. الجَوّ صافي.
It's sunny.	*ijjáww múšmis.*	الجَوّ مُشْمِس.
sun	*šámis (šmūs)*	شمِس (شْموس)
The sun has come out.	*ṭíl3at iššámis*	طِلْعت الشّمِس
The sun is shining.	*iššámis múšriqa.*	الشمِس مُشْرِقة.

darkness	*3ítma*	عِتْمة
It's dark.	*3áttamat iddínya.*	عتّمت الدِّنْيا
cloud	*ɣēma*	غِيْمة
It's cloudy. It's overcast.	*ijjáww mɣáyyim.*	الجوّ مْغيِّمِ.
rain	*šíta*	شِتا
It is raining. It's rainy.	*iddínya bitmáṭṭir.* *bitšátti.*	الدِّنْيا بِتْمطِّرِ. بِتْشتِّي.
It's started to rain.	*bádat tmáṭṭir.*	بدت تْمطِّرِ.
It's stopped raining.	*wággafat máṭar.*	وَقّفت مطر.
It is pouring.	*bitnággiṭ.*	بِتْنقِّط
rainbow	*qōs qúzaḥ (aqwās qúzaḥ)*	قوْس قُزح (أقْواس قُزح)
wind	*háwa* *rīḥ*	هَوا ريح
It's windy.	*háwa gáwi.* *rīḥ gáwi.*	هَوا قَوي. ريح قَوي.
to blow	*habb, yhibb*	هبَّ، يْهبَّ
snow	*tálij*	تلج
It's snowing.	*iddínya bittálij.*	الدِّنْيا بِتّلِّج.
Does it snow where you're from?	*bittálij 3índku?*	بِتّلِّج عِنْدْكو؟
Where I'm from, it snows a lot in the winter.	*bittálij 3ínna ktīr fi -ššíta.*	بِتّلِّج عِنّا كْتير في الشِّتا.
hail	*bárad*	برد
It's hailing.	*bitmáṭṭir bárad.*	بِتْمطِّر برد.
fog	*ḍabāb*	ضْباب

It's foggy.	iddínya ḍabāb. ijjáww ḍabāb.	الدِنْيا ضباب. الجّوّ ضباب.
storm	3āṣifa (3awāṣif)	عاصِفة (عواصِف)
There's a windstorm. It's stormy.	ijjáww 3awāṣif.	الجّوّ عَواصِف.
There's a rainstorm.	fī 3āṣifit máṭar.	في عاصِفةْ مطر.
sandstorm, dust storm	3āṣifa turābíyya	عاصِفة تُرابية
hurricane, typhoon, cyclone	i3ṣār (a3āṣīr)	إِعْصار (أعاصير)
tornado	i3ṣār qám3i	إعْصار قمْعي
dust devil	zōba3a (zawābi3)	زوْبعة (زَوابِع)
the eye of the storm	márkaz ilʔi3ṣār	مرْكز الاعْصار
lightning	bárig	برْق
There was a flash of lightning.	kān fī bárig.	كان في برِق.
Lightning struck the tree.	ilbárig ḍárab iššájara.	البرِق ضرب الشّجرة.
thunder	rá3id	رعِد
The thunder woke me up last night.	ṣōt irrá3id ṣaḥḥāni -mbāriḥ fi -llēl.	صوْت الرّعِد صحّاني إمْبارِح في اللّيْل.
weather forecast	innášra -jjawwíyya	النّشْرة الجّوّية
What's the forecast for tomorrow?	šū tawaqqu3āt ijjáww búkra?	شو تَوَقُّعات الجّوّ بُكْرا؟
Do you think it's going to rain?	bālak ḥatmáṭṭir?	بالك حتْمطِّر؟
It looks like (it's going to) rain.	šákilha ḥatmáṭṭir.	شكِلْها حتْمطِّر.
We're expecting a storm.	bnistánna 3āṣifa.	بْنِسْتنّى العاصِفة.
climate	munāx	مُناخ

arid, dry	*jāff* *nāšif*	جافّ ناشِف
humid	*ráṭib*	رطِب
tropical	*istiwāʔi*	اِسْتِوائي
The weather is quite changeable.	*ijjáww byitgállab.*	الجّوّ بِتْقلّب.
drought	*jafāf*	جفاف
flood	*fayaḍān*	فَيَضان

<table>
<tr><td>43</td><td colspan="2"># Animals</td></tr>
</table>

animal	ḥayawān	حَيَوان
pet	ḥayawān alīf	حَيَوان أليف
Do you have any pets?	3índak ḥayawānāt alīfa?	عِنْدك حَيَوانات أليفة؟
dog	kalb (klāb)	كَلْب (كْلاب)
cat	bíssa (bísas)	بِسَّة (بِسس)
I like cats, but I don't like dogs so much.	ána baḥíbb ilbísas bass baḥíbbiš liklāb ktīr.	أنا بحِبّ البسس بسّ بحِبِّش الكْلاب كْتير.
cage	gáfaṣ (gfāṣ)	قفص (قْفاص)
leash	silsílit kalb (salāsil kalb)	سِلْسِلِةْ كَلْب (سلاسِل كَلْب)
dog collar	ṭōg (ṭwāg)	طوْق (طْواق)
to train	dárrab, ydárrib	درّب، يْدرّب
(pet) food, feed	3álaf ákil ḥayawānāt	علف أكِل حَيَوانات

Both masculine and feminine noun forms exist for most animals. These are, of course, used when referring to animals of a specific gender. Otherwise, it is usually the masculine form that is used to refer to an animal. However, certain animals are more commonly referred to by their feminine forms. The more common form is listed below.

bear	dubb (díbaba)	دُبّ (دِببة)
beaver	qúndus (qanādis)	قُنْدُس (قنادِس)
buffalo	jāmūsa (jawāmīs)	جاموسة (جَواميس)
deer, gazelle	ɣazāla (ɣizlān)	غزالة (غِزْلان)
elephant	fīl (fíyala)	فيل (فيّلة)
fox	tá3lab (ta3ālib)	تعْلب (تعالِب)
giraffe	zarāfa	زرافة

hippopotamus	*fáras náhir (afrās náhir)*	فرس نهِر (أفْراس نهِر)
kangaroo	*kánɣar*	كنْغر
koala	*kwālā*	كْوالا
leopard, panther, cheetah	*fáhid (fhūd)*	فهِد (فْهود)
lion	*ásad (ʔsūd)*	أسَد (أُسود)
mouse; rat	*fār (fīrān)*	فار (فيران)
polar bear	*dubb qúṭbi*	دُبّ قُطبي
rabbit	*árnab (arānib)*	أرْنب (أرانِب)
rhinoceros	*waḥīd ilqárn*	وَحيد القرْن
skunk	*ẓurbān*	ظُرْبان
squirrel	*sinjāb (sanājīb)*	سِنْجاب (سناجِب)
tiger	*nímir (nmūra)*	نمِر (نمْورة)
wolf	*ðíʔib (ðiʔāb)*	ذِئِب (ذِئاب)

seal	*fúqma*	فُقْمة
sealion	*ásad ilbáḥar (ʔusūd ilbáḥar)*	أسَد البحر (أُسود البحر)
dolphin	*dulfīn (dalāfīn)*	دُلْفين (دلافين)
whale	*ḥūt (ḥītān)*	حوت (حيتان)

bird	*ṭēr (ṭyūr)*	طيْر (طْيور)
canary	*kinār*	كِنار
crow, raven	*ɣurāb*	غُراب
dove, pigeon	*ḥamāma*	حمامة
eagle, condor, vulture	*nísir*	نِسِر
hawk, falcon	*ṣágir (ṣgūr)*	صقِر (صْقور)
ostrich	*naʒāma*	نعامة
parrot	*babbaɣāʔ*	ببّغاء

peacock	*ṭāwūs (ṭawāwīs)*	طاووس (طَواويس)
penguin	*baṭrīq (baṭāriq)*	بطْريق (بطاريق)
seagull	*náwras (nawāris)*	نَوْرس (نَوارِس)
small bird (sparrow, finch, etc.)	*3aṣfūr (3ṣāfīr)*	عصْفور (عصافير)
stork	*láqlaq (laqāliq)*	لقْلق (لقالِق)
swallow	*sanáwnaw*	سنَوْنَو
swan	*báj3a*	بجْعة

reptiles	*zawāḥif* [pl.]	زواحِف
cobra	*kōbra*	كوْبْرا
crocodile	*timsāḥ (tamāsīḥ)*	تمِساح (تماسيح)
lizard	*siḥlíyya (saḥālī)*	سِحْلية (سحالي)
snake	*ḥáyya (ḥayāya)*	حيّة (حَيايا)
turtle, tortoise	*sulḥufā (salāḥif)*	سُلْحُفاة (سلاحِف)

frog	*ḍúfḍa3 (ḍafāḍi3)*	ضُفْدع (ضفادع)

fish	*sámak*	سمك
shark	*girš*	قِرْش
jellyfish	*gandīl*	قنْديل

insect, bug	*ḥášara*	حشرة
ants	*námil*	نمِل
bees	*náḥil*	نحِل
A bee stung me.	*garṣátni náḥla.*	قرْصتْني نحْلة.
bee-sting	*gárṣit náḥla*	قرْصِة نحْلة
beehive	*xálíyyit náḥil*	خلية نحِل

beetle	xúnfusa (xanāfis)	خُنْفُسة (خنافِس)
butterfly	farāša	فراشة
cockroach; cricket	ṣarṣūr (ṣarāṣīr)	صرْصور (صراصير)
flea	barɣūt (barāɣīt)	برْغوت (براغيت)
flies	dubbān dibbān	دُبّان دِبّان
grasshoppers, locusts	jarād	جراد
lice	gámil	قمِل
The child has head lice.	ilwálad mgámmal.	الوَلد مْقمِّل.
mosquito	ba3ūḍa	بعوضة
mosquito bite	gárṣit ba3ūḍa	قرْصِةْ بعوضة
A mosquito bit me.	garṣátni ba3ūḍa.	قرْصتْني بعوضة.
moth	farāša	فراشة
scorpion	3ágrab (3agārib)	عقْرب (عقارِب)
snail	ḥalazōn	حلزوْن
spider	3ankabūt (3anākib)	عنْكبوت (عناكِب)
spider web	šábakit 3ankabūt	شبكِةْ عنْكبوت
I'm afraid of spiders.	ána baxāf min il3anākib.	أنا بخاف مِن العناكِب.
wasp	dabbūr (dabābīr)	دبّور (دبابير)
worm	dūd	دود
beak, bill	mungār (manāgīr)	مُنْقار (مناقير)
claw, talon	máxlab (maxālib)	مخْلب (مخالِب)
feathers	rīš	ريش
fur	fáro	فُرْوْ
horn, antler	gárin (grūn)	قرِن (قْرون)

feeler, antenna	*garn istiš3ār* *garn ilḥášara*	قَرْن اِسْتِشْعار قَرْن الحشرة
paw, leg	*ríjil (rijlēn)*	رِجِل (رِجْلين)
tail	*dēl (dyūl)* *dánab (dnāb)*	دَيْل (دْيول) دنب (دْناب)
udder, teats	*ḍrū3*	ضْروع
wing	*janāḥ (ájniḥa)*	جناح (أُجْنِحة)

Plant Life

plant	zár3a	زَرْعة
tree	šájara	شجرة
bush, shrub	šujēra	شُجَيْرة
leaf	wárag (wrāg)	وَرق (وْراق)
branch	fíri3 (áfru3)	فِرِع (أَفْرُع)
trunk	jídir (jdūr) jídi3 (jdū3)	جِدِر (جْدور) جِدع (جْدوع)
bark	liħāʔ	لِحاء
bamboo	xēzarān	خَيْزران
palm tree	náxla (náxil, naxīl)	نخْلة (نخِل، نخيل)
oak tree	šájarit ilbalūṭ šájarit issindyān	شجرِةِ البلّوط شجرِةِ السِّنْدْيان
pine tree	šájarit liṣnōbar	شجرِةِ الصّنوْبر
royal poinciana tree	šájarit ilbōnsyāna	شجرِةِ البوْنْسْيانا
sycamore tree	šájarit ijjummēz	شجرِةِ الجُمَّيْز
willow tree	šájarit iṣṣufṣāf	شجرِةِ الصُّفْصاف
flower	wárda (wrūd)	وَرْدة (وْرود)
petal	šátla	شتْلة
stem, stalk	sāq	ساق
carnation	grúnful	قُرْنْفُل
daisy, mum, chrysanthemum	uqħuwān	أُقْحُوان
poppy	šaqāʔiq innu3mān xušxāš	شقائِقِ النُّعْمان خُشْخاش

rose	záhra (zhūr)	زهْرة (زُهور)
sunflower	3abbād iššámis dawwār iššámis	عبّاد الشمْس دوّار الشّمْس
tulip	xuzāma	خُزامى
violet	záharit ilbanáfsaj	زهرةْ البنفْسج
cactus	ṣabbār	صبّار
moss	ṭúḥlub (ṭaḥālib)	طُحْلُب (طحالِب)
vine	kárma	كرْمة
seed	bízra (bízir)	بِذْرة (بِذِر)
to plant (a seed), grow (a plant)	zára3 [7]	زرع
(a plant) to grow	kíbir [1]	كِبِر
This plant is really growing fast!	hādi -zzár3a gā3da btíkbar b-súr3a!	هادي الزّرْعة قاعْدة بْتِكْبر بْسُرْعة!
to water (a plant)	sága, yísgi	سقى، يِسْقي
to fertilize	zábbal, yzábbil ḥaṭṭ [55] zíbil	زبّل، يْزبِّل حطّ زِبِل
to weed (a garden)	3áššab, y3áššib	عشّب، يْعشِّب
plant pot	ḥōḍ	حوْض

color	lōn (alwān)	لوْن (ألْوان)

The cardinal colors below each have three forms listed as masculine and feminine separated by a comma and followed by the plural in parentheses. The feminine form is listed because it is not simply formed by adding ة -a as is done with most other adjectives.

black	áswad, sōda (sūd)	أسْوَد، سوْدا (سود)
white	ábyaḍ, bēḍa (bīḍ)	أبْيض، بيْضا (بيض)
blue	ázrag, zárga (zúrug)	أزْرق، زرْقا (زُرْق)
green	áxḍar, xáḍra (xúḍur)	أخْضر، خضْرا (خُضُر)
red	áḥmar, ḥámra (ḥúmur)	أحْمر، حمْرا (حُمُر)
yellow	áṣfar, ṣáfra (ṣúfur)	أصْفر، صفْرا (صُفُر)

Colors ending in ي -i and those borrowed from other languages are invariable (i.e. they do not have feminine or plural forms).

beige	bēj [invar.]	بيْج
brown	bínni	بِنِّي
fushia	fūši [m.], fūšya [f.]	فوشي، فوشْيا
gray	ramādi sákani	رمادي سكني
lemon-yellow	(áṣfar) lamūni	(أصْفر) لموني
navy blue	kúḥli	كُحْلي
olive	zēti	زيْتي
orange	ōrānj burtaqāli	أوْرانْج بُرْتْقاني
pink	záhri záhir [invar.]	زهْري زهِر

purple, violet	*banáfsaji* *mūv* [invar.]	بنفْسجي موف
turquoise	*tirkwāz*	تِركْواز
shade	*dáraja*	درجة
light	*fātiħ*	فاتح
light green	*áxḍar fātiħ*	أخْضر فاتح
dark	*ɣāmig*	غامِق
dark red	*áħmar ɣāmig*	أحْمر غامِق
colorful, multi-colored	*mláwwan*	مْلوّن

Shapes, Sizes, and Measurements

shape	šákil (aškāl)	شكِل (أشْكال)
circle	dāʔira (dawāʔir)	دائِرة (دوائِر)
circular	dāʔiri	دائِري
oval	bayḍāwi	بَيْضاوي
square; square(-shaped)	murábba3 mrábba3	مُربَّع مْربَّع

Notice that the word above is a passive participle with the prefix مـ, which may be pronounced with a sukuun (ْ) or damma (ُ). This is true for many such words, depending on personal preference, level of formality, and enunciation.

| rectangle; rectangular | mustaṭīl | مُسْتطيل |
| triangle; triangular | mutállat | مُتلَّت |

big, large	kbīr (kbār)	كْبير (كْبار)
small, little	ṣɣīr (ṣɣār)	صْغير (صْغار)
length; (person) height	ṭul	طول
long; (person) tall	ṭawīl (ṭwāl)	طَويل (طْوال)
short	gaṣīr (gṣār)	قصير (قْصار)
width	3arḍ	عرْض

measurement	gyās	قْياس
to measure	gās, yḡīs	قاس، يْقيس
size, volume	ḥájim (aḥjām)	حجِم (أحْجام)
surface area	masāḥa	مساحة
distance	masāfa	مسافة

millimeter	*millīmítir*	مِلّيمِتِر
centimeter	*sāntimitir*	سانْتيمِتِر
meter	*mítir (amtār)*	مِتِر(أمْتار)
kilometer	*kēlōmitir*	كيْلوْمِتِر
inch	*inš* *būṣa*	إنْش بوصة
foot	*qádam (aqdām)*	قدم (أقْدام)
mile	*mīl (amyāl)*	ميل (أمْيال)
square meter	*mítir murábba3*	مِتِر مُربّع
cubic meter	*mítir muká33ab*	مِتِر مُكعّب
weight	*wázin (awzān)*	وَزِن (أوْزان)
to weigh	*wázzan, ywázzin*	وَزّن، يْوَزِّن
gram	*grām*	غْرام
kilogram	*kēlōgrām* *kēlō*	كيْلوغْرام كيْلو
ton (metric)	*ṭunn (aṭnān)*	طُنّ (أطْنان)
ounce	*ōnṣa*	أوْنصة
pound	*pāwnd*	باوْنْد

every; all	*kull*	كُلّ
every child	*kull wálad*	كُلّ وَلَد
all of the children	*kull liwlād*	كُلّ الِوْلاد
most (of)	*áɣlab* *mú3ẓam*	أَغْلَب مُعْظم
most people	*áɣlab innās*	أَغْلَب النّاس
some	*ba3ḍ*	بَعْض
some people	*ba3ḍ innās*	بَعْض النّاس
no, none of	*wála wāḥad min*	وَلا واحد مِن
no students, none of the students	*wála wāḥad min iṭṭullāb*	وَلا واحد مِن الطُّلّاب
a lot of	*__ ktīr*	ـكْتير
a lot of money	*maṣāri ktīr*	مصاري كْتير
a lot of people	*nās ktīr*	ناس كْتير
a little __ a few __	*__ galīl* *šwáyyit __*	ـقليل شْوَيّة ـ
a little time	*wágit galīl*	وَقِت قليل
a little money	*šwáyyit maṣāri*	شْوَيّة مصاري
a few people	*šwáyyit nās*	شْوَيّة ناس
a couple of __	*jōz __* *-ēn*	جوْز ـ ـيْن

The dual suffix ـيْن *-ēn* expresses the idea of 'two.' See page 199.

a couple of months	*šahrēn* [dual]	شهْرَيْن

| several | *káza*
áktar min | كذا
أكْتر مِن |

Both words above are followed by a singular indefinite noun, as seen in the example below.

| several kinds | *káza nū3*
áktar min nū3 | كذا نوع
أكْتر مِن نوع |

number, numeral	*ráqam (arqām)*	رقم (أرْقام)
number (quantity)	*3ádad (a3dād)*	عدد (أعْداد)
to count	*3add, y3idd*	عدّ، يْعِدّ
odd	*fárdi* *múfrad*	فرْدي مُفْرد
even	*záwji*	زَوْجي
zero	*ṣífir*	صِفِر
cardinal number	*3ádad áṣli*	عدد أصْلي
one	__ *wāḥad* [m.], __ *wáḥda* [f.]	__واحد، __ واحْدة

واحد *wāḥad* and واحْدة *wáḥda* follow the noun they modify and agree with it in gender.

two	*tnēn*	تْنيْن

تْنيْن *tnēn* is generally not needed to modify a noun. Instead, the suffix يْن- *-ēn* is used, as in the example below.

two tables and two chairs	*ṭāwiltēn w kursiyyēn*	طاوِلْتيْن وكُرْسِييّيْن

The numbers 3-10 have two forms. The full form, ending in ة- *-a*, is used when not followed by a noun, most notably when counting: واحَد *wāḥad*, تْنيْن *tnēn*, ثلاثة *tlāta*, أرْبعة *árba3a* 'one, two, three, four…'. The shortened form, shown in parentheses, precedes the plural noun it modifies: سبع كُتُب *sába3 kútub* 'seven books.'

three	*talāta (tál(a)t __)*	ثلاثة (تلات__)
four	*árba3a (árba3 __)*	أرْبعة (أرْبع__)
five	*xámsa (xám(a)s __)*	خمْسة (خمس__)
six	*sítta (sitt __)*	سِتّة (سِتّ__)
seven	*sáb3a (sába3 __)*	سبْعة (سبع__)
eight	*tamānya (táman __)*	ثمانْية (تمن__)
nine	*tís3a (tísa3 __)*	تِسْعة (تِسع__)

| ten | 3ášara (3áš(a)r ___) | (___عشر) عشرة |

> Only the numbers 3-10 are followed by a plural noun in Arabic. The numbers 11+ are followed by a singular noun: ḥdā3iš ktāb حْداعِش كْتاب 'eleven books.'

eleven	ḥdā3iš	حْداعِش
twelve	tnā3iš	تْناعِش
thirteen	tlattā3iš	تْلتّاعِش
fourteen	arba3tā3iš	أرْبعْتاعِش
fifteen	xamstā3iš	خمسْتاعِش
sixteen	sittā3iš	سِتّاعِش
seventeen	saba3tā3iš	سبعْتاعِش
eighteen	tamantā3iš	تمانْتاعِش
nineteen	tisa3tā3iš	تِسعْتاعِش

> Compound numbers with 20, 30, etc., are literally phrased 'one and twenty,' 'two and twenty,' etc.

twenty	3išrīn	عِشْرين
twenty-one	wāḥad w 3išrīn	واحد وعِشْرين
twenty-two	tnēn w 3išrīn	تْنيْن وعِشْرين

> In compound numbers, the numbers 3-9 appear in their full forms.

twenty-three	talāta w 3išrīn	تلاتة وعِشْرين
thirty	talātīn	تلاتين
forty	arb3īn	أرْبعين
fifty	xamsīn	خمْسين
sixty	sittīn	سِتّين
seventy	sab3īn	سبْعين
eighty	tamānīn	تمانين
ninety	tis3īn	تِسْعين
one hundred	míyya	مية
two hundred	mītēn [dual]	ميتيْن

three hundred	talatmíyya	تلتْمية
four hundred	arba3míyya	أرْبعْمية
five hundred	xamasmíyya	خمسْمية
six hundred	sittmíyya	سِتْمية
seven hundred	saba3míyya	سبعْمية
eight hundred	tamanmíyya	تمنْمية
nine hundred	tisa3míyya	تِسعْمية
one thousand	alf	ألْف
two thousand	alfēn [dual]	ألْفيْن
three thousand	talattalāf	تلاتّلاف
four thousand	arba3talāf	أرْبعْتلاف
five thousand	xamastalāf	خمسْتلاف
six thousand	sittalāf	سِتّلاف
seven thousand	saba3talāf	سبعْتلاف
eight thousand	tamantalāf	تمنْتلاف
nine thousand	tisa3talāf	تِسعْتلاف
ten thousand	3ašartalāf	عشرْتلاف
eleven thousand	ḥdā3šir alf	حْداعْشر ألْف
twenty thousand	3išrīn alf	عِشْرين ألْف
one hundred thousand	mīt alf	مية ألْف
million	malyōn	ملْيوْن
billion	milyār balyōn	ملْيار بلْيوْن
arithmetic, calculation	ḥsāb	حْساب
to calculate, to work out	ḥásab, yíḥsib	حسِب، يِحْسِب
calculator	āla ḥāsba	آلة حاسْبة

How did you work that out in your head? I need a calculator!	*kēf ḥasábit hāda b-3áglak? ána bíddi āla ḥāsba.*	كَيْف حسبِت هادا بْعقْلك؟ أنا بِدّي آلة حاسْبة.
to add, add up	*jáma3, yíjma3*	**جمع، يِجْمع**
Add up the price of all the items to get the total.	*ijma3 ḥagg kull liɣrāḍ, biṭlá3lak ilmajmū3.*	اِجْمع حقّ كُلّ الغْراض، بِطْلعْلك المجْموع.
to subtract	* nággaṣ, ynággiṣ* *ṭáraḥ, yíṭraḥ*	**نقّص، يْنقّص** **طرح، يِطْرح**
Subtract the smaller amount from the larger to find the difference.	*nággiṣ irráqam liṣɣīr min likbīr 3ašān tí3rif ilfárg.*	نقّص الرّقم الصْغير مِن الكِبير عشان تِعْرِف الفرْق.
to multiply by	*ḍárab, yúḍrub*	**ضرب، يُضْرُب**
Multiply the length and width to find the area of the rectangle.	*úḍrub iṭṭūl fi -l3arḍ 3ašān tíḥsib masāḥit ilmustaṭīl.*	أُضْرُب الطّول في العرْض عشان تِحْسِب مساحِةْ المُسْتطيل.
to divide by	*gássam 3ála, ygássim 3ála*	**قسّم على، يْقسّم على**
Divide the total by the number of people to find the average.	*gássim ilmajmū3 3ála 3ádad innās 3ašān tí3rif ilmu3áddal.*	قسّم المجْموع على عدد النّاس عشان تِعْرِف المُعدّل.
to equal, be equal to	*sāwa, ysāwi*	**ساوى، يْساوي**
equals, is	*bisāwi* *byusāwi* *bíṭla3*	**بيساوي** **يُساوي** **بيطْلع**
plus, and	*zāʔid*	**زائِد**
Three plus two equals five.	*talāta zāʔid tnēn bisāwi xámsa.*	تلاتة زائِد تْنيْن بيساوي خمْسة.
minus	*nāgiṣ*	**ناقِص**
Ten minus nine equals one.	*3ášara nāgiṣ tís3a bíṭla3 wāḥad.*	عشرة ناقِص تِسْعة بيطْلع واحد.
times	*ḍarb*	**ضرْب**

Three times four equals twelve.	talāta ḍarb árba3a bisāwi tnā3iš.	تلاتة ضرْب أرْبعة بيساوي تْناعِش.
divided by	taqsīm	تقْسيم
Twenty divided by four equals five.	3išrīn taqsīm árba3a bisāwi xámsa.	عِشْرين تقْسيم أرْبعة بيساوي خمْسة.

ordinal number	3ádad tartībi	عدد ترْتيبي
first	áwwal [m.], ūla [f.]	أوّل، أُولى
second	tāni [m.], tānya [f.]	تاني، تانْية
third	tālit [m.], tālta [f.]	تالِت، تالْتة
fourth	rābi3 [m.], rāb3a [f.]	رابِع، رابْعة
fifth	xāmis [m.], xāmsa [f.]	خامِس، خامْسة
sixth	sādis [m.], sādsa [f.]	سادِس، سادْسة
seventh	sābi3 [m.], sāb3a [f.]	سابِع، سابْعة
eighth	tāmin [m.], tāmna [f.]	تامِن، تامْنة
ninth	tāsi3 [m.], tās3a [f.]	تاسِع، تاسْعة
tenth	3āšir [m.], 3āšra [f.]	عاشِر، عاشْرة

There are no unique ordinal forms for numbers over 10. The cardinal number is used. An ordinal number can be distinguished from a cardinal number because it follows the noun it modifies and usually takes the defininte article. Compare the following:

There are twenty books, and the twentieth book is mine.	fī 3išrīn ktāb w liktāb il3išrīn íli.	في عِشْرين كْتاب والكِتاب العِشْرين إلي.
the last __	āxir __	آخِر __

fraction	júzuʔ (ajzāʔ)	جُزْء (أجْزاء)
whole	kull	كُلّ
half	nuṣṣ (nṣāṣ)	نُصّ (نْصاص)

Two halves make a whole.	*innuṣṣēn bí3malu júzu? kāmil.*	النُّصيْن بيعْملوا جُزْء كامِل.
a third	*tult*	تُلْت
a fourth, a quarter	*rúbi3*	رُبِع
a fifth	*xums*	خُمْس
three fifths	*talt xmās*	تلْت خُماس

Fractions above 10 are formed with ordinal numbers separated by على *3ála* (or the shortened form عَ *3a*).

one twelfth (1/12)	*wāḥad 3a tnā3iš.*	واحد عَ تْناعِش.
three twentieths (3/20)	*talāta 3ála 3išrīn*	تلاتة على عِشْرين
percentage, portion	*nísba (nísab)*	نِسْبة (نِسب)
percent	*fi -lmíyya*	في المية
what percent(age) of	*gaddēš fi -lmíyya*	قدّيْش في المية
fifty percent of people	*xamsīn fi -lmíyya min innās*	خمْسين في المية مِن النّاس

49   Time

time	*wágit (awgāt)*	وَقِت (أوْقات)
day	*yōm (ayyām)*	يوْم (أيّام)
in the morning	*iṣṣúbiħ*	الصُّبِح
at noon	*iḍḍúhur*	الضُّهُر
in the afternoon	*ba3d iḍḍúhur* *il3áṣir*	بعْد الضُّهُر العصِر
in the evening	*ilmása*	المسا
at night	*fi -llēl*	في اللّيْل
at midnight	*b-nuṣṣ illēl*	بْنُصّ اللّيْل
three days ago	*min tálatt iyyām*	مِن تلاتّ إيّام
the day before yesterday	*áwwal imbāriħ*	أوّل إمْبارِح
yesterday	*imbāriħ*	إمْبارِح
yesterday morning	*imbāriħ iṣṣúbiħ*	إمْبارِح الصُّبِح
yesterday evening	*imbāriħ ilmása*	إمْبارِح المسا
last night	*imbāriħ fi- llēl*	إمْبارِح في اللّيْل
today	*ilyōm*	اليوْم
this morning	*ilyōm iṣṣúbiħ*	اليوْم الصُّبِح
this afternoon	*ilyōm ba3d iḍḍúhur* *ilyōm il3áṣir*	اليوْم بعْد الضُّهُر اليوْم العصِر
this evening	*ilyōm ilmása* *ilmása*	اليوْم المسا المسا
tonight	*illēla* *lyōm fi-llēl*	اللّيْلة اليوْم في اللّيْل

tomorrow	*búkra*	بُكْرا
tomorrow morning	*búkra -ṣṣúbiḥ*	بُكْرا الصُّبِح
tomorrow evening	*búkra -lmása*	بُكْرا المسا
tomorrow night	*búkra fi -llēl*	بُكْرا في اللّيْل
the day after tomorrow	*bá3id búkra*	بعِد بُكْرا
in three days	*kamān tálatt iyyām*	كمان تلاتّ إيّام
every day	*kull yōm*	كُلّ يوْم
every other day	*yōm bá3id yōm* *yōm āh yōm la?*	يوْم بعِد يوْم يوْم آه يوْم لا
all day	*ṭūl linhār*	طول النِّهار
week	*isbū3 (asabī3)*	إسْبوع (أسابيع)
weekday, work day	*yōm dawām*	يوْم دَوام
(on) the weekend	*āxir lisbū3*	آخِر الإسْبوع
Sunday	*ilʔáḥad*	الأَحَد
Monday	*litnēn*	الاِتْنيْن
Tuesday	*ittalāt*	التّلات
Wednesday	*ilʔárbi3a* *ilʔába3*	الأرْبِعا الأرْبِع
Thursday	*ilxamīs*	الخميس
Friday	*ijjúm3a*	الجُمْعة
Saturday	*issábit*	السّبِت
See you on Saturday!	*bašūfak yōm issábit!*	بشوفك يوْم السّبِت!
last week	*lisbū3 ílli fāt* *lisbū3 ilmāḍi*	الإسْبوع اللي فات الإسْبوع الماضي

this week	*lisbū3 hād*	الإسْبوع هاد
next week	*lisbū3 ijjāy*	الإسْبوع الجّاي
I'll tell you next week or the week after.	*bagúllak lisbū3 ijjāy aw ílli bá3du.*	بقُلّك الإسْبوع الجّاي أوْ اللي بعْدو.
month	*šáhir (ášhur)*	شهِر (أشْهُر)

Although months have proper names, Palestinians tend to refer to months by number.

January	*šáhir wāħad* [lit. month one] *kānūn ittāni*	شهِر واحد كانون التّاني
February	*šáhir tnēn* [lit. month two] *šbāṭ*	شهِر تْنيْن شْباط
March	*šáhir talāta* *āđār*	شهِر تلاتة آذار
April	*šáhir árba3a* *nīsān*	شهِر أرْبعة نيسان
May	*šáhir xámsa* *ayyār*	شهِر خمْسة أيّار
June	*šáhir sítta* *ħuzāyrān*	شهِر سِتّة حُزيْران
July	*šáhir sáb3a* *tammūz*	شهِر سبْعة تمّوز
August	*šáhir tamánya* *āb*	شهِر تمنْية آب
September	*šáhir tís3a* *aylūl*	شهِر تِسْعة أيْلول
October	*šáhir 3ášara* *tišrīn ilʔáwwal*	شهِر عشرة تِشْرين الأوّل

November	*šáhir ḥdā3iš* *tišrīn ittāni*	شهِر حْداعِش تِشْرين التّاني
December	*šáhir tnā3iš* *kānūn ilʔáwwal*	شهِر تْناعِش كانون الأوّل
I was born in December.	*ána -nwaládit fi šáhir tnā3iš.*	أنا انْوَلدِت في شهِر تْناعِش.
calendar	*taqwīm* *ruznāma*	تقْويم رُزْنامة
last month	*iššáhir ílli fāt* *iššáhir ilmāḍi*	الشّهِر اللي فات الشّهْر الماضي
this month	*iššáhir hād*	الشّهِر هاد
next month	*iššáhr ijjāy*	الشّهْر الجّاي
season	*fáṣil*	فصِل (فُصول)
spring	*irrabī3*	الرّبيع
summer	*iṣṣēf*	الصّيْف
fall, autumn	*ilxarīf*	الخريف
winter	*iššíta*	الشِّتا
I like to go to Jericho in the winter.	*baḥíbb arūḥ 3ála ʔarīḥa fi -ššíta.*	بحِبّ أروح على أريحا في الشِّتا.
holiday	*3īd (a3yād)*	عيد (أعْياد)
New Year's Eve	*lēlit rās issána*	ليْلِةْ راس السّنة
New Year's Day	*rās issána*	راس السّنة
Valentine's Day	*3īd ilḥúbb* *ilvālintāyn*	عيد الحُبّ الفالِنْتايْن
Halloween	*ilhālōwīn*	الهالوْوين
Thanksgiving	*3īd iššúkur*	عيد الشّكُر

Mother's Day (March 21)	3īd il?úmm	عيد الأُمّ
Children's Day (March 22)	3īd iṭṭúfil	عيد الطِّفِل
Labor Day (May 1)	3īd il3ummāl	عيد العُمّال
Nakba Day (May 15)	đíkra -nnákba	ذِكْرى النَّكْبة
Independence Day (November 15)	3īd il?istiqlāl	عيد الإِسْتِقْلال

Muslim holidays follow the Islamic lunar calendar, and thus may fall at various times of the year.

Ramadan	ramaḍān	رمضان
Eid Al-Fitr, the Lesser Eid (3 days)	3īd ilfíṭir il3īd liṣγīr	عيد الفِطِر العيد الصِّغير
Eid Al-Adha, the Feast of the Sacrifice, the Greater Eid (4 days)	3īd il?áḍħa il3īd likbīr	عيد الأَضْحى العيد الكِبير
Mawlid (birth of the Prophet Mohammad)	đíkra -lmáwlid innábawi	ذِكْرى المَوْلِد النَّبَوي
Christmas	3īd ilmīlād ilmajīd likrīsmās	عيد الميلاد المجيد الكْريسْماس
Epiphany	ilγaṭās	الغطاس
Easter	3īd ilfíṣiħ	عيد الفِصِح
year	sána (snīn)	سنة (سْنين)
twenty years **ago**	gábil 3išrīn sána	قبِل عِشْرين سنة
last year	issána -lli fātat issána ilmāḍya	السّنة اللي فاتت السّنة الماضْية
this year	issána hādi	السّنة هادي
next year	issána -jjāya	السّنة الجّايَة

in five years	*kamān xams snīn*	كمان خمْس سْنين
period, era, age	*3áṣir (3ṣūr)*	عصِر (عْصور)
decade	*3áqid (3qūd)* *3ašr snīn*	عقِد (عْقود) عشْر سْنين
in the 1980s	*bi-ttamānīnāt*	بالتّمانينات
century	*qárin (qrūn)*	قرِن (قْرون)
in the 19th century; in the 1800s	*bi-lqárn ittisa3tā3iš*	بِالقرْن التِسعْتاعِش
millennium	*alfíyya*	ألْفية
in the present	*bi-lḥāḍir*	بِالحاضِر
(right) now; just (now)	*táwwi* *halgēt* *halḥīn* *hássa*	توّي هلْقيْت هلْحين هسّا
I just went to the bank.	*ána táwwi rúḥit 3a -lbank.*	أنا توّي رُحِت عَ البنْك.
Okay, I'll do it right now!	*māši, halgēt bá3malu!*	ماشي، هلْقيْت بعْملو!
in the past	*fi -lmāḍi* *fi -zzammānāt*	في الماضي في الزمّانات
a long time ago, in the past	*zamān* *min zamān*	زمان مِن زمان
in the future	*fi -lmustágbal*	في المُسْتقْبل
right now, right away	*táwwi* *3a ṭūl*	توّي عَ طول
soon, in a bit	*kamān šwáyya*	كمان شْوَيّة
I'll go to bed soon.	*ḥanām kamān šwáyya.*	حنام كمان شْوَيّة.
later	*ba3dēn*	بعديْن

one day, some day	*márra* *fi yōm min ilʔiyyām*	مرّة في يوْم مِن الإيّام
hour	*sā3a*	ساعة
minute	*dgīga (dagāyig)*	دْقيقة (دقايِق)
second	*sānya (sawāni)*	ثانْيَة (ثَواني)
What time is it?	*gaddēš issā3a?*	قدّيْش السّاعة؟
It's one o'clock. (1:00)	*issā3a wāḥda.*	السّاعة واحْدة.
It's two o'clock. (2:00)	*issā3a tintēn.*	السّاعة تِنْتيْن.
It's three o'clock. (3:00)	*issā3a talāta.*	السّاعة تلاتة.
It's **five past** three. (3:05)	*issā3a talāta w xámsa.*	السّاعة تلاتة وخمْسة.
It's **ten past** three. (3:10)	*issā3a talāta w 3ášara.*	السّاعة تلاتة وعشرة.
It's **a quarter past** three. (3:15)	*issā3a talāta w rúbi3.*	السّاعة تلاتة ورُبِع.
It's **twenty past** three. (3:20)	*issā3a talāta w tilt.*	السّاعة تلاتة وتِلْت.
It's **twenty-five past** three. (3:25)	*issā3a talāta w nuşş ílla xámsa.*	السّاعة تلاتة ونُصّ إلّا خمْسة.
It's three **thirty**. (3:30)	*issā3a talāta w nuşş.*	السّاعة تلاتة ونُصّ.
It's **twenty-five to** four. (3:35)	*issā3a talāta w nuşş w xámsa.*	السّاعة تلاتة ونُصّ وخمْسة.
It's **twenty to** four. (3:40)	*issā3a árba3a ílla tilt.*	السّاعة أرْبعة إلّا تِلْت.
It's **a quarter to** four. (3:45)	*issā3a árba3a ílla rúbi3.*	السّاعة أرْبعة إلّا رُبِع.
It's **ten to** four. (3:50)	*issā3a árba3a ílla 3ášara.*	السّاعة أرْبعة إلّا عشرة.
It's **five to** four. (3:55)	*issā3a árba3a ílla xámsa.*	السّاعة أرْبعة إلّا خمْسة.
It's **almost** four o'clock.	*issā3a tagrīban árba3a.*	السّاعة تقْريباً أرْبعة.

The following expressions are the Arabic equivalents of 'a.m.' and 'p.m.' The hours for which each expression is commonly used is listed. There is some overlap or difference of opinion, allowing more than one expression for certain times of the day.

in the morning (4-11 a.m.)	*iṣṣúbiḥ*	الصُّبح
9 a.m.	*issā3a tís3a -ṣṣúbiḥ*	السّاعة تِسْعة الصُّبح
in the afternoon (12-3 p.m.)	*iḍḍúhur*	الضُّهُر
3 p.m.	*issā3a talāta -ḍḍúhur*	الساعة تْلاتة الضُّهُر
in the afternoon (3-6 p.m.)	*-l3áṣir*	العصِر
in the evening (5-7 p.m.)	*-lmáɣrib*	المغْرِب
at night (7 p.m. - 3 a.m.)	*fi -llēl*	في اللّيل
in the morning (3-6 a.m.)	*ilfájir*	الفجِر
what time, when	*3a -lʔákam* *wagtēš* *ayy sā3a*	عَ الأكم وَقْتيْش أيّ ساعة
What time do you get up?	*3a -lʔákam btíṣḥa?*	عالأكم بْتِصْحى؟
at __ o'clock	*issā3a __* *3a -l __*	السّاعة __ عَ الــ __
around __ o'clock	*tagrīban 3a -l__* *ḥawāli -ssā3a __*	تقريباً عَ الــ __ حَوالي السّاعة__
I usually get up around seven.	*ána bi-l3āda báṣḥa tagrīban 3a- ssáb3a.*	أنا بِالعادة بصْحى تقريباً عَ السّبْعة.
at __ o'clock sharp	*issā3a __ bi-ẓẓábiṭ*	السّاعة __ بِالظّبِط
early	*bádri*	بدْري

I went home early from school today.	*rawwáḥit min ilmádrasa 3a -ddār bádri -lyōm.*	روّحِت مِن المدْرسة عَ الدّار بدْري اليوْم.
late	*mit?áxxir*	**مِتْأخِّر**
I got home late at night.	*rjí3it 3a -ddār fi -llēl mit?áxxir.*	رْجِعِت عَ الدّار في الليل مِتْأخِّر.
since, for	*min*	**مِن**
I've been living in Gaza since 2010.	*ána 3āyiš fi ɣázza min il?alfēn w 3ášara.*	أنا عايِش في غزّة مِن الألْفيْن وعشرة.
until	*la-ḥádd* *la-ɣāyit __*	**لحدّ** **لغايِةْ**
I watched TV until eleven o'clock.	*(i)tfarrájit 3a -ttilfizyōn la-ḥádd issā3a ḥadā3iš.*	اِتْفرّجِت عَ التِّلْفِزْيوْن لحدّ السّاعة حْداعِش.

50 Pronouns

I	*ána*	أنا
we	*íḥna*	إحْنا
you	*ínta*	إنْتَ
you	*ínti*	إنْتي
you, you guys	*íntu*	إنْتو
he, it	*húwwa*	هُوَّ
she, it	*híyya*	هِيَّ
they	*húmma*	هُمَّ

this (these)	*hāda* [m.], *hādi* [f.] *(hadōl)*	هادا، هادي (هدوْل)
that (those)	*hadāk* [m.], *hadīk* [f.] *(hadōlāk)*	هداك، هديك (هدوْلاك)
this __, that __, these __, those __	*ha-l__*	هالـــ

everyone	*kull wāḥad*	كُلّ واحد
Everyone needs friends.	*kull wāḥad biḥtāj ṣḥāb.*	كُلّ واحد بيحْتاج صْحاب.
someone	*ḥáda* *ḥadd*	حدا حدّ
Someone is at the door.	*fī ḥáda 3a -lbāb.*	في حدا عَ الباب.
anyone	*ayy ḥáda* *ayy ḥadd*	أيّ حدا أيّ حدّ
Anyone can do it.	*ayy ḥáda bígdar yi3málha.*	أيّ حدا بيقْدر يِعْملْها.
no one	*fiš ḥadd* *wála ḥáda*	فِش حدّ وَلا حدا
No one lives forever.	*fiš ḥadd bi3īš la-lʔábad.*	فِش حدّ بيعيش للأبد.

everything	*kull íši*	كُلّ إشي
Everything is ready.	*kull íši jāhiz.*	كُلّ إشي جاهِز.
something	*íši*	إشي
I want to eat something sweet.	*bíddi ākul íši ḥílu.*	بِدّي آكُل إشي حِلو.
anything	*áyy íši*	أيّ إشي
What do you want to eat? – Anything is fine.	*šū bíddak tākul? – ayy íši.*	شو بِدّك تاكُل؟ – أيّ إشي.
nothing	*wála ʔíši*	وَلا إشي
What did you buy? – Nothing!	*šū -štarēt? – wála ʔíši.*	شو اشْتريْت؟ – وَلا إشي.

English	Transliteration	Arabic
what	šū	**شو**
What is that?	šū hād?	شو هاد؟
What do you want?	šū bíddak?	شو بِدّك؟
who	mīn	**مين**
Who told you that?	mīn gállak hēk?	مين قلّك هيْك؟
Who did you tell?	la-mīn gúlit?	لمين قُلت؟
which __	ayy ____	**أيّ___**
Which movie do you want to see?	ayy fílim bíddak tíḥḍar?	أيّ فِلِم بِدّك تِحْضر؟
where	wēn	**ويْن**
Where do you live?	wēn sākin?	ويْن ساكِن؟
when	wagtēš máta	**وَقْتيْش** **متى**
When are you going on vacation?	wagtēš bitʔájjiz?	وَقْتيْش بِتْأجِّز؟
how	kēf	**كيْف**
How do you usually get to work?	kēf bi-l3āda bitrūḥ 3a šúɣlak ?	كيْف بِالعادة بِتْروح عَ شُغْلك؟
why	lēš	**ليْش**
Why are you late?	lēš mitʔáxxir?	ليْش مِتْأخِّر؟
how many, how much; how long, how much time	gaddēš ákam kam	**قدّيْش** **أكم** **كم**
How many people are there in your family?	íntu kam wāḥad fi -l3ēla?	إنْتو كم واحد في العيْلة؟
How much does this cost?	gaddēš ḥággu? bákam hād?	قدّيْش حقّو؟ بكم هاد؟

How much water is there in the bottle?	*gaddēš fī máyya bi-ligzāza?*	قدّيش في ميّة بِالقْزازة؟
How long does it take you to get to work?	*gaddēš btāxud má3ak wágit la-tūṣal 3a -ššúɣul?*	قدّيش بْتاخُد معك وَقِت لتوصل عَ الشُّغُل؟
How long have you been married?	*gaddēš ílak midjáwwiz?*	قدّيش إلك مِتْجَوِّز؟
How long is this carpet?	*gaddēš ṭūl hādi -ssijjāda?*	قدّيش طول هادي السِّجّادة؟
how old	*gaddēš 3úmur*	**قدّيش عُمُر**
How old are you?	*gaddēš 3úmrak?*	قدّيش عُمْرك؟
how big	*gaddēš ḥájim* *gaddēš kúbur*	**قدّيش حجِم** **قدّيش كُبُر**
How big is your house?	*gaddēš ḥájim dārku?* *gaddēš kúbur dārku?*	قدّيش حجِم دارْكو؟ قدّيش كُبُر دارْكو؟
how far	*gaddēš ilmasāfa* *gaddēš b3īd*	**قدّيش المسافة** **قدّيش بْعيد**
How far is it from here to downtown?	*gaddēš ilmasāfa min hān la-lbálad?*	قدّيش المسافة مِن هان للبلد؟
how often	*kull gaddēš*	**كُلّ قدّيش**
How often do you exercise?	*kull gaddēš btíl3ab riyāḍa?*	كُلّ قدّيش بْتِلْعب رِياضة؟

slowly	bišwēš 3a máhil	بِشْوِيْش عَ مهِل
fast, quickly	b-súr3a	بْسُرْعة
at least	3a -lʔagáll agáll íši	عَ الأقلّ أقلّ إشي
almost, nearly, around, about	tagrīban ħawāli	تقْريباً حوالي
again	kamān márra márra tānya	كمان مرّة مرّة تانْيَة
alone	la-ħālu	لحالو
also	kamān	كمان
here	hān hína	هان هِنا
there	hināk	هِناك
everywhere	kull makān	كُلّ مكان
I see him everywhere.	bašūfu b-kull makān.	بشوفو بُكّلّ مكان.
somewhere	makān	مكان
We can eat somewhere else.	bnígdar nrūħ nākul b-makān tāni.	بْنِقْدر نْروح ناكُل بمْكان تاني.
anywhere	wēn makān ayy makān	وِيْن مكان أيّ مكان
We can go anywhere.	bnígdar nrūħ wēn makān.	بْنِقْدر نْروح وِيْن مكان.
nowhere	wála makān	وَلا مكان

Nowhere is safe.	wála makān fī amān. wála makān āmin.	وَلا مكان فيه أمان. وَلا مكان آمِن .
always	dāyman	دايْماً
She always does her homework.	dāyman bitḫáll wājíbha.	دايْماً بِتْحِلّ واجِبْها.
sometime	márra	مرّة
Let's have coffee sometime.	xallīna márra níšrab gáhwa.	خلّينا مرّة نِشْرب قهْوَة.
sometimes	marrāt aḫyānan	مرّات أحْياناً
I sometimes get up late.	marrāt bášḫa mitʔáxxir.	مرّات بصْحى مِتْأَخِّر.
anytime	ayy wágit	أيّ وَقِت
You can call me anytime.	btígdar tittíṣil fíyya b-ʔayy wágit.	بْتِقْدر تِتّصِل فِيّا بِأيّ وَقِت.
never	bi-lmárra ábadan wála márra	بالمرّة أبداً وَلا مرّة
I never eat breakfast.	ána bafṭáriš bi-lmárra.	أنا بفْطِرش بالمرّة.
They've never been to Egypt.	wála márra rāḫu 3a máṣir.	وَلا مرّة راحوا عَ مصِر .
usually	bi-l3āda 3ādatan	بِالعادة عادةً
I usually go to work by car, but I sometimes walk.	bi-l3āda barūḫ 3a -ššúɣul bi-ssayyāra bass marrāt barūḫ máši.	بالعادة بروح عَ الشُّغُل بالسّيّارة بسّ مرّات بروح مشي.
often	ktīr káza márra	كْتير كزا مرّة
I often see him at the café.	ktīr bašūfu bi-lkāfi.	كْتير بشوفو بِالكافي.

somehow	*kēf ba3rífiš* [lit. I don't know how] *b-ṭarīga 3ajība*	كيْف بعْرِفِش بْطريقة عجيبة
The cat somehow got in the house.	*ilbíssa dáxlat 3a -ddār, kēf ba3rífiš.*	البِسّة دخْلت عَ الدّار، كيْف بعْرِفِش.
very	*ktīr __*	كْتير__
very good	*ktīr mnīḥ*	كْتير مْنيح
__ enough	*__ la-dáraga* *__ kfāya*	__لدرجة __كْفايَة
big enough	*kbīr la-dáraga*	كْبير لدرجة
too __; too much, too many	*__ ktīr* *__ zyāda 3an illuzūm*	__كْتير __زْيادة عن اللّزوم
too big	*kbīr ktīr* *kbīr zyāda 3an illuzūm*	كْبير كْتير كْبير زْيادة عن اللُّزوم
too much money	*maṣāri ktīr*	مصاري كْتير
too many people	*nās ktīr*	ناس كْتير
well	*kwáyyis* *mnīḥ*	كْوَيِّس مْنيح
You speak Arabic well.	*ínta btíḥki 3árabi kwáyyis.*	إنتَ بْتِحْكي عربي كْوَيِّس.
still; (not)... yet	*líssa*	لِسّا
I'm still hungry.	*ána líssa ja3ān.*	أنا لِسّا جعان.
He isn't here yet.	*líssa mā wíṣliš.*	لِسّا ما وِصْلِش.
(not)... yet	*la-ḥátta -lʔān*	لحتّى الآن
He isn't here yet.	*la-ḥátta -lʔān mā wíṣliš.*	لحتّى الآن ما وِصْلِش.
already	*min gábil*	مِن قْبِل

I already told you!	gultíllak min gábil.	قُلْتِلَّك مِن قبِل.
I've already eaten lunch.	(i)tɣaddēt min gábil.	اِتْغدّيْت مِن قبِل.
just	táwwi gábil šwáyya	توّي قبْل شْويّة
I just ate.	táwwi akálit.	توّي أُكلِت.
inside	júwwa	جُوّا
It's hot today. Let's stay inside.	ilyōm šōb. xallīna júwwa.	اليوْم شوْب. خلّينا جُوّا.
outside	bárra	برّا
Let's sit outside.	xallīna núg3ud bárra.	خلّينا نُقْعُد برّا.
abroad, overseas	bárra (-lbálad)	برّا (البلد)

برّا *bárra,* literally 'outside,' is also used to mean 'abroad.' The context usually clears up any ambiguity in meaning; however, when you need to clarify that you mean 'abroad' and not 'outside', you can say برّا البلد *bárra -lbálad* 'outside of the country.'

He lives abroad.	húwa 3āyiš bárra.	هُوّ عايِش برّا.
I'm going abroad next week.	ána msāfar bárra lisbū3 ijjāy.	أنا مْسافر برّا الإسْبوع الجّاي.
upstairs	fōg	فوْق
Come upstairs!	íṭla3 fōg!	اِطْلع فوْق!
downstairs	táḥit	تحِت

53 Conjunctions

and	w	و
or	aw	أَوْ
but	bass	بسّ
whether, if	law íza	لَوْ إذا
that	ínnu	إنّو
because	3ašān la-ʔínn	عشان لإنّ
I'm tired today because I went to bed late last night.	ána ta3bān 3ašānni nímit mitʔáxxir imbāriḥ.	أنا تعْبان عشانيّ نِمِت مِتْأخِّر إمْبارِح.
I feel good because I exercise every day.	ḥāsis ḥāli mnīḥ la-ʔínni batmárran kull yōm.	حاسِس حالي مْنيح لإنّي بتْمرّن كُلّ يوْم.
so	3ašān hēk la-hēk	عشان هيْك لهيْك
I went to bed late last night, so I'm tired today.	(i)tʔaxxárit fi -nnōma -mbāriḥ, 3ašān hēk ta3bān ilyōm.	إتْأخّرِت في النّوْمة إمْبارِح، عشان هيْك تعْبان اليوْم.
so that, in order to	3ašān	عشان

When عشان 3ašān is followed by a bare imperfect verb, it means 'so that' or 'in order to.' Otherwise, it means 'because,' as shown a few lines above.

You have to study hard in order to learn Arabic well.	lāzim tígra mnīḥ 3ašān tit3állam 3árabi kwáyyis.	لازِم تِقرا مْنيح عشان تِتْعلّم عربي كْوَيِّس.
We had to leave home early to get there on time.	iḍtarrēna nítla3 min iddār bádri 3ašān nūṣal 3a -lwágit.	اِضْطرّيْنا نِطْلع مِن الدّار بدْري عشان نوصل عَ الوَقِت.
after	bá3id	بعِد

I had dinner after I got home last night.	(i)t3aššēt bá3id ma wṣílit 3a- ddār imbāriḥ.	اتِعشّيت بعِد ما وْصِلِت عَ الدّار إمْبارِح.
I always have dinner after I get home.	dāyman bat3ášša bá3id ma ʔáwṣal 3a -ddār.	دايماً بتْعشّى بعِد ما أوْصل الدّار.
I'll have dinner after I get home this evening.	ḥat3ášša bá3id ma ʔáwṣal 3a -ddār ilmása.	حتْعشّى بعِد ما أوْصل عَ الدار المسا.
before	gábil	**قبِل**
He opened the window before he went to bed last night.	húwwa fátaḥ iššubbāk imbāriḥ gábil ma ynām.	هُوَّ فتح الشُّبّاك إمْبارِح قبِل ما يْنام.
He always opens the window before he goes to bed.	dāyman bíftaḥ iššubbāk gábil ma ynām.	دايماً بيفْتح الشُّبّاك قبِل ما يْنام.
He'll open the window before he goes to bed tonight.	ḥayíftaḥ iššubbāk ilyōm gábil ma ynām.	حَيِفْتح الشُّبّاك اليوْم قبِل ما يْنام.
until, by the time	la-3índ ma la-ḥádd ma	**لعِنْد ما** **لحدّ ما**
I lived in Gaza until I graduated from university.	ána 3íšit fi ɣázza la-3índ ma -txarrájit min ijjām3a.	أنا عِشِت في غزّة لعِنْد ما إتْخرّجِت مِن الجّامْعة.
I'll stay in a hotel until I find an apartment.	ḥaḍáll gā3id bi-lfúndug la-ḥádd ma ʔalāgi šágga.	حضّل قاعِد بالفُنْدُق لحدّ ما ألاقي شقّة.
by the time	la-bēn ma la-ḥádd ma	**لبينْ ما** **لحدّ ما**
It was nine o'clock by the time he got up.	la-bēn ma ṣíḥi kānat issā3a tís3a.	لبينْ ما صِحي كانت السّاعة تِسْعة.
while	w bēn ma	**و** **بينْ ما**

I did my homework while I was watching TV.	ḥallēt ilwāgib w ána batfárraj 3a -ttilfizyōn.	حَلّيْت الواجِب وأنا بتْفرّج عَ التِّلْفِزْيوْن.
if	law	لَوْ
If I have enough money, I'll buy it.	law má3i maṣāri bikafū kān ištarētha.	لَوْ معي مصاري بيكفّوا كان اِشريْتْها.
If I had enough money, I'd buy it. / If I had had enough money, I would have bought it.	law kānu maṣāríyya bikafū kunt ištarētha.	لَوْ كانو مصاريّا بيكفّوا كُنْت شريْتْها.
when (time clause)	lámma wágit	لمّا وَقِت
When we got home from work, we went straight to bed.	lámma rjí3na 3a -ddār min iššúɣul, 3a ṭūl nímna.	لمّا رْجِعْنا عَ الدّار مِن الشُّغُل عَ طول نِمْنا.
when (introducing a noun clause)	wagtēš máta	وَقْتيْش متى
I don't know when they're coming.	bá3rifš wagtēš jāyyīn.	بعْرِفِش وَقْتيْش جايّين.
where	wēn	ويْن

Instead of introducing a noun clause with ويْن *wēn*, a synonymous expression such as المكان اللي *ilmakān ílli* or المطْرح اللي *ilmáṭraḥ ílli*, literally 'the place that,' can be used.

I can't remember where I put my keys.	miš zākir wēn ḥaṭṭēt mafātīḥi.	مِش زاكِر ويْن حطّيْت مفاتيحي.
why	lēš lē	ليْش ليْه
Do you know why he said that?	btí3rif lēš hēk gāl?	بْتِعْرِف ليْش هيْك قال؟
who	mīn	مين
I want to know who did it.	bíddi á3rif mīn 3ámal hēk.	بِدّي أعْرِف مين عمل هيْك.
what	šū	شو

I want to know what you did.	*bíddi ʔá3rif šū 3amálit.*	بِدّي أعْرِف شو عملِت.
I know what you did.	*bá3rif šū 3amálit.*	بعْرِف شو عملِت.

<table>
<tr><td>54 Prepositions</td></tr>
</table>

in; at	*fi* *b(i)-*	في بِـ
in the box	*fi -ṣṣandūg*	في الصّندوق
in, inside; into	*júwwa* *juwāt*	جُوّا جُوّات
outside of; out of	*bárra* *barrāt*	برّا برّات
on; onto; against	*3ála* *3a*	على عَ

عَ *3a* is a shortened form of على *3ála*. Both can be used interchangeably, but the shortened form is more commonly the one used before a definite article.

on the table	*3a-ṭṭāwla*	عَ الطّاوْلة

Prepositions are highly idiomatic, making them notoriously tricky to translate. Notice how 'against' is translated in the following English sentence literally as 'on' in Arabic.

The table is against the wall.	*iṭṭāwla 3a -lḥēṭ.*	الطّاوْلة عَ الحيْط.
He leaned against the car.	*sánad 3a -ssayyāra.*	سند عَ السّيّارة.
to	*3ála* *3a* *la-*	على عَ لـَ
The car is going to Gaza.	*issayyāra rāyḥa 3a γázza.*	السّيّارة رايْحة عَ غزّة.
from	*min*	مِن
from my house to school	*min dāri la-lmádrasa*	مِن داري للمدْرسة
above, over	*fōg*	فوْق
The painting is hanging over the sofa.	*illáwḥa m3állga fōg ilkánaba.*	اللّوْحة مْعلّقة فوْق الكنبة.

The airplane flew over the mountains.	ṭārat iṭṭayyāra fōg lijbāl.	طارت الطَّيّارة فوْق الجِبال.
He jumped over the fence.	naṭṭ fōg lisyāj.	نطّ فوْق السِياج.

under, beneath	*táḥit*	**تحِت**
under the table	*táḥt iṭṭāwla*	**تحْت الطَّاوْلة**
between	*bēn*	**بيْن**
The post office is between the bank and the supermarket.	máktab ilbarīd bēn ilbánk w -ssūbar mārkit.	مكْتب البريد بيْن البنْك والسّوْبر مارْكِت.
near, close to	*garīb min*	**قريب مِن**
My office is close to my brother's house.	máktabi garīb min dār axūyi.	مكْتبي قريب مِن دار أخوي.
far from	*b3īd 3an*	**بْعيد عن**
Nablus is far from Gaza.	nāblis b3īda 3an ɣázza.	نابْلِس بْعيدة عن غزّة.

قريب *garīb* and بْعيد *b3īd* are actually adjectives, and as such vary for gender. Notice the feminine form used in the sentence above as the subject, a city, is feminine.

next to; along	*jamb*	**جنْب**
There's a coffee shop next to my office.	fī kāfi jamb máktabi.	في كافي جنْب مكْتبي.
We walked along the river.	mašēna jamb innáhir.	مشيْنا جنْب النَّهِر.
in front of; across from, opposite	*guddām* *gbāl*	**قُدّام** **قْبال**
I sat down in front of the TV.	ga3ádit guddām ittilfizyōn.	قعدِت قُدّام التِّلْفِزْيوْن.
He sat across from the interviewer.	gá3ad guddām ílli bigābil.	قعد قُدّام اللي بيقابِل.
behind	*wára*	**وَرا**
I parked behind the house.	ṣaffēt wára -ddār.	صفّيْت وَرا الدّار.

around, surrounding	ḥawalēn dāyir maydūr	حَوَليْن دايِر مَيْدور
There's a fence surrounding the house.	fī syāj ḥawalēn iddār.	في سْياج حَوَليْن الدّار.

Prepositions are highly idiomatic, and often a verb in English that requires a preposition can be expressed by a verb that doesn't require a preposition in Arabic, as can be seen in the sentences below.

He <u>swam across</u> the river.	gáṭa3 innáhir sbāḥa. [lit. he crossed the river swimming]	قطع النّهِر سْباحة.
Don't <u>go down</u> the ladder.	mā <u>tínzil 3an</u> issíllam.	ما تِنْزِل عن السِّلّم.
The cat <u>climbed up</u> the tree.	ilbíssa <u>ṭíl3at 3a</u> -ššájara.	البِسّة طِلْعت عَ الشّجرة.
The train <u>went through</u> the tunnel.	ilgiṭār <u>3ábar</u> innáfag.	القِطار عبر النّفق.
down from; off	min 3an	مِن عن
The cat climbed down the tree.	ilbíssa nízlat 3an iššájara.	البِسّة نِزْلت عن الشّجرة.
The book fell off the table.	liktāb wígi3 3an iṭṭāwla.	الكِتاب وِقع عن الطّاوْلة.
past	min guddām	مِن قُدّام
I walked past the restaurant.	marágit min guddām ilmáṭ3am.	مرقِت مِن قُدّام المطْعم.
toward	3ála 3a bittijāh	على عَ باتِّجاه
He ran toward the door.	jára 3a- lbāb.	جرى عَ الباب.
with	ma3	مع
I had dinner with my friends.	(i)t3aššēt ma3 sḥābi.	اِتْعشّيْت مع صْحابي.
by, with	b(i)-	بـ

I came to work by bus.	*jīt 3a -ššúɣul bi-lbāṣ.*	.جيت عَ الشُّغُل بِالباص
She wrote the letter by hand.	*kátbat irrisāla b-ʔīdha.*	.كتْبت الرِّسالة بْإيدْها
She wrote the letter with a pencil.	*kátbat irrrisāla b-gálam rṣāṣ.*	.كتْبت الرِّسالة بْقلمِ رْصاص
without	*bidūn* *min ɣēr*	**بِدون** **مِن غيْر**
I can't live without you.	*bagdáriš a3īš min ɣērak.*	.بقْدرِش أعيش مِن غيرْك

The following common verbs did not fit neatly into other categories. If you cannot find a verb here, try the index in the back of the book to see if it is listed under another category.

to abandon, desert	*hájar, yúhjur*	هجر، يُهْجُر
to accept	*gíbil, yígbal*	قِبِل، يِقْبل
to accompany	*rāḥ ma3, yrūḥ ma3* *ája ma3, yīji ma3*	راح مع، يْروح مع أجا مع، ييجي مع
to adjust; fix	*zábbaṭ, yzábbiṭ*	زبّط، يْزبّط

زبّط *zábbaṭ* could also be spelled ظبّط, as in MSA, although it is always pronounced with *z* in Palestinian Arabic.

to admit	*i3táraf, yi3tírif*	اِعْترف، يِعْترِف
to advise, recommend	*náṣaḥ, yínṣaḥ*	نصح، يِنْصح
to affect	*ássar 3ála, yʔássir 3ála*	أثّر على، يْأثّر على
to allow	*xálla, yxálli* *sámaḥ la-, yísmaḥ la-*	خلّى، يْخلّي سمح لـ، يِسْمح لـ
to answer, respond, reply	*radd 3ála, yrudd 3ála* *jāwab 3ála, yjāwib 3ála*	ردّ على، يْرُدّ على جاوَب على، يْجاوِب على
to apologize for	*i3tázar 3ála, yi3tízir 3ála*	اِعْتذر على، يِعْتِذِر على
to appear	*báyyan, ybáyyin*	بيّن، يْبيّن
to appreciate	*gáddar, ygáddir*	قدّر، يْقدّر
to approve of	*wāfag, ywāfig*	وافق، يْوافِق
to arrange, organize	*náẓẓam, ynáẓẓim*	نظّم، يْنظّم
to ask	*sáʔal, yísʔal*	سأل، يِسْأل
to attend; watch, view	*ḥíḍir, yíḥḍar*	حِضِر، يِحْضر
to be	*kān, ykūn*	كان، يْكون

to be able to, can	gídir, yígdir 3írif, yí3rif	قِدِر، يِقْدِر عِرِف، يِعْرِف
Can you swim?	btí3rif tísbaħ?	بْتِعْرِف تِسْبح؟
I can't understand a word you said.	mā fhímtiš íši min ílli gúltu.	ما فْهِمْتِش اِشي مِن اللي قُلْتو.
to become, be; to happen	ṣār, yṣīr	صار، يْصير
to beg, plead	(i)trájja, yitrájja	اِتْرجّى، يِتْرجّى
to begin, start	báda, yíbda bállaš, ybálliš	بدا، يِبْدا بلّش، يْبلِّش
to behave	(i)tʔáddab, yitʔáddab	اِتّأدّب، يِتّأدّب
to bet	rāhan, yrāhin	راهن، يْراهِن
to blame __ for	lām __ 3ála, ylūm __ 3ála	لام ـــ على، يْلوم ـــ على
to bother, disturb	dāyag, ydāyig	ضايَق، يْضايِق
to break	kásar, yíksir	كسر، يِكْسِر
to bring, get	jāb, yjīb	جاب، يْجيب
to burn	ħárag, yíħrig	حرق، يِحْرِق
to care	ihtámm, yihtámm	اِهْتمّ، يِهْتمّ
to carry, lift, pick up	ħámal, yíħmil	حمل، يِحْمِل
She carried the box to the kitchen.	ħámlat iṣṣandūg la-lmáṭbax.	حمْلت الصّنْدوق للمطْبخ.
He lifted the child up.	ħámal ilwálad.	حمل الوَلد.
(transitive) **to change**	ɣáyyar, yɣáyyir	غيّر، يْغيّر
(intransitive) **to change**	(i)tɣáyyar, yitɣáyyar	اِتْغيّر، يِتْغيّر
to chase, pursue	lāħag, ylāħig ṭārad, yṭārid	لاحق، يْلاحِق طارد، يْطارِد
to cheat, deceive	ɣašš, yɣušš	غِشّ، يْغُشّ
to cheer, encourage	šájja3, yšájji3	شجّع، يْشجّع
to choose	ixtār, yixtār	اِخْتار، يِخْتار

to climb, ascend, go up	ṭíli3, yíṭla3	طِلع، بِطْلع
to close, lock	sákkar, ysákkir gáffal, ygáffil	سكَّر، يْسكِّر قفَّل، يْقفِّل
to come	ája, yīji	أجا، بيجي
to compare	qāran, yqārin	قارن، يْقارِن
to contact	(i)ttáṣal b(i)-, yittíṣil b(i)-	اِتَّصل بِـ، يِتّصِل بِـ
to continue	kámmal, ykámmil	كمَّل، يْكمِّل
to cut	gaṣṣ, yguṣṣ	قصّ، يْقُصّ
to decline	ráfaḍ, yúrfuḍ	رفض، يُرْفُض
to decrease, reduce	gall, ygill	قلَّ، يْقِلّ
to demand	ṭálab, yúṭlub	طلب، يُطْلُب
to deny	ánkar, yínkir	أنْكر، يِنْكِر
to descend, go down	nízil, yínzal	نزِل، يِنْزل
to describe	wáṣaf, yūṣif	وَصف، يوصِف
to design	ṣámmam, yṣámmim	صمَّم، يْصمِّم
to differ	ixtálaf, yíxtilif	اِخْتلف، يِخْتِلِف
to disappear	ixtáfa, yíxtifi	اِخْتفى، يِخْتِفي
to do, make	3ámal/3ímil, yí3mal	عمل/عِمِل، يِعْمل
to drop	wágga3, ywággi3	وَقَّع، يْوَقِّع
He dropped his book.	wágga3 ktābu.	وَقّع كْتابو.
to edit, correct	3áddal, y3áddil ṣállaḥ, yṣálliḥ	عدَّل، يْعدِّل صلَّح، يْصلِّح
to express	3ábbar 3an, y3ábbir 3an	عبَّر عن، يْعبِّر عن
to fall	wígi3, yūga3	وِقع، يوقع
to find	lága, ylāgi	لقى، يْلاقي

(intransitive) **to finish, come to an end;** (transitive) **to finish, end, complete, accomplish**	*xállaṣ, yxálliṣ*	خَلَّص، يْخَلِّص
to float	*ṭāš, yṭīš* *ṭáfa, yítfu*	طاش، يْطيش طفا، يِطْفو
The ball is floating in the water.	*ilkōra ṭāyša 3a -lmáyya.*	الكْوْرة طايْشة عَ الميّة.
to get, take, receive, obtain; pick up, grab	*áxad, yāxud*	أخد، ياخُد
He picked the book up from the table.	*áxad liktāb 3an iṭṭāwla.*	أخد الكِتاب عن الطّاوْلة.
to give	*á3ṭa, yá3ṭi*	أعْطى، يَعْطي
to go	*rāḥ, yrūḥ*	راح، يْروح
to have	*kān 3índu*	كان عِنْدو

عِنْدو *3índu* is a prepositional phrase used like a verb to mean 'have.' See the book Palestinian Arabic Verbs p. 106.

to help	*sā3ad, yْsā3id*	ساعد، يْساعِد
to hit	*ḍárab, yúḍrub*	ضرب، يُضْرُب
to imagine	*(i)txáyyal, yitxáyyal*	اِتْخَيِّل، يِتْخَيِّل
to intend to	*náwa, yínwi*	نَوى، يِنْوي
I intend to succeed at my job.	*ána nāwi Ɂánjaḥ b-šúɣli.*	أنا ناوي أنْجح بْشُغْلي.
to jump	*naṭṭ, ynuṭṭ*	نطّ، يْنُطّ
to leave; quit	*sāb, ysīb* *tárak, yútruk*	ساب، يْسيب ترك، يُتْرُك
to lie	*kázab, yíkzib*	كزب، يِكْزِب
to look	*šāf, yšūf* *iṭṭálla3, yiṭṭálla3*	شاف، يْشوف اِتْطلّع، يِتْطلّع
to lose	*xísir, yíxsar*	خِسِر، يِخْسَر
to mean	*gáṣad, yúgṣud*	قصد، يُقْصُد

(intransitive) **to move**	(i)tẖárrak, yitẖárrak	إتْحرَّك، يِتْحرَّك
(transitive) **to move**	ẖárrak, yẖárrik	حرَّك، يْحرِّك
I can't move my leg!	miš gādir aẖárrik ríjli.	مِش قادِر أحرِّك رِجْلي.
to offer	3áraḍ, yí3riḍ	عرَض، يِعْرِض
to open	fátaẖ, yíftaẖ	فتح، يِفْتح
to order, command	ámar, yúʔmur	أمر، يَأْمُر
to order, request	ṭálab, yúṭlub	طلب، يُطْلُب
to pass, go past	márag, yúmrug	مرق، يمُرْق
to pay	dáfa3, yídfa3	دفع، يِدْفع
to play	lí3ib, yíl3ab	لعِب، يِلْعب
to prepare	jáhhaz, yjáhhiz ẖáḍḍar, yẖáḍḍir	جهَّز، يْجهِّز حضَّر، يْحضِّر
to prohibit	mána3, yímna3	منع، يِمْنع
to punish	3āqab, y3āqib jāza, yjāzi	عاقِب، يْعاقِب جازى، يْجازي
to put, set (down)	ẖaṭṭ, yẖuṭṭ	حطَّ، يْحُطّ
He set down the book on the table.	ẖaṭṭ liktāb 3a-ṭṭāwla.	حطَّ الكِتاب عَ الطّاوْلة.
to return, go back	ríji3, yírja3	رِجِع، يِرْجع
to say, tell	gāl, ygūl	قال، يْقول
to show	wárja, ywárji fárja, yfárji	وَرْجى، يْوَرْجي فرْجى، يْفَرْجي
to sink	yírig, yíɣrag	غِرِق، يِغْرق
The Titanic sank over a hundred years ago.	ittāytānik yírgat gábil áktar min mīt sána.	التّايْتانِك غِرْقت قبل أكْتر مِن مية سنة.
to sit	gá3ad, yúg3ud	قعد، يِقْعُد
to stay	ḍall, yḍall	ضلّ، يْضلّ

(transitive) **to stop, make stop**; (intransitive) **to stop**	*wággaf, ywággif*	وَقَّف، يْوَقِّف
(intransitive) **to stop; to stand**	*wígif, yūgaf*	وِقِف، يوقف
to succeed	*níjiħ, yínjaħ*	نِجِح، يِنْجح
to suggest, propose	*iqtáraħ, yiqtíriħ*	إقْترح، يِقْترِح
to talk	*ħáka, yíħki*	حكى، يِحْكي
to tear	*mázza3, ymázzi3* *xáxxag, yxázzig*	مزّع، يمْزِّع خزّق، يْخزِّق
to thank	*šákar, yúškur*	شكر، يُشْكُر
to tie	*rábaṭ, yúrbuṭ*	ربط، يُرْبُط
to touch	*lámas, yílmis*	لمس، يِلْمِس
to try, attempt	*ħāwal, yħāwil*	حاوَل، يْحاوِل
to try, try out	*járrab, yjárrib*	جرّب، يْجرِّب
to turn off, extinguish	*ṭáfa, yíṭfi*	طفى، يِطْفي
to use	*istá3mal, yistá3mil* *istáxdam, yistáxdim*	إسْتعمل، يِسْتعْمِل إسْتخْدم، يِسْتخْدِم
to wait	*istánna, yistánna* *intázar, yintízir*	إسْتنّى، يِسْتنّى إنْتظر، يِنْتِظِر
to walk, go, leave	*máša, yímši*	مشى، يِمْشي
to wash	*ɣásal, yíɣsil*	غسل، يِغْسِل
to watch, view	*itfárraj 3ála, yitfárraj 3ála*	إتْفرّج على، يِتْفرّج على
to welcome, greet	*istágbal, yistágbil*	إسْتقْبل، يِسْتقْبِل

The following common adjectives did not fit neatly into other categories. If you cannot find an adjective here, try the index in the back of the book to see if it is listed under another category.

good	mnīḥ (mnāḥ)	مْنيح (مْناح)
bad	miš mnīḥ sáyyiʔ	مِش مْنيح سيِّئ
hard	gāsi	قاسي
soft	ṭári	طري
difficult, hard	ṣí3ib	صِعِب
easy	síhil	سِهِل
important	muhímm	مُهِمّ
necessary	ḍarūri	ضروري
strong	gáwi (ágwiya)	قَوي (أقْويا)
weak	ḍ3īf (ḍ3āf)	ضْعيف (ضْعاف)
deep	yamīg 3amīg	غميق عميق
shallow	sáṭḥi	سطْحي
long; (person) tall	ṭawīl (ṭwāl)	طَويل (طْوال)
He's very tall.	húwwa ṭawīl ktīr.	هُوَّ طَويل كْتير.
short	gaṣīr (gṣār)	قصير (قْصار)
She's quite short.	híyya gaṣīra ktīr.	هِيَّ قصيرة كْتير.
old, ancient	gadīm (gdām)	قديم (قْدام)
new	jdīd (jdād)	جْديد (جْداد)
clear, obvious	wāḍiḥ	واضِح
His answer was very clear.	jawābu kān ktīr wāḍiḥ.	جَوابو كان كْتير واضِح.

unclear	*miš wāḍiḥ*	مِش واضِح
clean	*nḍīf (nḍāf)*	نْضيف (نْضاف)
dirty	*wísix*	وِسِخ
heavy	*tgīl (tgāl)*	تْقيل (تْقال)
light	*xafīf (xfāf)*	خفيف (خْفاف)
ready	*jāhiz*	جاهِز
Are you ready yet?	*ínta jāhiz wálla líssa?*	إنْتَ جاهِز وَلّا لِسّا؟
I'm ready!	*ána jāhiz!*	أنا جاهِز!
right (person)	*má3u ḥagg*	معو حقّ
Yes, you're right!	*ṣaḥḥ, má3ak ḥagg!*	صحّ، معك حقّ!
wrong (person)	*ɣalṭān*	غلْطان
I think you're wrong (about that).	*aẓúnn ínnak ɣalṭān.*	أظُنّ إنّك غلْطان.
slow	*baṭīʔ*	بطيء
fast, quick	*sarī3*	سريع
hot	*súxun*	سُخُن
warm	*dāfi*	دافي
cool, cold	*sāgi3* *bárid*	ساقِع بارِد
famous	*mašhūr*	مشْهور (مشاهير)
independent	*mustaqíll*	مُسْتقِلّ
busy	*mašɣūl*	مشْغول
empty; (person) available, free	*fāḍi*	فاضي
Are you free tomorrow?	*fāḍi búkra?*	فاضي بُكْرة؟
full	*malyān*	ملْيان
useful	*mufīd*	مُفيد

useless	*malūš fāyda* *mā ʔílu luzūm*	ملوش فايْدة ما إلو لُزوم
careful, cautious	*ḥarīṣ*	حريص
careless	*múhmil*	مُهْمِل
absent-minded	*sarḫān* *šārid*	سرْحان شارِد
open	*maftūḫ*	مفْتوح
closed	*msákkar*	مْسكّر
wet	*mablūl*	مبْلول
dry	*nāšif*	ناشِف
quiet	*hādi*	هادي
noisy	*múz3ij*	مُزْعِج
rough	*xíšin*	خِشِن
smooth	*nā3im*	ناعِم
narrow; tight	*ḍíyyig*	ضيّق
wide; loose	*wāsi3*	واسِع
dark	*m3áttim*	مْعْتّم
bright, light	*mnáwwir*	مْنوّر
sharp	*ḥādd*	حادّ
blunt	*ḫāfi*	حافي
additional	*zyāda* [invar.] *kamān* [invar.] *idāfi*	زيادة كمان إضافي
the same __	*nafs il-__*	نفْس الــ
similar	*zayy bá3aḍ*	زيّ بعض
different	*ɣēr* *mixtílif*	غيْر مِخْتِلِف

| possible; probable, likely | *múmkin*
ma3gūl | مُمْكِن
مَعْقول |
| impossible | *mustaḥīl* | مُسْتحيل |

57 Social Expressions

yes	ā ná3am	آه نعم
no	laʔ/lā	لا
Excuse me, ...	3an íznak	عن إذْنك
Please.	law samáḥit.	لَوْ سمحِت
Here you are!; Go ahead!; You first!	tfáḍḍal!	تْفضّل!
Thank you.	šúkran	شُكْراً
You're welcome.	3áfwan	عفْواً
I'm sorry!	āsif!	آسِف!
I apologize!	ba3tízir!	بعْتِزِرا!
Hi!; Hello!	márḥaba! hála! salāmāt!	مرْحبا! هلا! سلامات!
Good morning!	şabāḥ ilxēr!	صباح الخيْر!
How are you?	kēf ḥālak?	كيْف حالك؟
I'm fine.	ilḥámdu lillāh tamām b-xēr	الحمْدُ لله تمام بْخيْر
Hi! How are you? It's been a long time since I've seen you!	márḥaba, kēf ḥālak? min zamān mā šúftak.	مرْحبا، كيْف حالك؟ مِن زمان ما شُفتك.
What's up?	šū -lʔaxbār?	شو الأخْبار؟

Goodbye!	*bāy!* *salām!*	باي! سلام!
Good night!	*tíşbaɧ 3ála xēr!*	تِصْبح على خيْرا!
Have a nice day!	*yōmak sa3īd!* *nhārak sa3īd!*	يوْمك سعيد! نْهارك سعيد!
Hope to see you soon!	*bašūfak 3an garīb!*	بشوفك عن قريب!
See you later!	*bašūfak ba3dēn!*	بشوفك بعْديْن!
Have a good trip!	*tūşal bi-ssalāma!*	توصل بِالسَّلامة!
Take care!	*intíbih 3a ɧālak!*	اِنْتِبِهْ عَ حالك!
Welcome!	*áhla w sáhla!*	أهْلا وسهْلا!
May God be with you! (farewell)	*álla ykūn má3ak!*	الله يُكون معك.
Welcome home! We really missed you!	*áhla w sáhla! ištagnālak ktīr!*	أهْلا وسهْلا! اِشْتقْنالك كْتير.
I miss you!	*ištágtillak!*	اِشْتقْتِلَّك!
It's nice to meet you.	*(i)tšarráfit b-ma3ríftak.*	اِتْشرَّفْت بِمَعْرِفْتك.
Congratulations!	*mabrūk!* *mubārak!*	مبْروك! مُبارك!
Congratulations on graduating!	*mabrūk ittáxxaruj!*	مبْروك التَّخرُّج!

English	Transliteration	Arabic
Thank you. (response to congratulations)	*álla ybārik fīk.*	الله يْبارِك فيك.
Congratulations! (on an engagement, marriage, etc.)	*mabrūk, álla ytammimílkum 3a xēr.*	مبْروك، الله يِتمِّمِلْكُم عَ خيْر.
Thank you. (response if the congratulator is married)	*álla ybārik fīk.* *3ugbāl la-ʔawlādak.*	الله يْبارِك فيك. عُقْبال لأوْلادك.

Thank you. (response if the congratulator is single)	3ugbāl 3índak. 3ugbālak.	عُقْبال عِنْدك. عُقْبالك.
Congratulations! (on opening a shop)	mabrūk ilʔiftitāḥ.	مبْروك الافْتِتاح.
Congratulations! (on having a baby)	mabrūk, yitrábba b-3ízzak.	مبروك، يِتْرَبَّ بْعِزَّك.
Thank you!	tíslam. šúkran	تِسْلَم. شُكْراً.
Thank you! (response if the congratulator is single)	3ugbāl 3índak. 3ugbālak.	عُقْبال عِنْدك. عُقْبالك.
Good luck!	álla ywáffgak. bi-ttawfīg.	الله يْوَفّْقك. بالتَّوْفيق.
(utterance when someone has finishes performing one of the five daily prayers)	taqábbal allāh.	تقبّل الله.
(response)	mínna w mínkum.	مِنّا ومِنكُم.
Welcome back from your pilgrimage! (greeting to someone who has recently returned from hajj)	ḥíjja magbūla. ḥijj mabrūr.	حِجّة مقْبولة. حِجّ مبْرور.
My condolences. (to someone who has lost a relative)	ilbagíyya b-ḥayātak.	البقية بْحَياتك.
Thank you. (response to condolences)	t3īš. ḥayātak ilbāgya.	تْعيش. حَياتك الباقْية.
(utterance when hearing that somone has passed away)	álla yṣábbir áhlu.	الله يْصبرّ أهْلو.
R.I.P. May <u>he</u> rest in peace!; May <u>she</u> rest in peace!	álla yírḥamu. álla yirḥámha.	الله يِرْحمو . الله يِرْحمْها.

Get well soon!	*álla yišfīk.*	الله يِشْفيك.
(greeting to someone who has just had a shower or returned from the hammam)	*na3ēman.*	نعيْماً.
(utterance before starting to eat)	*b-ismi-llāh.*	بِاسْم الله.
(uttereance when after finishing eating)	*ilḥámdu lillāh.*	الحمْدُ لله.
(utterance to someone who has finished eating)	*dāyma.* *súfra 3āmra.*	دايْمة. سُفْرة عامْرة .
(uttereance of appreciation to someone who helps or does you a favor)	*ya3ṭīk il3āfya.*	يَعْطيك العافيْة.
Thank you! (response)	*álla y3āfīk.*	الله يْعافيك.
(greeting to someone who has just come back home from the hospital)	*ilḥamdílla 3a salāmtak.*	الحمْدِ لله عَ سلامْتك.
Bless him! (when talking about a child)	*mā šāʔ allāh.* *álla yxallī la-ʔáhlu.*	ما شاء الله. الله يْخلّيه لأهْلو.
May God bless you!	*allāh ybārik fīk.*	الله يْبارِك فيك.

Notebook

section	English	Pronunciation	Arabic

complexion 22
composition 75
computer 85
computer program 85
concrete 99
condiments 58
condom 83
condor 187
conference 146
congested 80
congestion 80
congratulations 241
conjugate 167
conjugation 168
consciousness 151
consonant 169
constipated 81
constitution 138
construction 99
construction worker 99
contact 232
contact lenses 35
contagious 83
continent 177
continue 232
convict 141
cook 42, 68, 109
cook book 43
cookie 55
cooking 42
cool 237
coolness 182
coop 147
copy 73
corn 148
corner 97
corpse 3
corral 147
correct 72, 232
correcttest 75
cosmos 179
cost 106
cotton 34
cotton candy 55

couch 41
cough 19, 81
council 145
count 199
counter 103
country 170
couple 10, 197
coupon 107
courgette 57
courier bag 30
court 141
courtyard 47
cousin 8
cow 147
coworker 65
crab 61
cracker 55
craft 67
crash 96
crazy 152
cream 54
cream soup 62
cricket 189
crime 140
criminal 140
criticism 157
criticize 157
crochet 114
crocodile 188
cross walk 91
cross-eyed 16
crossstreet 91
crow 187
crowd 117
cruel 155
crustaceans 61
cry 17, 153
cubic meter 196
cucumber 56
culture 170
cumin 59
cup 52
cup one's ear 18
cupboard 42
cure 82
curly hair 20

currency 143
curriculum 72
curry 59
curtain 38
cushion 44
customer 108
customer service representative 68
customs 132
customs officer 132
cut 42, 82, 232
cut in half 42
cut up 42
cute 28
cuttlefish 61
cyclist 90
cyclone 184
Czech Republic, Czech 173
dad 5
Dair Al Balah 175
dairy products 54
daisy 191
dance 121, 122
dancer 122
dark 194, 238
dark brown hair 20
dark red 194
dark-skinned 22
darkness 183
darling 10
darn 114
dashboard 93
date 10
dates 57
dating 10
daughter 5
dawn prayer 162
day 205; one ~ 211; some ~ 211; the ~ before yesterday 205
day off 110
day shift 65
dead 3
Dead Sea 176

deaf 18
death 3
death sentence 142
debt 101
decade 210
deceased 3
deceive 231
December 208
decide 151
decision 151
declare 132
declare war on 149
declension 168
decline 167, 232
decrease 232
deep 236
deer 186
defecate 26
defend 149
defense 142, 149
definite 168
degree 77
delayed 134
delete 85
delicious 50
delivermail 103
demand 232
democracy 138
democratic 138
demolish 99
demon 161
demonstrate 139
demonstration 139
demonstrator 139
Denmark 172
dent 95
dental floss 47
dentist 68, 84
dentistry 78
deny 232
depart 135
department 76, 137
deposit 102
descend 232
descendents 9
describe 232

Visit our website for information on current and upcoming titles,

free excerpts, and language learning resources.

www.lingualism.com